Media Diversity Law

Schriften zum Medien-, Urheber- und Wirtschaftsrecht

Herausgegeben von Prof. Dr. Georgios Gounalakis

Band 23

PL ACADEMIC RESEARCH

Georgios Gounalakis / Greg Taylor (eds.)

Media Diversity Law

Australia and Germany Compared

PL ACADEMIC RESEARCH

Bibliographic Information published by the Deutsche Nationalbibliothek
The Deutsche Nationalbibliothek lists this publication in the Deutsche Nationalbibliografie; detailed bibliographic data is available in the internet at http://dnb.d-nb.de.

Library of Congress Cataloging-in-Publication Data
Names: Gounalakis, Georgios, editor. | Taylor, Greg, (Law teacher), editor.
Title: Media diversity law : Australia and Germany compared / Georgios Gounalakis, Greg Taylor (eds.).
Description: Frankfurt am Main : Peter Lang GmbH Internationaler Verlag der Wissenschaften, 2016. | Series: Schriften zum medien-, urheber- und wirtschaftsrecht ; Band 23
Identifiers: LCCN 2016010014 | ISBN 9783631660751
Subjects: LCSH: Mass media--Law and legislation--Australia. | Mass media--Law and legislation--Germany. | Mass media policy--Australia. | Mass media policy--Germany.
Classification: LCC K4240 .M4323 2016 | DDC 343.4309/9--dc23 LC record available at http://lccn.loc.gov/2016010014

ISSN 1867-1012
ISBN 978-3-631-66075-1 (Print)
E-ISBN 978-3-653-05461-3 (E-Book)
DOI 10.3726/978-3-653-05461-3

PL Academic Research is an Imprint of Peter Lang GmbH.

Peter Lang – Frankfurt am Main · Bern · Bruxelles · New York · Oxford · Warszawa · Wien

This publication has been peer reviewed.

www.peterlang.com

Foreword

This collection of essays owes its origin to a grant in the "Go8 - Germany Joint Research Cooperation Scheme" jointly operated by the Australian Group of Eight Universities[1] and the *Deutscher Akademischer Austauschdienst* under the title "Approaches to Media Diversity Law: Australia and Germany Compared". The contributing authors warmly thank those bodies for their generosity!

The project was conceived in the conviction that media diversity is of the first importance for democratic societies such as Australia and Germany that thrive on open discussion. Despite all recent technological developments, it is still the case that the ownership of media (print and electronic) brings with it substantial power in the marketplace of ideas. For this reason, both Germany and Australia have created mechanisms specifically designed to ensure that undue concentration of media ownership is avoided and to promote media diversity in general. If a diversity of viewpoints is not present in the media, the democratic debate will be severely compromised, as will public scrutiny of non-state actors with significant societal power such as big business, lobby groups and indeed media organisations themselves.

The project also was conceived with an eye to the similarities and differences between both countries. Both countries are liberal Western capitalist societies strongly committed to the rule of law, individual freedoms and democratic values and principles. Both countries also face similar economic, social and technological challenges. Yet there also are important differences between Australia and Germany that make a comparison of how Australia and Germany regulate for media diversity profitable. Each country's media regulation was forged under very different circumstances and in the face of very different challenges: Germany in the shadow of National Socialism; Australia in a period of relative prosperity with economy-of-scale challenges. In Germany, media diversity is mandated by constitutional principles, but in Australia there is only the implied right to political communication, which contains no such mandate. In Germany, the federal States are heavily involved in this area of law (largely through the Inter-State Agreement on Broadcasting), whereas all relevant rules of law in Australia are federal.

The book's chapters reveal that notwithstanding these important differences, both countries have evolved similar legislative regimes comprising media specific regulation designed to promote media diversity and general competition/cartel

1 The Group of Eight (Go8) comprises Australia's eight leading research universities.

laws that can be applied to control the accumulation and abuse of market power in media markets. Professor Georgios Gounalakis and Dr Simon Rößß have provided a masterful comparison of the provisions of Australian and German law on media diversity in their chapter, which is a model of the comparative law method and concludes with recommendations based on experience in both countries to improve the law of each. Professor Gounalakis is a member of the German Commission on Concentration in the Media and his expertise has enabled him to write, with Dr Röß, a most valuable comparison with Australia that provides at once both the detail and the overview.

Professor Gounalakis' and Dr Röß's analysis is complemented by Dr John Duns' examination of media diversity from the viewpoint of Australian competition law compared with European Union (EU) law, Dr Sharon Rodrick's examination of Australia's media ownership and control rules, with a particular focus on cross-media ownership, and Professor Michael Kling's review of the application of EU, German and Australian merger control regulation to print media. While these examinations reveal some interesting contrasts between Australian, German and EU law, for the most the similarities of the legislative frameworks far outweigh their differences.

Dr Eric Windholz's thoughtful and interesting contribution provides some explanations for this state of affairs. Dr Windholz traces the evolution of German and Australian media law and the economic, social and political forces that have shaped it. Dr Windholz concludes that despite the differences between the countries – in particular Germany's constitutionally guaranteed communication freedoms and the quasi-legislative role played by the German Constitutional Court – two important similarities appear to have held sway: the power of private broadcasters and the role of politics. A common challenge in both countries is that politicians are both the prime target of media scrutiny and also in charge of setting the rules, along with the often close informal connexions between the rule-setters and those subject to the rules. Dr Windholz concludes that, in both countries, the vested interests of media owners have influenced the design of regulatory regimes favourable to their interests, thereby potentially undermining attempts to enforce media diversity and the social and democratic values that lie behind it.

Politics and the role of constitutional principles in this field also are themes of Professor Greg Taylor's examination of how political appointments to the boards of public broadcasters can undermine their independence and threaten the diversity of news and opinion they bring to public and political debates. Professor Taylor observes that while there would appear to be some truth in the somewhat shopworn and superficial idea that civil-law systems proceed by positing all-encompassing theories and engaging in top-down reasoning from them, unlike the methodology of common-law countries,[2] both systems operate in environments in which there are societal and political pressures that tend to distort even the finest set of principles. Accordingly the constitutional principles in Germany which call for diversity even within one public broadcaster as part of the state's positive duty to promote the freedom of the media do not have the salutary effect that an Australian unacquainted with the practical realities might hope for: in Germany too, party politics and the need for efficiency as well as diversity in the running of public broadcasters combine to render the situation roughly comparable with that in Australia, in which no such fine constitutional principles apply.

Another similarity found amongst the contributions to this volume is the conclusion that both countries' media laws have failed to prevent a concentration of media ownership, and have failed to keep pace with changing technology. The need for reform permeates the pages. Dr Duns in his chapter explores whether the solution lies in leaving the promotion of media diversity solely to competition law, and whether competition law could be adjusted in some fashion to be effective in this role. Dr Duns concludes that while there is some merit in this proposal, on balance it is not one that should be pursued – a conclusion also reached by Professor Gounalakis and Dr Rößß, Professor Kling and Dr Rodrick in their chapters. Rather, these authors make a number of interesting and insightful suggestions for how media diversity laws might be reformed. Of these, Dr Rodrick's call for 'root and branch' reform of Australia's media laws is arguably the most adventurous.

Looming over all this is a factor of great importance for both countries, as everywhere in the world: the rise of the Internet. Internet-based technologies have fundamentally changed the media landscape. They also have revealed that core concepts underpinning the prevailing legal regime – "media" and "diversity" – individually and combined – are complex, contested and ever changing. It seems obvious that media diversity is a good thing, but in order to understand the concept and its potential and limitations it is essential to work out what exactly is meant by diversity. It is diversity of ownership, opinion or programming? And has the internet increased media diversity? It is certainly true that there have been a few successes in electronic-only media as a result of the Internet: "In Daily" is one

2 The reference here is to statements such as : '[t]o the lawyer whose mind has been moulded by civilian influences, the theory may come first, and the source of the theory may be the writings of jurists not the decisions of Judges. However, that is not the way in which a system based on case law develops; over time, general principle is derived from judicial decisions upon particular instances, not the other way around' : *Roxborough* v. *Rothmans of Pall Mall* (2001) 208 CLR 516, 544.

example in Australia. But aside from such outstanding exceptions, the Internet has not yet reached its full potential. Many well-patronised websites belong to existing media proprietors, while others struggle to have their voices heard above the clamour of opinion. All this makes reaching agreement on what is diversity, and then measuring it, increasingly problematic, an issue explored in a number of chapters. The lack of agreement on these issues risks making diversity, as a legislative goal, an elusive and contested concept.

So quickly has technology moved that there is no longer agreement as to what constitutes "media". There has been an explosion in the number of possibilities for expressing one's own opinion. Moreover, news and current affairs are no longer simply broadcast or published to a passive public. Increasingly they sit on the Internet waiting to be found by people employing private search engines, and who are increasingly being asked to pay for it. To what extent does the challenge this poses to traditional media (print, radio and television) require re-thinking of the Australian and German approaches to media diversity? At present, any answers to these questions can be only preliminary as the potential of the Internet is still unfolding – but it is nevertheless a field in which thoughtful comparison from various angles is very fruitful, as Romy Nicole Fleischer's essay examining the application of EU anti-trust law to online search engines amply demonstrates. This theme also is picked up by Professor Justin Malbon who examines the impact of discriminatory geo-pricing (also known as differential or dynamic pricing) of digital media products on the consumers of those products (and the diversity of media they choose to consume), and asks the question what, if anything, policy makers, legislators and regulators should do about it. Ms Fleischer's and Professor Malbon's chapters also bring into focus the great power the new media landscape has placed in the hands of the intermediaries that provide the tools for searching and finding content, but whose potential to impact upon media diversity remains largely unregulated.

The rise of the internet also emphasises both the convergence of traditional and new media, and the significant differences that exist among them. This arguably is most pronounced in the realm of traditional newspapers, as revealed by Professor Kling's detailed and informative analysis of EU, German and Australian legislation and case law on merger control in the print media sector. Professor Kling's examination reveals the outcome of individual merger investigations in Germany is sometimes different from the outcome in Australia, even though the legislation and cases seem at first sight to be quite similar. Professor Kling insightfully explains that the reason for this is to be found in the facts, not the law. For historical, economic and social reasons, Germany's local and regional media has flourished and been protected in a manner that Australia's has not. The geographical vastness of Australia combined with its small population and high population concentration mean that the network of local newspapers that characterises Germany to this day has, in Australia, been largely absent for many decades. Moreover, German regionalism has survived in most fields of social life. As Professor Kling points out, Germany is a 'country of regions'; Australia is much less regionally diverse. Thus there are several cities of a million or more people in Australia in which only one locally printed newspaper circulates. Similar factors also have limited the variety of television and radio services that can be provided.

Finally, a note should be added about the different writing and citation styles evident in this collection. In a book dealing with two legal systems written by authors from two different legal cultures, it is inevitable that there will be a diversity of styles. This is not at all a matter for regret, however. First, it is something that arises naturally in comparative law; some lack of uniformity is inevitable. Second, it is something that ought to be celebrated in a book about the value of diversity, and the need to protect and promote it. As a result, the decision was taken not to insist on any great degree of uniformity in writing and citation styles among the authors. Little if anything would be achieved, and something of value may have been lost, by doing so.

The editors wish to make special mention of Christian Sunke, who very ably and efficiently assisted with the preparation of the manuscript for publication.

Greg Taylor and *Eric Windholz*
Marburg and Melbourne, January 2016

Contents

Georgios Gounalakis & Simon Rößl[1]

Cross media ownership:

A comparison of the legal framework of Australia and Germany

1 Professor Dr. Georgios Gounalakis holds a chair and is head of an institute conducting research in the fields media law, international private law, comparative law and private law at the Marburg Law School of the Philipps-University Marburg in Germany. He is also an expert working for the commission evaluating the permissibility of mergers in the media sector ("Kommission zur Ermittlung der Konzentration im Medienbereich"). Dr. Rößl works as a law tutor and research fellow at the above mentioned institute.

Abstract: Australian and German media concentration laws display an astonishing degree of structural conformity despite being based on quite different historical backgrounds. The following essay compares their approaches regarding the prevention of predominant media power and elaborates necessary improvements in order to prepare media concentration laws for present and future challenges.

The essay compares the legal framework of Australia and Germany with a particular focus on cross media ownership because this type of economic concentration can lead to an especially worrying influence on public opinion. Therefore, it is necessary to limit the extent of cross media ownership by both competition law and specific media regulation.

A. Types of concentration

It is important to understand the economic background of media concentration in order to assess the effectiveness of the current legal framework. Private broadcasting companies are commercial enterprises that are subjected to market forces and, consequently, strive for a dominant market position. They can achieve this goal both by growing faster than their competitors (internal growth) or by merging with other enterprises (external growth).[2] Mergers can lead to horizontal, vertical and conglomerate cross-media concentration – the entire development being supported by the convergence of media.

2 *Müller*, Konzentrationskontrolle zur Sicherung der Informationsfreiheit (2004), p 150.

I. Horizontal concentration

Horizontal concentration entails merging of companies belonging to the same stage of production, for example, combinations of two broadcasting companies, or two newspaper publishers. These enterprises benefit from economies of scale and decreasing contact costs. Economies of scale concern rationalisation effects in the area of acquisition, production, distribution and financing. A peculiarity of the broadcasting sector is that the costs of production and broadcasting remain the same no matter how large the audience is. The unit cost advantage increases significantly with the audience reach.[3] Furthermore, the advertising industry focuses on the audience rate when allocating advertisement slots. Therefore, an increase in the audience rate – while keeping production costs stable – does not only lower the expenses per recipient, but also augments the advertising revenues. This phenomenon fosters large broadcasting groups. The flipside is high barriers for new entrants that are less attractive for advertising clients due to their lower audience reach.[4] Finally, we have to address the impacts of horizontal concentration on media pluralism. Groups of channels can use contents multiple times, and the audience might subjectively perceive a variety of information, although being presented with the same information though different outlets. A few or even one media group would then be in the position of dominating public opinion.[5]

II. Vertical concentration

Vertical concentration involves merging of media companies belonging to the upstream or downstream production stage. The production stage includes, for example, production of movies or documentaries, broadcasting through free- and pay-TV, publishing newspapers, maintaining websites, and technical infrastructure. Media companies can save high transaction costs comprising, among other things, expenditures for research, contract formation and the dealer's margin.[6] Additionally, vertical integration can lower marketing risks, which are quite significant because the marketing of products is characterised by great uncertainty

---

3 *Gounalakis/Zagouras*, Medienkonzentrationsrecht (2008), p 195; *Heinrich*, Medienökonomie, Band 2: Hörfunk und Fernsehen (2002), p 241.

4 *Janik*, AfP 2002, p 104 (107); *Helwig*, Die Kompetenz der Europäischen Gemeinschaft zur Schaffung eines Europäischen Medienkonzentrationsrechts (2009), pp 24, 26–28; *Müller*, Konzentrationskontrolle, p 152; *Heinrich*, Medienökonomie, p 241.

5 *Helwig*, Europäisches Medienkonzentrationsrecht, p 32; *Trafkowski*, Medienkartellrecht (2002), pp 12–13.

6 *Heinrich*, Medienökonomie, pp 245–246; *Janik*, AfP 2002, p 104 (108).

about consumers' preferences. This makes it very difficult to assess whether a purchased Hollywood movie or a self-produced TV show will be more successful. The success of a broadcaster highly depends on attractive, but also extremely expensive, media content. Hence engaging in the trade of programme rights as well as in movie production can provide a significant competitive advantage.[7]

The main concern regarding vertical concentration is the control of distribution channels. A media entity that integrated a large part of the supply chain not only possesses market power, but also a dominant influence on public opinion. Special risks for media pluralism emerge in the case that a company also controls the infrastructure for the distribution of media content, since it can both prefer its own productions and exclude other broadcasters. This control constitutes a gate-keeper position.[8]

III. Cross-media concentration

Cross-media concentration describes the cooperation of enterprises being part of different types of media, for example, a newspaper publisher purchasing a TV channel. Again these companies profit from multiple usages of information and from a competitive advantage in the advertising market, especially by offering combined rates for cross-media advertisements. These enterprises also have the options of advertising their own products through different media and of internal cross-subsidising of unprofitable media sectors.[9]

The downsides of such a strong market position for the diversity of opinions are quite obvious. First, the range of opinions will be reduced in the long term because of the elimination of small, independent undertakings and because of higher entry barriers for new entrants.[10] Secondly, conglomerate concentration promotes homogeneous reporting and a decrease of intermedia criticism, additionally enabling the merged companies to report negatively about competitors in

7 *Müller*, Konzentrationskontrolle, pp 153–154.

8 *Gounalakis*, AfP 2004, p 394; *Janik*, AfP 2002, p 104 (108); *Helwig*, Europäisches Medienkonzentrationsrecht, pp 32–33.

9 *Müller*, Konzentrationskontrolle, pp 154–155; *Janik*, AfP 2002, p 104 (108); *Helwig*, Europäisches Medienkonzentrationsrecht, pp 29–30, 33–35; *Gounalakis/Zagouras*, Medienkonzentrationsrecht, pp 196–197.

10 *Kübler*, Medienverflechtung (1982), pp 96–99; *Janik*, AfP 2002, p 104 (109).

a subtle way.[11] What is more, the audience often does not recognise this interaction, thus attributing a higher credibility to information being reported several times.[12]

IV. The impact of media convergence

All these effects are reinforced by the convergence of media, meaning the approximation of different types of media especially due to digitisation.[13] There is, first, technical convergence and, secondly, content-related convergence. Technical convergence is characterised by a convergence of distribution channels enabling, for instance, the transmission of information for TV, radio, and internet by the same cable network.[14] In addition, the former separation of devices has become obsolete, since computers can nowadays be used to watch TV programmes and TVs are able to connected directly to the internet. Technical convergence also facilitates the convergence of contents because the same piece of information can be used multiple times in several different media at no great expense – for example, by marketing a weather forecast in a newspaper, on the radio, TV, and the internet. This can optimise the marketing chain, but also lead to homogeneous media coverage.[15]

B. Provisions against media concentration

The risks associated with media concentration are twofold: economic power and a prevalent influence on public opinion. Accordingly, both Germany and Australia have implemented two legal regimes addressing these concerns. On the one hand, special broadcasting regulations restrict links between different media companies. On the other hand, general competition laws focus on the economic aspects of mergers.

---

11 *Mailänder*, Konzentrationskontrolle zur Sicherung von Meinungsvielfalt im privaten Rundfunk (2000), pp 184–185; *Bender*, Cross-Media-Ownership (1997), pp 79–80; *Janik*, AfP 2002, pp 104 (108–109).

12 *Renck-Laufke*, ZUM 2000, p 369 (374); *Helwig*, Europäisches Medienkonzentrationsrecht, pp 33–34.

13 *Gounalakis*, Konvergenz der Medien (2002), p 12.

14 *Rossen-Stadtfeld*, ZUM 2000, p 36 (37); *Zagouras*, Konvergenz und Kartellrecht (2002), pp 9–10.

15 *Helwig*, Europäisches Medienkonzentrationsrecht, pp 37–38; *Zagouras*, Konvergenz und Kartellrecht, pp 11–12.

I. Australia

Publications regarding German media law regularly start by highlighting the particular constitutional role and protection of the press and the broadcasters. The German parliament is obliged by the constitution to provide a legal framework that guarantees media diversity. On the contrary, most of the Australian articles focus primarily on ordinary laws. The Australian Constitution does not contain an explicit constitutional right for newspaper publishers and broadcasting companies and hence no constitutional foundation for media concentration provisions.[16] Instead the High Court has recognised the existence of an implied freedom of political communication forming an important part of the representative democracy.[17] Yet it only encompasses a freedom from government restraint without directly conferring a right on individuals.[18] The decisive question is whether this different starting point of Australian and German media law also results in a different level of protection against media concentration, which will be recognisable towards the end of this essay.

Australia subjects its media entities both to a sector-specific legal framework (*Broadcasting Services Act* 1992 = BSA) and to the general competition law provisions (Australian *Competition and Consumer Act* 2010 = CCA). The CCA provides restrictions on media companies that are not covered by the BSA print media.[19] Apart from that, the spheres of application of the BSA and the CCA overlap, raising the question about the relationship between these legal regimes. According to s 77 of the BSA its ownership and control provisions "have effect notwithstanding the *Competition and Consumer Act* 2010". The Federal Court interpreted this section as subjecting media transactions to both legal systems;[20] in other words, a merger might comply with the CCA but violate the BSA. Moreover, the CCA applies to the print media for which no specific diversity provisions exist.[21] The following paragraphs outline the specific prerequisites of the BSA before turning

---

16 *Sawer/Abjorensen/Larkin*, Australia: The state of democracy (2009), pp 208–209; *Leonard*, Making Converged Regulation Possible, Communications Law Bulletin Vol. 31.2 (June 2012), Convergence Review Special Edition, p 1. This author criticises the lack of a broader constitutional guarantee.

17 *Nationwide News Pty Ltd v Wills* (1992) 177 CLR 1; *Australian Capital Television Pty Ltd v the Commonwealth* (1992) 177 CLR 106; *McCloy v New South Wales* [2015] HCA 34, [30].

18 *Lange v Australian Broadcasting Corporation* (1997) 189 CLR 520.

19 *Butler/Rodrick/McNamara/Fitzgerald*, Australian Media Law (2012), p 895.

20 *Austereo Ltd v Trade Practices Commission* (1993) 41 FCR 1.

21 *Butler/Rodrick/McNamara/Fitzgerald*, Australian Media Law, p 896.

to the more general competition rules. Finally, Australian restrictions on foreign investments are addressed.

1. *Broadcasting Services Act*

a) *Substantive law*

The following chapter will provide an overview of the Australian media concentration provisions. All of them try to address the control which one media entity exercises over another, which is why the term "control" gains a key role. Therefore, the concept of control will be explained first, before this essay looks at the prohibited control-based connections between different media companies.

aa) The concept of control

"Control" is the decisive prerequisite triggering the below mentioned restrictions on media mergers; the Australian Communications and Media Authority (ACMA) is in charge of making this assessment. S 6(1) of the BSA basically defines control as being the result of trusts, agreements, arrangements, understandings and practices, whether or not having legal or equitable force and whether or not based on legal or equitable rights. This definition focuses on the manner in which control is obtained. The content of control is outlined by Schedule 1 of the BSA.[22] However, the ways in which control can emerge are so diverse that an exhaustive definition cannot realistically be formulated. A flexible understanding of control better reflects reality.[23] According to the Federal Court the term "control" refers to the power to direct or restrain what a company may do on any substantial issue. Consequently, even a veto power can be sufficient.[24] A very important practical tool for assessing the existence of control is the assumption contained in Part 3 of Schedule 1 of the BSA. Accordingly, a person is deemed to be in a position to exercise control over a company if his company interests exceed 15%.[25] A company interest can, for example, relate to shareholdings, voting rights, dividends and the later winding-up of a company. Each of these interests is explained in s 8 of the BSA. What makes it even more difficult to appraise the control of a company is

---

22 *Butler/Rodrick/McNamara/Fitzgerald*, Australian Media Law, p 882.

23 Explanatory Memorandum to the Broadcasting Services Bill 1992, Part 5 – Control of commercial broadcasting licences, available on https://www.comlaw.gov.au/Details/C2004B01820/Explanatory%20 Memorandum/Text.

24 *CanWest Global Communications Corporation v Australian Broadcasting Authority* (1998) 153 ALR 47 at 77, 82.

25 *Rolph/Vitins/Bannister*, Media Law: Cases, Materials and Commentary (2010), p 137.

the fact that other companies can be used as an intermediary. Therefore, Part 4 of Schedule 1 provides a method for tracing company interests through a chain of companies, the so-called fractional tracing method. It basically multiplies the interests a person has in several companies. If a person has a company interest to the extent of 30% in company A and company A again has an interest in the amount of 10% in company B (the target company), then the fractional tracing method suggests multiplying 3/10 and 1/10, thus resulting in a 3%-interest of that person in the target company B. However, this method leads to outcomes that do not sufficiently reflect reality. For example, Part 4 of Schedule 1 assigns a company interest of 8% to a person having a company interest of 80% in undertaking A, which again possesses an interest of 10% in the target company B. This figure is too low given the fact that the person in question can fully control the first company A with an interest of 80% and is able to fully exercise his 10% interest in the target company B. The fractional tracing method should grade the different interests instead of applying a schematic formula. If a company interest exceeds 50%, then there should be an assumption of a 100% interest in this very company. This would also reduce the contrast between Part 3 and Part 4 of Schedule 1 caused by the above-mentioned assumption in Part 3 of Schedule 1 according to which a company interest of 15% is enough to control a company.

bb) Horizontal concentration

Mergers of television companies are confined by s 53(2) of the BSA, which limits a television broadcasting company to one television licence per licence area. The licence areas are defined by the ACMA. Furthermore, s 53(1) of the BSA provides an audience reach restriction by prohibiting a person from exercising control of commercial television broadcasting licences across the country that reach more than 75% of the Australian population. However, the allocation of licence areas seems outdated nowadays because broadcasts can also be received via the internet which does not face the same geographical restraints as traditional transmission technologies.[26]

Horizontal mergers of radio broadcasting companies are similarly restricted. Pursuant to s 54 of the BSA, a person is not allowed to exercise control of more than two commercial radio broadcasting licences in the same licence area. This provision tries to strike a balance between the necessity of economies of scale and the prevention of an undesirable concentration of ownership. In contrast

26 *Butler/Rodrick/McNamara/Fitzgerald*, Australian Media Law, pp 872–873.

to commercial television, the BSA does not impose an audience reach limit on radio broadcasters.[27]

There is no specific piece of legislation restricting mergers between publishers in order to guarantee the diversity of the Australian press. Yet those undertakings have to comply with the requirements of competition law[28], which will be addressed later.

cc) Cross-media concentration

The reform of the BSA in 2006 significantly changed the legal framework for cross-media ownerships. Before this amendment a media company was limited to one type of media; in other words, a television broadcasting company was not allowed to acquire a radio broadcaster or newspaper publisher, if the radio broadcaster's licence area or newspaper's primary circulation was within the television broadcaster's licenced service area.[29] This restriction was relaxed and nowadays there are two safeguards against cross-media concentration: a prohibition of transactions leading to an "unacceptable media diversity situation"[30] or to an "unacceptable three-way control"[31].

(1) Unacceptable media diversity situation

The requirements of an unacceptable media diversity situation depend on whether the affected licence area is a metropolitan or a regional one. Mainly State capital cities qualify as metropolitan licence areas, whereas the remaining licence areas fall within the second category. The relevant licence areas are those of commercial radio because they better reflect the likely influence of a given media company on public opinion than the quite large and geographically diverse television licence areas.[32] If a merger is about to occur on a national scale, the parties have to analyse the impact on each affected radio licence area.[33] An unacceptable media diversity situation regarding a metropolitan radio licence area requires that the number of "points" in the licence area is less than five, while this threshold is reduced to four

---

27 *Rolph/Vitins/Bannister*, Media Law, p 134; *Butler/Rodrick/McNamara/Fitzgerald*, Australian Media Law, pp 874–875.

28 *Butler/Rodrick/McNamara/Fitzgerald*, Australian Media Law, p 896.

29 *Rolph/Vitins/Bannister*, Media Law, pp 127–130.

30 S 61AB of the BSA.

31 S 61AEA of the BSA.

32 *Butler/Rodrick/McNamara/Fitzgerald*, Australian Media Law, p 876.

33 *Butler/Rodrick/McNamara/Fitzgerald*, Australian Media Law, p 878.

"points" regarding regional licence areas.[34] This test is therefore often referred to as the 5/4 rule. A point represents an independent media "voice" in a given licence area which could consist of an independently controlled commercial television or radio broadcasting licensee or of a newspaper *associated* to the relevant licence area. A newspaper is associated with a certain licence area if at least 50% of its circulation takes place within this very area. Consequently, national newspapers are not included in the diversity test despite their large circulation, since their circulation is not specifically associated with any licence area.[35] However, subscription licensees, magazines and online content do not count as a "voice" for the purpose of this test. S 61AC of the BSA and its table specify what qualifies as a point.[36] If e.g. one media company exercises control over another, then the BSA allocates only one point to both media operations.[37] The ACMA maintains a Register of Controlled Media Groups presenting the ownership and control of media groups in each licence area in order to enable compliance with the cross-media ownership restrictions.[38] However, this register does not constitute an accurate list of the total number of points in a licence area, since its focus is on controlled media groups without mentioning independent media groups. If a prospective buyer wants to obtain further information, he has to consult the Media Control Database displaying all – controlled and independent – media operations in each commercial radio licence area. This database also contains an estimate of the total number of points in each licence area.[39]

The Australian ownership regulations have three major downsides: First, all media operators are treated as equally influential despite significant differences. A media group owing a daily newspaper, a television and two radio stations in a licence area accounts for only one point just like a radio station with a small listening audience. In addition, the legal framework does not take into account whether a certain media outlet provides information of public concern or just aims at entertaining its audience.[40] The Government actually considered a qualitative test weighing the impact of a merger on the "news culture". Yet this approach faced the difficulty that there are no objective methods for measuring media diversity,

34 S 61AB of the BSA.

35 *Butler/Rodrick/McNamara/Fitzgerald*, Australian Media Law, p 880.

36 *Rolph/Vitins/Bannister*, Media Law, p 133.

37 Item 1 of the table within the BSA.

38 *McGill*, (2007) 30 UNSW Law Journal 280, 281, 283; *Butler/Rodrick/McNamara/Fitzgerald*, Australian Media Law, p 876.

39 *Butler/Rodrick/McNamara/Fitzgerald*, Australian Media Law, p 877.

40 *Butler/Rodrick/McNamara/Fitzgerald*, Australian Media Law, p 878.

thus resulting in legal uncertainty about the potential outcome of the analysis.[41] Secondly, the cross-media provisions do not cover all relevant media. Among print media the BSA only takes into account newspapers in English that are published at least four days a week. Moreover, a newspaper must be associated with a certain licence area and at least 50% of the circulation of a newspaper must be by way of sale. Hence, national and freely distributed newspapers and magazines are not captured by the cross-media ownership rules.[42] This is quite precarious, since especially national newspapers and political magazines have a major influence on shaping people's opinion. The same is true for freely available newspapers because of their potential to reach a large audience.[43] Further on, subscription broadcasting and online services are not included in the cross-media ownership test either, clearly showing that the reform in 2006 did not manage to prepare the diversity test for current and future challenges caused by the increasing social and political interaction via online platforms.[44] Thirdly, choosing radio licence areas as a benchmark for the diversity provisions seems even more outdated because the programme of radio and TV broadcasters is available nationwide via the internet.[45]

(2) Unacceptable three-way control

The above-mentioned test is supplemented by the prohibition of the combined ownership of three types of media in a radio licence area. An unacceptable three-way control situation exists if a person has control of (a) a commercial television broadcasting licence significantly overlapping with the relevant radio licence area, (b) a commercial radio broadcasting licence and (c) a newspaper associated with the relevant radio broadcasting licence area.[46] This restriction displays similar shortcomings as the 5/4 rule by not taking into account national and freely available newspapers or magazines.[47] It cannot prevent a media group from obtaining a television broadcasting licence in Australia's major licence areas enabling it to reach 75% of the population, and from controlling two radio licences in every

---

41 Explanatory Memorandum to the Broadcasting Services Amendment (Media Ownership) Bill 2006, pp 21–22.

42 *Butler/Rodrick/McNamara/Fitzgerald*, Australian Media Law, p 878; *Rolph/Vitins/Bannister*, Media Law, p 133.

43 Also critical: *Butler/Rodrick/McNamara/Fitzgerald*, Australian Media Law, p 879.

44 *Butler/Rodrick/McNamara/Fitzgerald*, Australian Media Law, p 878.

45 Similar criticism: ACMA, Broken concepts: The Australian communications legislative landscape (2011), p 23.

46 S 61AEA of the BSA.

47 *Butler/Rodrick/McNamara/Fitzgerald*, Australian Media Law (2012), pp 879–880.

radio broadcasting licence area (no 75% limit) in combination with a national newspaper. The current legal safeguards are clearly insufficient and do not avert a further increase of the already very advanced media concentration.

(3) Disclosure of cross-media links

Media entities are not only subjected to restrictions in terms of cross-media ownerships, but also to certain disclosure duties after the implementation of such connections. Television and radio broadcasters as well as newspaper publishers are obliged to disclose the existence of cross-media relationships when they report about the business affairs of a cross-controlled media company. This is called the "business affairs disclosure method". Radio broadcasters have a choice: They can either opt for the business disclosure method or for the "regular disclosure method". The latter requires them to regularly broadcast a statement describing the cross-media relationship.[48] The statement has to be mentioned in a way that brings the relationship to the attention of a reasonable person.[49] This requirement means for radio broadcasters that they have to indicate the cross-media relationship during prime-time hours if they choose the regular disclosure method.[50] A newspaper has to mention this connection within the same edition.[51] It is important to point out that for broadcasters compliance with the disclosure obligation constitutes a licence condition, and for newspapers an infringement amounts to a criminal offence.[52] This duty of disclosure is a very positive instrument for counteracting one of the risks assigned to cross-media ownerships: a homogeneous reporting of news by the same media group through different outlets (e.g. TV and newspaper) that could be perceived as very trustworthy by the audience. However, it is less effective than it might seem at first sight, as the key requirement triggering the business disclosure method is quite vague. Pursuant to s 61BH(1) of the BSA matter or material that is about the business affairs of a cross-controlled media entity includes a reference to matter or material, where it would be reasonable to conclude that the object, or one of the objects, of the matter or the publication of the material was to promote or otherwise influence members of the public to view, listen or read that matter. When making this assessment regard is to be made to the nature of the matter or material and the way in which it is presented.

48 S 61BE(2) of the BSA.
49 Ss 61BB(6), 61BE(6), 61BF(6).
50 S 61BE(6) of the BSA.
51 S 61BF(2) of the BSA.
52 S 61BF(8) of the BSA.

dd) Vertical concentration

There are no specific provisions in the BSA addressing vertical concentration. This problem is left entirely to the competition authority.

b) Enforcement

The ACMA is vested with the powers of enforcing the ownership and control rules. Media companies are obliged to provide the ACMA with information regarding the control of media assets and directorships pursuant to ss 62 to 65B of the BSA. These notification duties are supposed to guarantee that the ACMA obtains the relevant information. An infringement of these requirements can result in substantial pecuniary fines.[53] If an envisaged transaction infringes one of the above-mentioned impermissible media concentration provisions, the concerned person can apply to the ACMA for a temporary approval of this breach. An approval may be granted if the ACMA is satisfied that the infringement is incidental to the objectives of the transaction which is the case if it is a subsidiary and relatively immaterial element of the overall transaction.[54] In addition, the applicant has to ensure that the breach ceases after a specified time. Undertakings by the applicant can be enforced in the Federal Court, e.g. by issuing a payment order in favour of the ACMA.[55] If the ACMA finds out about an intended unlawful transaction before its completion, it can seek an injunction from the Federal Court to stop the transaction.[56] A person, who actually manages to complete a transaction, without having obtained a prior approval of the infringement, commits an offence. The ACMA then has the discretion to issue a notice requiring the affected person to remedy this breach. Provided that the breach persists, the offender can be prosecuted.[57]

2. Competition and Consumer Act

a) Substantive law

As mentioned earlier in this chapter the CCA has a broader sphere of application than the BSA in that it restricts the mergers of subscription television and radio broadcasting companies and of newspaper publishers. The key provision is s 50 of the CCA prohibiting the acquisition of shares or assets by a corporation or a

---

53 *Butler/Rodrick/McNamara/Fitzgerald*, Australian Media Law, p 893.

54 *McGill*, (2007) 30 UNSW Law Journal 280, 286.

55 *Butler/Rodrick/McNamara/Fitzgerald*, Australian Media Law, p 890.

56 S 205Q of the BSA.

57 *Butler/Rodrick/McNamara/Fitzgerald*, Australian Media Law, pp 891–892.

person if this would have the effect, or be likely to have the effect, of substantially lessening competition in a market.[58] Pursuant to s 4E of the CCA the term "market" refers a market in Australia and, when used in relation to any goods or services, includes a market for those goods or services and other goods or services which are substitutable for, or otherwise competitive with, the first-mentioned goods or services. The market concept basically subdivides into the product and geographic market. Both categories aim at delimiting the products that effectively compete with each other. The product market is mainly defined by the properties of a product determining which products might be regarded as interchangeable by the consumer. The geographic market delineates the area in which competition of these interchangeable products takes place.[59] The Australian Competition and Consumer Commission (ACCC)[60] deploys the SSNIP-test for defining the relevant market. This test is based on the hypothetical scenario that a producer imposes a *small* but *significant* and *non-transitory increase* in *price* on a product (A). If enough customers then switch to a different product (B) and make the price rise unprofitable, both products are regarded as interchangeable and belong to the same market. Conversely, if the producer retains a significant amount of its customers and the price rise proves to be profitable, product A already constitutes the relevant market.[61] After having defined the relevant market the Australian Competition and Consumer Commission (ACCC) has to analyse whether the merger will substantially lessen competition within that market. S 50(3) of the CCA provides a non-exhaustive list of assessment criteria such as barriers to entry, the level of concentration, countervailing buyer power and the extent of vertical integration.

The definition of the relevant market has proved crucial for the admissibility of an intended merger.[62] The accurate market delineation decides whether the

58 *Griggs/Duke/Nielsen/Cejnar*, Competition Law in Australia (2012), p 120.

59 Market definitions highlighting the criterion of substitution were used in the following cases: *Queensland Co-operative Milling Association Ltd/Defiance Holdings Ltd, Re Proposed Merger with Barnes Milling Ltd (1976) ATPR 40–012*; for a more general explanation of the concept of the relevant market: *Griggs/Duke/Nielsen/Cejnar*, Competition Law in Australia, pp 42–43; *Butler/Rodrick/McNamara/Fitzgerald*, Australian Media Law, p 896. These books also mention the criteria "function" and "time" which are less relevant for our analysis.

60 More information about the ACCC can be found in: *Griggs/Duke/Nielsen/Cejnar*, Competition Law in Australia, p 52.

61 ACCC, Merger Guidelines (2008), pp 17–18; also see: *Griggs/Duke/Nielsen/Cejnar*, Competition Law in Australia, p 126.

62 The importance of market definition was highlighted in *Queensland Wire Industries v. Broken Hill Proprietary* (1989) 167 CLR 177, 188.

competition rules will effectively prevent an increasing concentration in the media market.[63] There has been a significant shift in the ACCC's attitude regarding market definition. Until 2006 it viewed television, radio, newspapers and online media as distinct product markets. This had the negative side-effect that competition law played a minor part in securing diversity in terms of cross-media ownership.[64] But also diversity on a horizontal level was not sufficiently protected by the competition provisions, as the example of the newspaper market reveals. The ACCC focused on the geographic coverage of newspapers and limited the market for capital city daily newspapers to their metropolitan territories. As a consequence, newspapers published in different cities would likely belong to separate markets despite potentially sharing a considerable amount of common content.[65] What is more, even if the geographic reach of newspapers significantly overlaps, their different content (e.g. local versus national focus) can cause their allocation to separate markets. Therefore, the ACCC was not able to obviate a high concentration of Australia's print media.[66] The ACCC adjusted its practice for cross-media ownerships. In its paper "Media Mergers" it admits that due to the convergence of media the different forms of media cannot be regarded as belonging to different markets anymore. The focus is more on the actual product, e.g. advertising slots and content, instead of distribution channels. Products can be offered across several delivery platforms. Nowadays the ACCC differentiates among the supply of advertising possibilities, the supply of content to consumers and the acquisition of content from content providers.[67] However, one issue is still not entirely settled: the importance of non-economic aspects. Is the ACCC entitled to take into account how a merger will impact on media diversity? S 50 of the CCA focuses on economic criteria and does not contain public interest criteria which could operate as a means of considering social, cultural and political consequences of mergers. The ACCC has declared that it will factor in repercussions on media diversity[68] - even though the Explanatory Memorandum to the BSA indicates otherwise[69].

---

63 *Butler/Rodrick/McNamara/Fitzgerald*, Australian Media Law, p 899.

64 *Butler/Rodrick/McNamara/Fitzgerald*, Australian Media Law, p 899.

65 House of Representatives Select Committee on the Print Media, Parliament of Australia, News and Fair Facts: The Australian Print Media Industry (1992), para 4.18.

66 *Butler/Rodrick/McNamara/Fitzgerald*, Australian Media Law, p 900.

67 ACCC, Media Mergers (2006), para 21.

68 ACCC, Media Mergers (2006), para 12.

69 Explanatory Memorandum to the Broadcasting Services (Media Ownership) Amendment Bill 2006 (Cth), p 10, para 34; available on: http://parlinfo.aph.gov.au/parlInfo/

b) Enforcement

Although there is no need for a prior approval of a merger, it is recommendable to contact the ACCC in advance to find out whether the merger faces any objections, since the ACCC can bring a court action challenging a merger, and a violation of competition provisions may have severe consequences.[70] There are three different ways to (partially) ensure that a merger will not be challenged afterwards: informal reviews, formal clearances and authorisations.[71] An informal review provides the parties to a merger with an estimate by the ACCC of whether the merger in question might breach s 50 of the CCA. However, even if the ACCC does not articulate any concerns during the informal review, this prevents neither the ACCC nor third parties from taking legal actions later, although the informal procedure does provide some assurance that it is unlikely that the transaction might be challenged by the ACCC. If the ACCC finds for an infringement, the parties can offer enforceable undertakings to the ACCC in order to alleviate its concerns. More legal certainty can be gained by applying for a formal merger clearance. In the event of a successful outcome neither the ACCC nor third parties can take legal action against the merger as long as it is carried out in accordance with the clearance decision. The competition authority has 40 business days to make its decision. If it fails to comply with this time limit, the application is regarded as being refused. The parties to a merger can challenge a rejection or an imposed modification before the Australian Competition Tribunal. The third option consists of an application for a merger authorisation by the Australian Competition Tribunal. However, an authorisation – unlike a clearance – does not confirm the compliance with the s 50 of the CCA but represents an exemption from this provision based on public benefit grounds. The discretionary decision of the Competition Tribunal is not appealable.[72]

If an intended merger breaches competition provisions and the parties to the merger do not offer sufficient remedies, the ACCC can apply to the Federal Court for an injunction to stop the merger. Beyond that, the ACCC can request the

---

download/legislation/ems/s527_ems_e5dd9ce3-3335-4e59-9bd4-9fba85f050ef/upload_pdf/305117em.pdf;fileType=application%2Fpdf.

70 *Griggs/Duke/Nielsen/Cejnar*, Competition Law in Australia, p 122.

71 *Butler/Rodrick/McNamara/Fitzgerald*, Australian Media Law, p 897.

72 *Griggs/Duke/Nielsen/Cejnar*, Competition Law in Australia, pp 122–124; *Butler/Rodrick/McNamara/ Fitzgerald*, Australian Media Law, pp 897–899. The informal merger review is explained in details in the ACCC's Merger Review Process Guidelines of July 2006 which are available on https://www.accc.gov.au/ system/files/Merger%20Review%20Process%20Guideline%20July%202006.pdf.

divestiture of shares or assets or apply for penalties if the transaction has already been advanced.[73]

3. *Restrictions on foreign investments*

Foreign investments in television and subscription television broadcasting services, but not in the print media, were restricted until the implementation of the *Broadcasting Services Amendment (Media Ownership) Act* 2006. These restrictions were abolished and foreign investments in the media sector are now only subjected to the general foreign investment provisions comprising the *Foreign Acquisitions and Takeovers Act* 1975, *the Foreign Acquisitions and Takeovers Regulations* 1989 and the government's foreign investment policy.[74] In addition, US investors and broadcasting services providers benefit from the free trade agreement between Australia and the US, but are subjected to the Australian provisions in terms of the broadcasting sector.[75] Foreign investments in "sensitive sectors" require prior notification and approval by the Treasurer advised by the Foreign Investment Review Board. The media sector is considered "sensitive" and an investment in this sector must not conflict with "national interests". However, there are no hard and fast criteria for this assessment. Decisions are made on a case-by-case basis.[76] The Foreign Investment Review Board considers, among others, impacts on the national security, competition, the economy and on other Government policies (including taxation).[77] The national interest test proves to be of little relevance in reality, since only three out of 24,105 applications decided in the period 2013–2014 were rejected.[78] A rejection by the Treasurer can be challenged in the Federal Court, albeit the chances of such an appeal are questionable because of the discretionary nature of this assessment.[79] All in all, the restrictions on foreign investments regarding cross-media ownerships are of limited practical importance.

---

73 ACCC, Merger Review Process Guidelines, p 4, at para 3.5.

74 *Rolph/Vitins/Bannister*, Media Law, pp 156–157; *Butler/Rodrick/McNamara/Fitzgerald*, Australian Media Law, p 903.

75 Australia-United States Free Trade Agreement, p 48, available on http://www.sice.oas.org/TPD/USA_AUS/ Studies/AUSFTAguide_e.pdf.

76 *Rolph/Vitins/Bannister*, Media Law, pp 157–158.

77 Foreign Investment Review Board, Annual Report 2013–2014, p 21.

78 Foreign Investment Review Board, Annual Report 2013–2014, p 22.

79 *Butler/Rodrick/McNamara/Fitzgerald*, Australian Media Law, p 905.

II. Germany

Germany similarly has two legal frameworks for coping with media concentration: the Inter-State Broadcasting Agreement (Rundfunkstaatsvertrag, abbreviated as RStV) – pendant to the Australian *Broadcasting Services Act* – and the competition law which again splits up into German and European components. However, there is no a corresponding European Broadcasting Services Act, which is why mergers on a European scale lack an important regulatory instrument, a shortcoming that will be picked up again towards the end of this essay. As in Australia, there does not exist any special regulation only for press diversity. Restrictions on foreign investments in the media sector by member states of the European Union (EU) are not possible because they would thwart the EU's objective of an internal market without frontiers. Additionally, the EU member states' legislative power for restrictions regarding investors from non-European countries is limited pursuant to Articles 63 and 64(2) of the Treaty on the Functioning of the EU (TFEU).

1. *Inter-State Broadcasting Agreement*

First, we will explain the sector-specific requirements of mergers regarding media companies and, secondly, a case will illustrate their practical application.

a) *Abstract outline*

To understand German broadcasting provisions, their underlying constitutional principles and concerns it is important to unearth the historical background constituting the particular constitutional role of broadcasting companies. Broadcasters possess a particular role because they are considered very vulnerable to abuse after having been used for propaganda purposes during the Second World War.[80] The German Constitutional Court attributed fundamental significance to the freedom of broadcasting enshrined in Article 5 (1) of the German Constitution ("Grundgesetz").[81] In the middle of the 20th century the number of broadcasting companies was very small due to the high expenses for founding a broadcasting company. TV programmes, especially, were produced only by state funded corporations until the end of the 1970s. The German constitution and the Inter-State Broadcasting Agreement guarantee the independence of broadcasting companies

80 *Gounalakis/Zagouras*, Medienkonzentrationsrecht, pp 10–12, 49–50, 73–74.

81 BVerfGE 35, 202 (219); 117, 244 (258).

towards state authorities.[82] On the other hand, there are hardly any regulations for the press because there has always been a great number of competing newspaper publishers.[83]

The RStV is a legally binding inter-State agreement concluded between the sixteen states of Germany, and regulates broadcasts which are available nationwide.[84] A federal law on media diversity is not feasible at the moment because of a lack of federal legislative power.[85] On the contrary, broadcasting companies with a regional or local audience reach do not fall within the scope of the RStV, but are subjected to special state media laws.[86] The media diversity provisions within the RStV basically codify the case-law of the German Constitutional Court.[87] The final assessment whether a merger would result in an impermissible media concentration is taken by the "Kommission zur Ermittlung der Konzentration im Medienbereich" (abbreviated as KEK),[88] which can be regarded as an equivalent to the ACMA. Ss 25 ff. of the RStV focus on the commercial television sector and only take other types of media into account as far as they strengthen the influence on public opinion exercised by television broadcasts.[89] S 25(1) of the RStV lays down the general objective that commercial broadcasts should reflect the plurality of opinions. This is obtained by allowing the major political, ideological and social forces and groups an adequate opportunity for presenting their opinions. Minority opinions shall also be considered adequately. The core element is to prevent a single social group from misusing the power of television broadcasts for their own ends.[90]

The restrictions for ensuring the achievement of the above-mentioned goal is contained in s 26 of the RStV. S 26(1) of the RStV operates as a general provision

---

82 *Ricker/Schiwy*, Rundfunkverfassungsrecht (1997), pp 26–27, 37, 40–41; see also: *Helwig*, Europäisches Medienkonzentrationsrecht, pp 51–54.

83 *Gounalakis/Zagouras*, Medienkonzentrationsrecht, pp 50, 61.

84 S 26(1) of the RStV refers to nationwide available broadcasts.

85 BVerfGE 12, 205. More information about the failed attempt of the federal government to implement a federal law in the 1950s can be found in: *Ricker/Schiwy*, Rundfunkverfassungsrecht, pp 33–36.

86 See for example s 33(1) of the State Media Law ("Landesmediengesetz") of North Rhine/Westphalia. For further information on the delimitation of the RStV and the state media laws: *Hesse*, Rundfunkrecht (2003), p 246, and in general the whole chapter 5.

87 *Gounalakis/Zagouras*, Medienkonzentrationsrecht, p 73.

88 S 36(4)(1) of the RStV.

89 *Gounalakis/Zagouras*, ZUM 2006, 716 (719–720); *Gounalakis/Zagouras*, Medienkonzentrationsrecht, p 75.

90 BVerfGE 12, 205 (262); *Gounalakis/Zagouras*, Medienkonzentrationsrecht, p 77.

prohibiting a broadcasting company to achieve a prevalent influence on public opinion alone or in combination with other companies. Such a prevalent influence on public opinion is presumed according to s 26(2)(1) if a media company achieves an average audience rate of 30% or more during a year due to its TV programmes. Moreover, pursuant to s 26(2)(2) a dominant influence on public opinion is also assumed if a media enterprise exceeds an audience rate of 25%, provided that one of the following two conditions is met: Either this company possesses a dominant role in another media-related market, or its influence on public opinion is equivalent to the one of a company with a television audience reach of 30%. The latter assessment is based on an overall consideration of the company's activities regarding the television sector and media-related markets.

The audience reach limit in s 26(2)(1) RStV contains an absolute limit of media power regarding nation-wide available TV programmes and counteracts horizontal concentration.[91] The supplementary regulations in s 26(2)(2) RStV address the problems of vertical concentration and cross-media ownerships.[92]

b) *The failed merger of Springer and ProSiebenSat.1*

The failed merger of the newspaper publisher Axel Springer and the TV channels ProSiebenSat.1 in 2006 illustrates how s 26(2) operates and the mechanism used to assess cross-media ownerships. ProSiebenSat.1 possessed an audience share of about 22% which is neither enough to fulfil the thresholds of s 26(2)(1) – 30% – nor of s 26(2)(2) – 25%. The KEK based its rejecting decision on s 26(1), the general provision, by arguing that the influence of the merged entity on media-related markets would be strong enough to compensate for the low audience reach.[93] The KEK converted the merged company's bearing on media-related markets into a fictitious broadcasting audience rate by comparing the influence of a television broadcast on public opinion with the influence wielded, for example, by a newspaper. This very conversion is based on the criteria of suggestive power, actuality, and reach. Axel Springer published the newspaper "Bild" which, at that time, had a market share of 26%. The influence of the "Bild" on public opinion was converted into a fictitious television "audience" share of 17%. The suggestive power of newspapers and hence their influence on public opinion was considered less strong due to the fact that people are more influenced by motion pictures than

91 *Mestmäcker*, in: Immenga/Mestmäcker, Kommentar zum Gesetz gegen Wettbewerbsbeschränkungen (2001), Vor § 35 para 109.

92 *Trute*, in: Hahn/Vesting, Rundfunkrecht: Rundfunkstaatsvertrag (2012), § 26 para 49.

93 KEK, reference number: 293 – 1 bis 5, pp 84–87 – Axel Springer AG.

text.[94] The KEK also took into account that the Springer media group owned TV programme guides. Their influence on public opinion was considered to amount to 1/7 of that of a television broadcast. This assessment was based on the fact that magazines are less up-to-date and that their suggestive power is quite low. However, they can have a very large reach, and in addition are often read several times. TV guides have an appreciable influence on the programme selection, as they contain evaluations and offer the possibility of advertising certain channels.[95]

The KEK regarded the potential bearing of online activities on the public's attitude as half of that of television broadcasts. This evaluation proved to be very difficult because in 2006 hardly any reliable findings with regard to the impact of the online available media content on the users' attitude existed. The KEK estimated the audience reach as being quite limited, since the internet was not already accessible at any time by the wide-spread usage of internet-capable mobile phones. An important factor of the evaluation was the high level of actuality. The KEK regarded the suggestive power of online available content as relatively low, an assessment that would surely be made differently today because of the highly increased range of on-demand videos. The KEK still considered the internet as a medium only supplementing press products and broadcasts. Media companies would regularly reuse the contents they have already produced for the classical media outlets by putting it online. They primarily use their websites for cross-promotion and less as an independent information provider. The KEK weighted the influence of the merged entity ProSiebenSat.1 and Springer on public opinion through online services at 6%, and subsequently converted this influence into a fictitious television audience reach of 3% because of the assumed lower suggestive power and reach of online services compared to television broadcasts.[96] The KEK investigated the influence of the merging undertakings in every relevant media sector and converted this influence into a fictitious broadcasting audience reach, which in the end amounted to 25%. The overall audience share, after having added the real (22%) and the fictitious figures (25%) – reached 47%. This influence on public opinion was deemed too strong by the KEK and led to the prohibition of the merger.[97]

Its decision was heavily criticised. On the one hand, it was argued that the assumed dominant influence by the merging companies on the public's attitude

94 KEK, 293 – 1 bis 5, pp 88–91 – Axel Springer AG.

95 KEK, 293 – 1 bis 5, pp 92–94 – Axel Springer AG.

96 KEK, 293 – 1 bis 5, pp 96–98 – Axel Springer AG; *Gounalakis/Zagouras*, Medienkonzentrationsrecht, pp 146–147.

97 KEK, 293 – 1 bis 5, p 99– Axel Springer AG.

was not supported by scholarly findings because reliable and precise media-specific research results were not available for this assessment.[98] However, the fact that media academics are not capable of providing the necessary findings cannot lead to the permissibility of all types of cross-media concentrations.[99] Also the criticism that the KEK's approach lacked transparency has to be contested, since it clearly and comprehensively explained its method, the relevant steps and the final outcome. The KEK should not be blamed for having adapted a new procedure because this type of cross-media merger did not fit into the normal thresholds and categories.[100] However, in the end the German Supreme Administrative Court ("Bundesverwaltungsgericht") overturned the KEK's decision. It held that the real audience reach of ProSiebenSat.1 was too far removed from the legal thresholds in s 26(2) of the RStV. The legislator had attributed a high significance to these thresholds and placed the broadcasting audience reach in the centre of the assessment, whereas the influence on media-related markets only plays a subordinate role. Therefore, the explicitly mentioned thresholds must not be circumvented too easily by having recourse to a company's influence on media-related markets. However, the general approach of converting the influence on related markets into a fictitious broadcasting audience rate was not considered impermissible. This method can still be applied provided that the thresholds in s 26(2) of the RStV have already been met.[101] But considering the development of the last decades it seems quite unlikely that a broadcasting company in Germany will obtain an audience share exceeding 25%. As long as this threshold is not fulfilled, broadcasters can theoretically expand their cross-media shareholdings to an unlimited extent, e.g., by acquiring several newspaper publishers, and hereby obtain a very large influence on public opinion. The current lack of an effective regulatory tool for preventing such a development is deeply worrying.[102]

2. *Competition Law*

Mergers of media companies can fall within the scope of European or German competition provisions. If the merging undertakings are quite big and the merger thus achieves a Community dimension, the European Council Regulation on

98 *Paschke/Goldbeck*, ZWeR 2007, 49 (72).
99 *Gounalakis/Zagouras*, Medienkonzentrationsrecht, p 151.
100 *Gounalakis/Zagouras*, Medienkonzentrationsrecht, pp 152–153.
101 BVerwGE 149, 52–65 = NVwZ-RR 2014, 473–477.
102 See also the opinion of the KEK: 17. Jahresbericht, 2013/2015, p 138.

control of mergers (ECMR)[103] is applicable. A Community dimension is given pursuant to Art 1(2) of the ECMR if the combined aggregate worldwide turnover of all the undertakings concerned exceeds 5,000 million and the aggregate Community-wide turnover of each of at least two of the undertakings concerned is more than 250 million, unless each of the undertakings concerned achieves more than two-thirds of its aggregate Community-wide turnover within one and the same member state. These quantitative thresholds are lowered and refined in Art 1(3) of the ECMR. However, there is no need to go into details, since media mergers in Europe normally do not fulfil the thresholds of the ECMR. The substantive assessment of the European and German competition provisions does not actually differ, since the competition provisions of the EU member states are often modelled on the ECMR.

a) European competition law

The ECMR is enforced by the EU Commission (pendant to the ACCC). Mergers (the ECMR uses the broader term "concentration" including both mergers and the acquisitions of shares etc.[104]) with a Community dimension require prior notification and approval by the Commission.[105] Contrary to the Australian provisions, a merger falling within the scope of the ECMR is not allowed to proceed without the prior approval of the Commission[106] and a violation of this formal requirement triggers a severe financial fine amounting up to 10% of the aggregate turnover of the undertakings concerned.[107] A merger that is not compatible with the common market can also be reversed subsequently.[108] The procedure is based on the idea of a "one-stop-merger control" meaning that mergers with a Community dimension are only investigated by the Commission and not by national competition authorities.[109] However, even though a merger has a Community dimension, it can be investigated by a national competition authority if the member state can prove a legitimate interest for the purpose of Art 21(4) of the ECMR. Such a legitimate interest can be the preservation of media plurality.

---

103 Council Regulation (EC) No 139/2004 of 20 January 2004 on the control of concentrations between undertakings.
104 Art. 3(1) of the ECMR.
105 Art. 4(1) of the ECMR.
106 Art. 7(1) of the ECMR.
107 Art. 14(2) of the ECMR.
108 Art. 8(4) of the ECMR.
109 Art. 21(2) of the ECMR. See also *Whish/Bailey*, Competition Law (2012), pp 844–845.

Yet this exemption provision is rarely applied.[110] The examination is divided into two phases. Phase 1 contains a summary assessment of the intended transaction and is normally limited to 25 working days[111]. At the end of phase 1 the Commission can declare the concentration compatible with the common market, accept commitments by the parties or open a phase 2 investigation. However, it cannot block the transaction at this procedural stage.[112] Phase 2 allows the Commission to conduct an in-depth investigation of the transaction for which it regularly has 90 working days[113]. At the end of phase 2 the Commission can either accept commitments, clear or block the transaction.[114] As part of its substantive test the Commission has to assess whether a concentration would "significantly impede effective competition" in the common market or in a substantial part of it, in particular as a result of the creation or strengthening of a dominant position.[115] This test slightly differs from the one the Australian competition authority applies which is the "substantial lessening of competition". The Australian test has the same wording as the one enshrined in the UK *Enterprise Act*.[116] The term "substantial lessening of competition" is commonly regarded as being a bit wider than the EU requirement of a significant impediment to effective competition by creating or strengthening a dominant position, since the EU merger control has a stronger focus on dominance. However, the practical implications of these theoretical differences – if there are any at all – are hard to identify.[117] The EU competition provisions, like the Australian ones, assign a high importance to the definition

---

110 *Whish/Bailey*, Competition Law, p 852.

111 Art 10(1)(1) of the ECMR. This time limit can be extended to 35 working days pursuant to Art 10(1)(2), e.g., if the parties offer commitments.

112 Art 8(2) of the ECMR.

113 Art 10(3)(1) of the ECMR. The time period for the phase 2-investigation can be increased to 105 working days if the undertakings concerned offer commitments at a late stage of the procedure.

114 Art 8(3) of the ECMR.

115 Art 2(3) of the ECMR.

116 S 22(1)(b) of the UK *Enterprise Act* 2002.

117 The theories of harm counteracted by the UK and EU competition provisions are the same: unilateral, coordinated, vertical and conglomerate effects. See for example: *Whish/Bailey*, Competition Law, pp 866–867, 932; *Rodger/MacCulloch*, Competition Law and Policy in the EU and UK (2015), pp 275–276. The assessment criteria used by the EU Commission are similar to the ones adduced in Australia: *Griggs/Duke/Nielsen/Cejnar*, Competition Law in Australia, 125 et seqq.

of the relevant market and the resultant determination of market shares.[118] The EU competition law also subdivides the market into a product and a geographic market. In doing so it deploys the same criteria for delimiting the product market such as the interchangeability of products due to their characteristics,[119] and even the SSNIP-test.[120] If the EU Commission has competitive concerns, the merging undertakings can offer commitments, referred to as "remedies",[121] to alleviate them.[122] These remedies play a significant role and many mergers were cleared as a consequence of such remedies, whereas it is quite rare for the Commission to block a merger completely.[123] Undertakings can directly appeal against rejecting decisions to the European Court of Justice.[124]

b) *German competition law*

aa) Abstract outline

The German merger provisions can be found in ss 35–43 of the "Gesetz gegen Wettbewerbsbeschränkungen" (GWB). The "Bundeskartellamt" (pendant to the ACCC) is responsible for the enforcement of the GWB. Intended mergers meeting the later mentioned thresholds have to be notified in advance,[125] and the competition authority has one month to inform the parties whether it will start an in-depth investigation[126] for which it has a time period of four months[127]. If one of these deadlines is not adhered to, the merger can proceed.[128] Media entities are generally subjected to the same competition provisions as any other undertaking, except for the thresholds that trigger the application of the German merger provisions. The

118 EU Commission, Horizontal merger guidelines, para 14. See also *Whish/Bailey*, Competition Law, p 868.

119 ECJ, 6/72 - Continental Can (1973), ECR 215, para 14; *Whish/Bailey*, Competition Law, 27 et seqq.

120 Only the European Commission, not the ECJ, applies the SSNIP-test: Commission Notice on the definition of the relevant product market for the purposes of Community competition law (97/C 372/03), para 17. However, the fact that the ECJ does not use this test makes no recognisable difference: *Rodger/MacCulloch*, Competition Law, p 96.

121 Commission Notice on remedies 2008/C 267/01, para 2.

122 Art 8(2)(2) of the ECMR.

123 *Whish/Bailey*, Competition Law, p 884.

124 Art. 16 of the ECMR.

125 s 39(1) of the GWB.

126 s 40(1)(1) of the GWB.

127 s 40(2)(2) of the GWB.

128 GWB: S 40(1)(1) – first deadline – and s 40(2)(2) – second deadline.

normal threshold for merging companies is quite high. The combined aggregate worldwide turnover of the undertakings concerned has to exceed €500 million. Additionally, at least one of the undertakings concerned must achieve a domestic turnover of more than €25 million, and the domestic turnover of another undertaking concerned has to be more than €5 million. Media companies hardly ever reach these figures and would often not be caught by the merger provisions. Therefore, the legislator decided to multiply their turnover.[129] For the publication, production and distribution of newspapers and magazines the *eight-fold* (before 2013: twenty-fold) amount of the turnover shall be taken into account, whereas for the production, distribution and broadcasting of radio and television programmes and the sale of radio and television advertising time as much as the *twenty-fold* amount of the turnover is taken as a basis.[130] The thresholds for the press sector were lowered in 2013 because this industry faces strong competition by online providers, and the legislator considered a higher level of concentration to be conducive to safeguarding the future existence of a sufficient number of newspaper publishers.[131] The German competition authority applies the same market definition and the same substantive test ("significant impediment to effective competition") as the EU Commission,[132] and the approach does not differ significantly from the one of the ACCC[133]. When delineating the relevant product market the focus is clearly placed on the advertising market. There is no market especially for "broadcasts", since the reception of television and broadcasting services – unlike the acquisition of press products – is normally free of any direct charge and therefore lacks an exchange of performances, which again constitutes a main requirement for a market.[134] As a consequence, the competition provisions do not capture restrictions which affect the actual contents of the broadcasted programme.[135] This is the reason why content diversity in the media sector cannot effectively be safeguarded by merger regulations. Plurality of the media does not currently amount to an assessment criterion, and the task of protecting media diversity is clearly assigned to the sector-specific authorities, the

---

129 *Gounalakis/Zagouras*, Medienkonzentrationsrecht, pp 55–56.

130 S 38(3) of the GWB.

131 Regierungsbegründung für ein Achtes Gesetz zur Änderung des Gesetzes gegen Wettbewerbsbeschränkungen, BT-Drucks. 17/9852, p 29 (Nummer 21 Buchstabe a); *Lettl*, WuW 2013, 706 (708).

132 The "significant impediment to effective competition" criterion entered German competition law in 2013. *Körber*, WuW 2014, 250.

133 B. II. 2. a).

134 *Parlasca*, WuW 1994, 210 (214–215); *Trafkowski*, Medienkartellrecht, pp 32–33.

135 *Schmidt*, ZUM 1997, 472; *Trafkowski*, Medienkartellrecht, pp 35–36.

KEK.[136] The insufficient protection afforded by competition rules can be seen in the press sector. There are no press-specific diversity provisions and the competition regulations are obviously not apt for filling this gap. An analysis in 2006 showed a high concentration in the newspaper market. At that time about 73% of the former West German areas were dominated by one local newspaper, and similarly only one newspaper existed in about 55% of the East German areas.[137] The fact that the concentration in the broadcasting sector has not advanced this far is due to the strict regulations of the German broadcasting services provisions.

bb) The failed merger of Springer and ProSiebenSat.1

The German competition authority BKA blocked the merger of ProSiebenSat.1 and Springer owing to competitive concerns, showing that the economic analysis can make a contribution – albeit limited – to the protection of media diversity. The BKA held that even prior to the intended cross-media merger there had been an oligopoly consisting of ProSiebenSat.1 and another broadcasting family (RTL) regarding the market for nationwide broadcasted television commercials. It was concerned that this oligopoly would extend its market power after the merger because ProSiebenSat.1 and the publisher Springer could then provide a one-stop shop for cross-media advertising campaigns.[138] Additionally, the BKA proved a positive correlation between the reports in one of Springer's newspapers, the "Bild", and the readers' choice of TV programmes. The "Bild" was therefore assumed to possess a significant influence on the television broadcasting sector.[139] Furthermore, a study revealed that a very high percentage of "Bild" readers above 14 also watched the programmes Sat.1 (approx. 90%) and ProSieben (about 80%).[140] As a result, the broadcasting family ProSiebenSat.1 and the publisher Springer can promote each other very effectively and, thus, expand their prevailing market power.[141] This type of cross-promotion is especially worrying from the media diversity perspective if it is presented in a subtle way that the readers of the newspaper or the television audience do not realise the interconnection between the two media.[142] Unlike in

136 *Gounalakis*, AfP 2004, 394 (396).

137 *Seufert/Schulz/Brunn*, Gegenwart und Zukunft des lokalen und regionalen Fernsehens in Ostdeutschland (2008), p 31.

138 Bundeskartellamt, reference number: B 6-92202-Fa – 103/05, pp 38–40, 62–63.

139 Bundeskartellamt, B 6-92202-Fa – 103/05, p 51.

140 Bundeskartellamt, B 6-92202-Fa – 103/05, pp 47–48.

141 Bundeskartellamt, B 6-92202-Fa – 103/05, pp 51–58.

142 *Gounalakis/Zagouras*, NJW 2006, pp 1624 (1625–1626); *Gounalakis/Zagouras*, Medienkonzentrationsrecht, p 196.

the Australian *Broadcasting Services Act* there are no obligations to disclose this interdependence. The competition authority scrutinised other markets as well, such as the market for nationwide distributed newspapers where Springer held a dominant position (80% market share) by virtue of the above-mentioned newspaper Bild, which again could also be reinforced by the merger.[143] It finally rejected the merger because it found for too many competitive concerns.

III. Comparison of the competition and the broadcasting provisions

One might question the necessity of two regulatory instruments in Germany and Australia especially considering the burden for media companies that are involved in two different law suits. In Germany, the Academic Advisory Board of the Federal Ministry of Economics once proposed the integration of the specific broadcasting provisions into the competition law.[144] However, we should not overlook the fact that both legal assessments have a different focus and supplement each other. Therefore, we want to highlight four major differences illustrating the necessity of retaining the broadcasting-specific restrictions.

First, competition provisions aim at hindering the creation or strengthening of a dominant position as a result of a merger; this development is also referred to as *external growth*. The reason for this is the fact that such a transaction does not create new economic capacities, but only changes the control over already existing ones. On the contrary, growth by its own efforts (*internal growth*) can have a positive connotation, since it proves the competitiveness of a company and the increase of its resources.[145] However, the broadcasting services provisions have a very different perception of internal growth, meaning in this context the increase of audience share, as this development can result in a prevalent influence on public opinion and represent a threat to the pluralism of opinions.[146] The broadcasting

---

143 Bundeskartellamt, B 6-92202-Fa – 103/05, p 43.

144 Proposal of the Academic Advisory Board of the Federal Ministry of Economics, paper "Offene Medienordnung", 29 et seqq., available at: http://www.bmwi.de/BMWi/Redaktion/PDF/Publikationen/Medienordnung1,property=pdf,bereich=bmwi2012,sprache=de,rwb=true.pdf. See for a critical analysis of this proposal: *Kübler*, ZRP 2000, 131.

145 *Kling/Thomas*, Grundkurs Wettbewerbs- und Kartellrecht (2004), p 460; *Gounalakis/Zagouras*, Medienkonzentrationsrecht, p 185.

146 *Gounalakis/Zagouras*, Medienkonzentrationsrecht, pp 181–182; *Helwig*, Europäisches Medienkonzentrationsrecht, p 78.

provisions limit the absolute audience reach and thus the potential for internal growth to 30% (Germany)[147] or 75% (Australia).[148]

Secondly, competition law in general – regardless whether one refers to German, European or Australian provisions – is based on a very accurate delineation of the relevant market. This can lead to the definition of very small markets, e.g., the German competition authority once identified a separate market for fishing magazines.[149] If the product characteristics are very particular, it is quite difficult for the consumer to find a substitute, which again results in the definition of a very narrow market. It is obvious that this narrow perspective is not apt to capture cross-media ownerships. From a (narrow) economic perspective a television broadcast and a newspaper might not be interchangeable, but from the (broader) media diversity perspective they can form a complementary unit for exerting a decisive influence on public opinion and must be regarded as a whole.[150]

Thirdly, the German broadcasting provisions very much reflect the case-law of the Constitutional Court, which is why they reflect the legislator's reaction to certain decisions rather than an overall political concept. As a result of this, the clauses of the German broadcasting Act, especially the more general ones, have to be interpreted in the light of the German Constitution.[151] This statement needs to be relativised in terms of the Australian *Broadcasting Services Act* that is not underpinned by a broad constitutional guarantee of freedom of media.[152]

Fourthly, competition provisions in both jurisdictions focus on the advertising market and do not consider the audience share as a market of its own, since the advertisement-funded free-to-air TV does not require any exchange of services between the viewers and broadcasters. But it is precisely the audience share that reveals the real bearing on the public's attitude that a media company has obtained. For securing plurality of opinions the audience share is the most crucial factor, and the fact that the competition provisions leave it completely aside evidences their inability to protect the media-based democracy.[153] The broadcasting services provisions are therefore indispensible.

---

147 S 26(2)(1) of the RStV.

148 S 53(1) of the BSA.

149 Bundeskartellamt, B 6 - 88/00, WuW/E DE-V, 370 (371).

150 *Kübler*, ZRP 2000, 131 (133); *Helwig*, Europäisches Medienkonzentrationsrecht, p 80.

151 *Mailänder*, AfP 2007, 297 (298); *Gounalakis/Zagouras*, Medienkonzentrationsrecht, p 181.

152 *Sawer/Abjorensen/Larkin*, Australia: The state of democracy, pp 208–209.

153 *Frey*, ZUM 1998, 985 (989); *Schüll*, Schutz der Meinungsvielfalt im Rundfunkbereich durch das europäische Recht unter besonderer Berücksichtigung des europäischen

IV. Comparison of the German and the Australian legal system

Germany and Australia subject mergers in the media sector to two control systems in order to prevent market and media power. Regarding the substantive competition law there are no material differences. However, German competition law lowers the turnover thresholds for media companies. This has a major impact on mergers of publishers because in both countries they are restricted only by competition law. The fact that mergers require prior notification and approval under the German and European regime is a procedural difference without significant practical impact on the accumulation of media power.

Both legal systems focus too much on the traditional broadcasting system. They neither provide an overall approach including all types of media for the purpose of a real media concentration regime, but adhere to their narrow broadcasting-centred perspective. German provisions place the television audience share in the centre of the analysis and regard the influence on other types of media as an ancillary factor. A broadcasting company's influence on publishers and online services providers is merely converted into a fictitious audience share, instead of accepting the important role of the other types of media and seeing their combined strength. However, the German provisions better address the problem of cross-media mergers than the Australian *Broadcasting Services Act*. Online services are not caught at all by the Australian regulation despite their increasing significance, while the German Broadcasting Act at least takes account of them by converting their influence into a fictitious television audience share. The Australian prohibition of an unacceptable three-way control situation is clearly not sufficient because the combined ownership of two different media can already amount to a worrying dominance. The current cross-media review system is too undifferentiated. There should be at least an assessment of the importance and size of the remaining media company in order to avoid the merger of two very influential companies, e.g., the only newspaper in a certain area and the only television broadcasting corporation while leaving only one independent radio broadcaster with a very small audience reach and a purely entertainment programme. The Australian laws should include more qualitative factors instead of a pure quantitative assessment. The same is true for the 5/4 rule, which suffers the additional downside of being based on radio licence areas. Using radio licence areas as the benchmark for assessing a company's influence on the public's attitude is no longer up-to-date and belies reality, since

---

Wettbewerbsrechts (2006), p 296. The fact that gratuitous services are not sufficient for constituting a market in Australia can be concluded from the following passage: *Griggs/Duke/Nielsen/Cejnar*, Competition Law in Australia, p 126.

the internet is not divided into licence areas. Furthermore, nationwide newspapers are not caught by the licence-based system although their influence exceeds that of local newspapers being associated to a particular licence area. The whole licence-based approach strongly differs from the German one. However, the Australian system includes an obligation to disclose cross-media links, which is very positive because it obviates the risk that a recipient might assign a higher credibility to a piece of information provided through two formally different but interconnected outlets. This can be seen as a role model for reforming the German broadcasting supervision. On the contrary, the Australian audience reach limit of 75% is much too high and shows a much more uncritical approach compared to the German limit of 30%. This different attitude might be based on the negative historical experience during the Second World War when broadcasting companies were abused for propaganda purposes. Still, every democracy should show a particular sensitivity towards media concentration especially of the horizontal variety.

V. Recommendable Improvements

1. Germany

The media concentration review in Germany has two major shortcomings. First, it focuses too much on television broadcasts instead of providing a more comprehensive regulation – a real media concentration law. Second, there are no broadcasting provisions on a European scale and the European competition law is neither designed nor apt for safeguarding media diversity, especially since – contrary to the German competition provisions – it does not even lower the thresholds for media mergers. Consequently, there is a major supervisory gap that should be filled by a European media concentration controls. However, the question whether the European Treaties provide for a legislative power for such an ambitious goal is very controversial and the following section will give some insight into this complex legal matter.

a) Improvements of the German diversity provisions

First, having two separate authorities for competition and broadcasting regulations makes mergers for media companies quite onerous. In the end, they may have to appeal against two rejecting decisions. A one-stop shop would be more advantageous and encouraging for investors.[154]

154 *Gounalakis*, NJW-Beilage 23/2002, 20 (23); *Koenig*, K&R 2000, 1 (2).

Secondly, the audience reach limits in the German broadcasting statutes only consider German-speaking programmes[155], which obviously seems outdated considering the increasing consumption of English-speaking information via the internet. It also encourages German television broadcasting corporations to merge with broadcasters from another European country.[156] This enables those companies to benefit from synergy effects such as common exploitation of intellectual property licences and common information sources like internationally operating news agencies. All these advantages can be realized even if the final programme is distributed in different languages. The above-mentioned failed merger of ProSiebenSat.1 and Springer is a good illustration of this increasing international focus of German media companies because ProSiebenSat.1 was then sold to the investor group Permira and Kohlberg Kravis Roberts.[157] Kohlberg Kravis Roberts also invests in the Australian media sector.[158] The above-mentioned development regarding European media entities underlines the necessity of a European regulation for media diversity.[159]

Thirdly, the present focus on television broadcasting companies and their audience rate is not appropriate for coping with different kinds of media concentration. A dominant position in a media-related market is only taken into account as far as it impacts on the television sector, thus not providing a comprehensive protection. Therefore, we need a media law addressing all kinds of concentration and not a mere television broadcasting law.[160] The importance of this concern is also emphasised by the recent development including the increase of the threshold for mergers in the press sector and the decision of the Supreme Administrative Court regarding the merger of ProSiebenSat.1 and Springer. The German Competition Act lowered the threshold for mergers in the press sector by two and a half times in 2013, enabling a lot of mergers to proceed without a review by the competition authority. This risks a serious amount of concentration in the press sector, and is especially worrying in combination with the decision of the Supreme Court from 2014 regarding the failed merger of ProSiebenSat.1 and Springer: provided that

155 S 27(1) of the RStV.

156 *Helwig*, Europäisches Medienkonzentrationsrecht, pp 82–83.

157 *Hess/Jury-Fischer*, AfP 2007, 103 (104).

158 *Rolph/Vitins/Bannister*, Media Law, pp 124 and 158.

159 *Gounalakis/Zagouras*, ZUM 2006, 716 (723).

160 *Bretschneider*, ZUM 2010, 418 (422); *Gounalakis/Zagouras*, ZUM 2006, 716 (717, 719–720); *Schwartmann*, Konvergentes Konzentrationsrecht für konvergente Medien, in: Krautscheid/Schwartmann (ed.), Fesseln für die Vielfalt? – Das Medienkonzentrationsrecht auf dem Prüfstand (2010), pp 18–19.

a television broadcasting company does not reach an audience share of at least 25%, even a very strong influence on other media – converted into a fictitious television audience reach – is not enough to finally fulfil the threshold triggering a review.[161] As a consequence, a broadcaster with an actual audience share not exceeding 25% can theoretically acquire an unlimited number of newspaper publishers and strengthen its media power.[162] Since newspaper publishers are subjected only to the competition law – which also relaxed its review criteria by raising the thresholds – huge conglomerates consisting of publishers and broadcasters might emerge in the coming years. This process has proven very difficult – politically and legally – to reverse, and can cause lasting damage to media plurality. The German Constitutional Court has often expressed its worries about the combined power of publishers and broadcasters, and highlighted the necessity to obviate such a development from the beginning because of the factual impossibility to correct such a negative development ex post.[163] If the failed merger of ProSiebenSat.1 and Springer had been brought in front of the German Constitutional Court, this court would certainly have established stronger restrictions for cross-media ownerships.

b) *Necessity and feasibility of a European media concentration control*

Nowadays we are facing the challenge of mergers between private media companies on a European scale. The existing laws can not tackle this problem because the national State Broadcasting Treaties only address national influence of media companies on public opinion, and the European competition law merely covers economic aspects. As a media company might already have achieved a dominant bearing on public opinion prior to offending the European Competition Law, transnational mergers are hardly limited.

Here the question arises whether it is possible to implement a European media law. However, there is no explicit legislative power within the Treaty on the functioning of the European Union (TFEU) allowing the EU to pass such a law.[164] What is more, media affairs are cultural matters coming under national sovereignty.[165] Nevertheless, the former European Community (EC) regulated fields not directly related to their legislative powers, and the European Court of Justice (ECJ) had no objections because it interpreted the legislative powers of the EC

---

161 BVerwGE 149, 52–65 = NVwZ-RR 2014, 473–477.

162 KEK: 17. Jahresbericht, 2013/2015, 138.

163 BVerfGE 73, 118 (175) = AfP 1986, 314.

164 *Helwig*, Europäisches Medienkonzentrationsrecht, p 287.

165 *Ress/Bröhmer*, Europäische Gemeinschaft und Medienvielfalt (1998), p 31.

very broadly. For instance, there is no explicit legislative power to regulate human health, but according to the ECJ the EU was allowed to limit tobacco advertisements. Although the first paragraph of Article 168 of the TFEU excludes any harmonisation of laws and regulations of the member states designed to protect and improve human health, harmonising measures adopted on the basis of other provisions of the Treaty can have an impact on the protection of human health. The approximation of national laws on the advertising and sponsorship of tobacco products was based on Articles 114, 53 and 62 of the TFEU. Article 114 (1) of the TFEU empowers the Council to adopt measures for the approximation of provisions in member states that prioritise the establishment and functioning of the internal market. Provided that the conditions of the aforementioned Articles are met, the protection of human health can be a decisive factor.[166]

A European media law could be based on Articles 53 (1) and 62 of the TFEU. These Articles empower the EU to coordinate provisions concerning the taking-up and pursuing of activities as self employed individuals and covering the freedom to provide services within the Union. The freedom of establishments is affected once a media company transfers its registered office to another Member State, whereas the freedom to provide services is concerned once a TV programme is broadcasted transnationally. The different national regulations addressing media concentration could have a negative impact on either freedom – for instance, if the Member States provide different regulations regarding admitted audience rates, reader rates, or mergers between media companies.[167] For example, while there are no laws covering media concentration and cross-media mergers in Denmark and Finland, Estonia prohibits cooperation between the press, radio stations, and TV corporations.[168] An approximation of the criteria for mergers and cooperation would further the internal market.

Moreover, according to the case law of the ECJ, a measure must genuinely prioritise the improvement of the conditions for the establishment and functioning of the internal market. A mere finding of disparities between national rules and the abstract risk of hindering fundamental freedoms or of distorting competition is not sufficient.[169] These premises are fulfilled due to the significant disparities concerning national media laws.[170]

---

166 ECJ, C-376/98 - Tobacco Advertising I, EuGHE 2000, I-8419, para 88.

167 *Gounalakis/Zagouras*, JZ 2008, 652 (656–657); *Gounalakis/Zagouras*, Medienkonzentrationsrecht, pp 215–218.

168 KEK, Dritter Konzentrationsbericht (2006), p 404.

169 ECJ, C-376/98 – Tobacco Advertising I, EuGHE 2000, I-8419, para 84–86.

170 *Gounalakis/Zagouras*, Medienkonzentrationsrecht, pp 217–218.

Finally, the principle of subsidiarity in Article 5 (3) of the Consolidated Version of the Treaty of the European Union (EUT), the principle of proportionality in Article 5 (4) of the EUT, and the cultural clause in Article 167 (5) TFEU do not limit the exercise of powers. Pursuant to Article 167 (5) of the TFEU the EU is not empowered to harmonise laws and regulations of the Member States concerning cultural matters. Consequently, critics contend that the EU is confined to regulating the economic aspects of broadcasting, such as TV commercials, whereas the protection of media pluralism does not fall within its legislative powers.[171] However, Article 167 (5) of the TFEU is intended only to prevent the EU from replacing or harmonising national cultural policies.[172] Protection of media pluralism on a European level would not constrain the cultural independence of the member states, but protect it from a co-ordinated reporting by a European oligopoly forming public opinion.[173] Additionally, Article 11 (2) of the European Charter of Fundamental Rights postulates media pluralism and has been binding since the Treaty of Lisbon pursuant to Article 6 (1) EUT.[174]

The principles of subsidiary and of proportionality do not confine the exercise of powers because it is evident that the Member States are not capable of fighting transnational influence on public opinion.

2. Australia

The Australian legislator should abolish the licence-based assessment of the *Broadcasting Services Act*, and should no longer adhere to a system that assigns importance to the transmission route. Instead, the real impact on public opinion based on the reach of a media and its contents ought to form the focus of attention, regardless of whether the information is transferred online or terrestrially. The derogation of the licence-based system should likewise resolve the contradiction that a local newspaper is more likely to be taken into account than one distributed nationwide. There is no point in trying to limit the assessment to newspapers which are associated with a certain radio licence area, since the predominant media power of a newspaper is not limited to these areas and, conversely, a nationwide newspaper is much more influential. However, the idea behind the prohibition of

---

171 *Hain*, AfP 2007, 527 (532); *Dörr/Schiedermair*, Ein kohärentes Konzentrationsrecht für die Medienlandschaft in Deutschland (2007), 35–39.

172 *Zagouras*, Pluralismus in Europa (2009) p 79.

173 *Gounalakis/Zagouras*, ZUM 2006, 716 (718); *Gounalakis/Zagouras*, JZ 2008, 652 (659–661).

174 *Helwig*, Europäisches Medienkonzentrationsrecht, pp 286–287.

a three-way control goes into the right direction, but should be improved by introducing a qualitative assessment of the media power of the remaining independent media company. This additional assessment criterion should include, among others, the audience reach and contents. As long as these factors are clearly defined by the *Broadcasting Services Act* there is no any risk of legal uncertainty. One of the most important amendments ought to address the television audience reach limit which is currently much too high (75%) considering that horizontal concentration represents the most significant and immediate risk to the diversity of opinions. It allows one television broadcasting company to control most of the reporting done by the media with the highest suggestive power. All in all, the Australian media diversity rules are not yet sophisticated enough to catch the present and future perils for media diversity.

C. Conclusion

The Australian and German media diversity rules still have some way to go in order to be prepared for the challenge created by the increasing consumption of television broadcasts via the internet. Likewise cross-media ownerships are not sufficiently regulated. The co-existence of two legal frameworks – competition and broadcasting provisions – proves to be a valuable interaction that prevents media power despite causing a considerable burden for media companies. This onus can be alleviated by enhancing the cooperation of both authorities and eventually by uniting the separate administrative procedures to a single one. Yet it might prove difficult to gain a political majority for these fundamental reforms especially for the implementation of a future European media concentration law.

Sharon Rodrick

Regulating media diversity in Australia:
Where to next?

Abstract: This chapter describes how Australian governments have sought to secure diversity of ownership and control across different forms of media, argues that a change in approach is required in view of the changes that have occurred in the industry since the inception of the cross-media ownership rules and outlines and evaluates three options for reform.

A. Introduction

The dissemination of information about a range of topics of public interest, as well as access to an assortment of opinions and viewpoints concerning those topics, is regarded as crucial to civic life in a robust, liberal democracy. Through coverage of a wide variety of issues from a number of perspectives, all sides of an argument are likely to be ventilated, political policies comprehensively analysed, governments, politicians and public institutions held to account, harmful and deceptive business practices exposed and corporate self-interest revealed.

The media play a unique role in providing the public with 'the information, education and quality entertainment they need to participate in political and social life' and in reflecting 'the range of views and experiences which are present in a democratic society'.[1] As Hitchens observed:

> There is an intimate relationship between democratic debate and the media. Governments, politicians, and public figures are rarely able to gain access to citizens in sufficiently large numbers except through the media. The media have become the town square. For citizens, the media are a major source for information and commentary on public issues .... To be an effective contributor to this democratic process, the media, as a channel for ideas and information and generator of debate, must be able to offer a variety of voices and views, and operate independently, without undue dominance by public or private power.[2]

In similar vein, the Council of Europe Committee of Ministers recognised 'the crucial contribution of the media in fostering public debate, political pluralism and awareness of diverse opinions, notably by providing different groups in society – including cultural, linguistic, ethnic, religious or other minorities – with an opportunity to receive and impart information, to express themselves and to exchange ideas.'[3]

---

1 Rhonda Jolly, 'Media Ownership Deregulation in the United States and Australia: in the Public Interest?' (Research Paper No 1, Parliamentary Library, Parliament of Australia, 2007–8) 10. See also: European Commission, 'A Free and Pluralistic Media to Sustain European Democracy' (The Report of the High Level Group on Media Freedom and Pluralism, 2013) http://ec.europa.eu/digital-agenda/sites/digital-agenda/files/HLG%20Final%20Report.pdf.

2 Lesley Hitchens, *Broadcasting Pluralism and Diversity: A Comparative Study of Policy and Regulation* (Oxford: Hart Publishing, 2006) 31–2.

3 Council of Europe, Recommendation CM/Rec (2007) 2 of the Committee of Ministers to Member States on Media Pluralism and Diversity of Media Content https://wcd.coe.int/ViewDoc.jsp?id=1089699.

There are a plethora of ways in which information and viewpoint diversity can be fostered. They include:

- strong free speech protection, which ensures that views and opinions can be lawfully expressed and that speech is restricted only in compelling circumstances. Unlike most western democracies, Australia lacks explicit protection of free speech in its federal *Constitution*. While the High Court has recognised that the *Constitution* embodies, by necessary implication, an implied freedom of political and government communication,[4] the implied freedom is limited in that it is not a personal right but a constitutional restriction on legislative power.[5] Moreover, the occasions on which legislation has been struck down or common law doctrines altered as a result of this implied freedom have been few and far between, rendering it of little practical assistance to free speech defenders;
- making full use of new technologies, which allow for different ways of disseminating information.[6] Technological advances have taken us from the printing press, to radio and television, and, more recently, to the internet, mobile phones and social media, and will undoubtedly continue to provide citizens with new and innovative ways of accessing and disseminating information. Australian governments have not always been quick to exploit new technologies; indeed, government policies have at times hampered their take-up;[7]

4 The implied freedom was first recognised in *Australian Capital Television Pty Ltd v Commonwealth (No 2)* (1992) 177 CLR 106; *Nationwide News Ltd v Wills* (1992) 177 CLR 1. The freedom was found to be implicit in ss 7 and 24 of the *Australian Constitution*, which provide, in essence, that the members of the two houses of parliament must be 'directly chosen by the people'.

5 This point was most recently reiterated in *McCloy v New South Wales* [2015] HCA 34 (7 October 2015) [30]. This is in contrast to the First Amendment to the United States' *Constitution*, which does confer a personal right.

6 Whether new technologies have delivered an abundance of diversity is discussed at length below.

7 Subscription television is a prime example. It was subject to a government moratorium for many years. When the moratorium was finally lifted, the government proceeded to bungle the licensing process, thereby retarding its development even further: Kim Jackson, 'Pay Television' (Background Paper No 22 of 1994, Parliamentary Research Service, Parliamentary Library, Parliament of Australia, 1994) https://www.aph.gov.au/binaries/library/pubs/bp/1994-95/95bp22.pdf. The conversion of the national and commercial television broadcasters from analogue to digital transmission was also strictly regulated by legislation. Unrestrained by government intervention, subscription television converted

- not imposing unjustified regulatory restrictions on entry to the media.[8] Australia has a poor track record on this issue, at least in respect of the electronic media. Entry to broadcasting has always been controlled by a rigorous licensing regime and governments have consistently protected the incumbent commercial television broadcasters;[9]
- subsidising local media outlets and community media in order to encourage diverse content;
- licensing different categories of broadcasters as a means of ensuring diverse content;
- imposing content requirements on broadcasters. The prime example in Australia is the Australian content rules, which require minimum amounts of Australian drama and documentaries to be broadcast on commercial television. Other examples include localism requirements, designed to ensure that regional interests are catered for, and children's television standards that aim to ensure that children have access to quality television programming that informs, entertains and educates;
- having a well-funded public broadcaster that is required by its charter to broadcast programs that are in the public interest.[10] Australia has two public broadcasters: the Australian Broadcasting Corporation (A.B.C.) and the Special Broadcasting Service (S.B.S.);
- imposing behavioural requirements such as editorial independence and rights of reply;[11]
- enacting laws that restrict media ownership and control.

---

to digital transmission far more quickly and seamlessly than its national and commercial counterparts.

8 It is conceded that high barriers to entry might exist for reasons other than government intervention. For example, the cost of establishing hard-copy newspapers poses a high barrier to entry. Spectrum scarcity in the analogue era also posed barriers to entry. Today, exclusive deals between content providers and those who provide the delivery platform may make it difficult for new entrants to obtain attractive content.

9 Governments cannot, however, control entry to the internet.

10 Rhonda Jolly, 'Media Ownership Deregulation in the United States and Australia: in the Public Interest?' (Research Paper No 1, Parliamentary Library, Parliament of Australia, 2007–8) 50.

11 These are targeted at 'internal plurality': Alison Harcourt, 'Observations on the House of Lords Select Committee on Communications Report on Plurality' (2014) 6(1) *Journal of Media Law* 1, 4.

It is the latter method of securing diversity that is the concern of this chapter, with a particular focus on how diversity can be secured across different forms of media.

I. Promoting diversity via media ownership restrictions

Whereas ownership diversity within industries is ordinarily valued for its contribution to competition, which generally results in lower prices for consumers, in the media context, diversity of ownership is primarily valued as an indirect means of securing diverse content and opinion. Conversely, it is generally considered that undue media concentration limits public access to diverse sources of news, information and opinion. In its 2001 *Report into Broadcasting*, the Australian Productivity Commission stated that:

> … the likelihood that a proprietor's business and editorial interests will influence the content and opinion of their media outlets is of major significance. The public interest in ensuring diversity of information and opinion, and in encouraging freedom of expression in Australian media, leads to a strong preference for more media proprietors rather than fewer. This is particularly important given the wide business interests of some media proprietors.[12]

The human rights group, Article 19, which campaigns for freedom of speech around the world, has catalogued some of the dangers of concentrated ownership of the main instruments of mass communication:

- "A reduced number of media owners can result in a reduced diversity of viewpoints being permitted to express themselves through the media.[13]
- If several media outlets are acquired by the same corporation, that corporation may decide to save money by simply using the same stories in each of its outlets. As a result, the news on the television will become identical to that in the newspaper and on the radio, and there will be little news of specific local or regional interest.
- The economies of scale achieved by large media conglomerates also mean that competing smaller publications have to reduce their expenditures, and are no longer able to create carefully investigated news items.

12 Productivity Commission, *Broadcasting Inquiry* (Report No 11, 2000) 314.

13 The risk is that 'some political views or forms of cultural expression (i.e. those favoured by predominant owners) will be overrepresented while others are sidelined or left out of the mainstream media': Gillian Doyle, 'What's 'New' about the Future of Communications? An Evaluation of Recent Shifts in UK Media Ownership Policy' (2002) 24(5) *Media Culture and Society* 715, 722.

- Advertisers will choose to go with the largest media conglomerates, further adding to the predicament of smaller competitors.[14]
- Lack of competition may lead to a reduced level of innovation and, in the long run, higher prices for consumers."[15]

Furthermore, the greater the concentration of media ownership the greater the risk that powerful media moguls will be in a position to influence government policy on media ownership, either by endorsing favourable ownership policies with auspicious coverage, or by resisting policies and laws that threaten to undermine their privileged position.[16] This power has implications for editorial and journalistic independence.

The proposition that diverse media ownership will deliver diverse content and viewpoints – and the converse proposition that a concentrated media will result in homogenous content and a reduction in viewpoint diversity – has not gone uncontested.[17] It has been noted that competitive markets might have a tendency to deliver homogenous output with little product differentiation because media owners want to maximise their market share, whereas if two outlets are controlled by one owner, that person has an incentive to differentiate between the outlets so that they do not cannibalise each other.[18] Moreover, as observed by the Article 19 organisation, 'an excessively fragmented media sector can … be highly detrimental to the interests of freedom of expression, for example because no outlet can muster sufficient staff and capital to undertake thorough journalistic research',[19] whereas in markets where there are less voices and less competition, media organisations will be more profitable and, therefore, in a position to devote more

14 There is also a danger that media companies might allow advertising priorities to influence their coverage for fear of losing advertising revenue.

15 Article 19, 'Concentration' https://www.article19.org/pages/en/concentration.html.

16 The response of the United Kingdom press to the damning Leveson inquiry report - Right Hon Lord Justice Leveson, *A Report into the Culture, Practices and Ethics of the Press* (2012) - and to subsequent attempts at reform is a telling example.

17 Australian Government, Department of Communications, 'Media Control and Ownership', (Policy Background Paper No 3, 2014) 7. See also Productivity Commission, *Broadcasting Inquiry* (Report No 11, 2000) 309–314 for a discussion of whether diversity of information and opinion requires diversity of ownership or control as a necessary prerequisite.

18 Bernard Keane, *Media Ownership: 'Controlling the News' in a Fragmenting Industry*, Crikey, 28 February 2013 http://www.crikey.com.au/2013/02/28/media-ownership-controlling-the-news-in-a-fragmenting-industry/.

19 Article 19, 'Concentration' https://www.article19.org/pages/en/concentration.html.

resources to innovation and investigative journalism or to use the profits of their greatest financial successes to subsidise their less well performing titles or outlets. However, since there is no way of ensuring that additional profits will not just be distributed to the organisation's executives and shareholders,[20] profitability is not a guarantee of diversity.

Although diverse media ownership will not inexorably produce information and viewpoint diversity, for the reasons outlined above it is reasonable to assume that 'ownership restrictions act as an effective "proxy" for plurality'[21] and this chapter proceeds on that basis.

II. Media ownership in Australia

Successive Australian governments have sought to achieve diverse media ownership and control through the imposition of specific statutory restrictions complemented by the operation of general competition laws. Indeed, one of the express objects of the Broadcasting Services Act 1992 (cth) (BSA) is to encourage diversity in the control of the more influential broadcasting services.[22] Examples of the former that are currently in force include: an audience reach restriction, which prohibits a person from being in a position to exercise control of commercial television broadcasting licences whose combined licence area populations exceed 75% of the Australian population; restrictions on the number of commercial television and radio stations that can be commonly owned or controlled within a particular geographic service area; and media diversity rules which seek to secure a minimum number of voices within geographic service areas and to restrict cross-media ownership and control rule in those areas.[23] The restrictions are all quantitative in nature and are monitored and enforced by the Australian Communications and Media Authority (ACMA), Australia's specialist media regulator. General competition law prohibits mergers that substantially lessen competition in a market. These laws are not quantitative; they require Australia's competition watchdog - the Australian Competition and Consumer Commission (ACCC) - to assess the likely impact of mergers on a case by case basis.

---

20 Lesley Hitchens, 'Australian Media Reform: Discerning the Policy' (2007) 30(1) *University of New South Wales Law Journal* 246, 254.

21 Right Hon Lord Justice Leveson, *An Inquiry into the Culture, Practices and Ethics of the Press* (2012) Vol. 1 [2.5].

22 *Broadcasting Services Act 1992* (Cth) s 3(c).

23 These restrictions are discussed in greater depth below.

The purpose of this chapter is to describe how Australian governments have traditionally attempted to secure diversity of ownership and control across different forms of media, to consider whether a change in approach is required and, if so, to propose some options for reform. To that end, it will explain the genesis of cross-media ownership rules, describe their current form and consider whether they remain appropriate in view of the changes that have occurred in the media industry since their inception. The chapter will then outline and evaluate three broad options for reform. Any assessment of the current laws and proposals for reform need to accommodate the changes wrought by technological convergence, which has been responsible for a move from:

> 'siloed' production and delivery – where services are produced and delivered by vertically integrated providers using a particular platform to a particular consumer device – to one of a 'layered' IP-based service delivery model which is 'agnostic' to infrastructure and distribution, and consumption potentially taking place on multiple devices, with multiple interactions in real-time (e.g. Twitter).[24]

Examples of technological convergence abound. Newspaper publishers invariably have websites that contain the same articles that appear in their hard-copy newspapers (often updated or slightly altered), as well as material that might not be included in the hard copy;[25] radio stations stream their programs live over the internet; television stations allow viewers to watch programs on their internet sites that have already been broadcast free-to-air;[26] and most media organisations have

---

24 Australian Government, Department of Communications, 'Deregulation in the Communications Portfolio' (Policy Background Paper No 1, 2013) 7. The ACMA has defined media convergence as 'the phenomenon where digitisation of content, as well as standards and technologies for the carriage and display of digital content, are blurring the traditional distinctions between broadcasting and other media across all elements of the supply chain, for content generation, aggregation, distribution and audiences': ACMA, 'Digital Australians—Expectations About Media Content in a Converging Media Environment: Qualitative and Quantitative Research Report', (October 2011) 7. See also: Select Committee on Communications, *Media Convergence*, House of Lords Paper 154, 2nd Report of Session 2012–13 (2013) ch 1.

25 Some online newspapers are accessible to the public free of charge; others are behind a pay wall.

26 These catch up programs can usually be accessed from the web site for a set period of time after they have been broadcast free-to-air. Australian viewers who have a certain type of receiver, good digital reception and a broadband connection can also access FreeviewPlus, which is a television service delivered via broadband that provides access to catch-up television across all free-to-air networks. In 2016 some commercial television networks will live stream all of their programs.

a social media presence.[27] The challenge for an Australian government seeking to reform the existing ownership and control regime is to accommodate these realities within a revised regulatory framework in a manner that can keep pace with ongoing technological change.

B. The genesis of cross media ownership rules

Cross media ownership rules were first introduced in Australia in 1987 when they were inserted into the *Broadcasting Act 1942* (Cth) by the *Broadcasting (Ownership and Control) Act 1987* (Cth).[28] They initially pertained only to television markets and formed one part of the Hawke Government's comprehensive legislative reform package. The main focus of that package was the abolition of the long-standing two-station rule, which prohibited a person from holding a prescribed interest in more than two commercial television licences,[29] and its replacement by the 60% audience reach rule,[30] which allowed a person to control interests in any number of commercial television licences provided they did not collectively serve more than 60% of the Australian population. However, it was not permissible to be in control of more than one television licence in the same licence area. The audience reach rule facilitated a significant increase in the number of prescribed interests that could be held by a person in commercial television licences. The Hawke Government took the view that to raise the national television ownership limit without imposing corresponding limits on cross-media ownership would

---

27 It goes without saying that these changes are not peculiar to Australia. For a discussion of some of the challenges and opportunities for media companies that are moving from being single sector suppliers of content to digital multi-platform suppliers see: Gillian Doyle, 'Multi-platform Media and the Miracle of the Loaves and Fishes (2015) 12(1) *Journal of Media Business Studies* 49.

28 Prior to 1987, cross-media ownership was common. See: Jock Given, 'Cross-media Ownership Laws: Refinement or Rejection?' (2007) 30(1) *University of New South Wales Law Journal* 258, 258–9.

29 The two-station rule had been in operation since 1956, when commercial television first commenced in Australia. Its purpose was to ensure that ownership of television licences in Australia was widespread.

30 The figure of 60% was chosen in order to prevent metropolitan networks from expanding into regional Australia and to enable the establishment of smaller regional networks which, in turn, would encourage local program production: House of Representatives Joint Select Committee on Broadcasting Legislation, Parliament of Australia, *Three Broadcasting Reform Proposals* (June 2013) [1.16].

result in an unacceptable level of media concentration in television service areas. According to the then Minister for Communications, cross-media ownership:

> can limit public access to diversity of opinion, information, news and commentary. It can inhibit competition, produce monopolies, and affect employment opportunities.[31]

Cross-media ownership rules were therefore introduced in order to:

> '(a) Support competition policy;
>
> (b) discourage concentration of media ownership in local markets;
>
> (c) enhance public access to a diversity of viewpoints, sources of news, information and commentary'.[32]

The rules enacted in 1987 restricted the common ownership of commercial radio and television licences within the service area of the commercial television licence,[33] and the common ownership of a commercial television licence and an 'associated newspaper', which was a newspaper whose primary circulation was within that television licensee's service area.[34] As then Treasurer Paul Keating famously said at the time, these rules would force media moguls to choose between being a 'queen of the screen' or a 'prince of the print'.

---

31 Commonwealth, *Parliamentary Debates*, House of Representatives, 29 April 1987, 2193 (Mr Duffy).

32 Commonwealth, *Parliamentary Debates*, House of Representatives, 29 April 1987, 2194 (Mr Duffy).

33 The legislation prohibited a person from holding a 'prescribed interest' in a commercial television licence and a 'prescribed interest' in a commercial radio licence where the radio licence had 'an area of monopoly' anywhere within the service area of the television licence. A 'prescribed interest' and an 'area of monopoly' were both defined in complex terms.

34 The legislation prohibited a person from having a 'prescribed interest' in a commercial television licence and a 'prescribed interest' in a newspaper that is associated with the service area of the associated television licence. Basically, a person owning a television licence 'could not own more than 15 per cent of a newspaper published 4 days per week which had more than 50 per cent of its circulation in the same area as that of the licence. However, a newspaper proprietor was restricted to owning just 5 per cent of a television licence in the same area': John Gardiner-Garden and Jonathan Chowns, 'Media Ownership Regulation in Australia' (E-Brief: Online Only, Parliamentary Library, Parliament of Australia, issued 22 October 2001; updated 26 March 2002; updated 16 June 2003; updated 30 May 2006).

In 1988, the television/ radio cross ownership restriction was refined[35] and a radio/newspaper restriction was introduced[36] in tandem with new radio ownership rules, with the appellation 'rajah of the radio' being added to 'queen of the screen' and 'prince of the print'. The cross-media ownership rules were complemented by cross-media directorship restrictions.

It is important to note that these cross-media ownership restrictions were all local in character; that is, they only prohibited combinations of ownership between newspapers and commercial television and radio licences that served the same geographic area. In reality, however, the rules entrenched a distinction between print, radio and television on a wider level. In fact, Treasurer Keating's words turned out to be prescient; the rules spawned a significant increase in concentration of ownership within industries. For example, Rupert Murdoch's News Ltd 'moved from being the smallest newspaper company to publishing more than 60% of the nation's newspapers and holding a monopoly in four capital cities.'[37] The repeal of the two-station rule and introduction of the audience reach rule led to the creation of the three metropolitan television networks – the Seven, Nine and Ten networks – that persist today. Other policies were responsible for the

---

35 *Broadcasting (Ownership and Control) Act 1988* (Cth). The phrase 'area of monopoly' was repealed and replaced with the phrase 'substantial market in common'. That is, a person could not have a prescribed interest (essentially an interest of 15% or more) in both a commercial television licence and a commercial radio licence if the two licences had a substantial market in common. A pair of licences had a substantial market in common if the Minister made a declaration to that effect by notice published in the *Gazette*. Such a declaration could not be made unless the service areas of the licences overlapped and more than 30% of the population of one service area was also within the other service area.

36 The restriction was in similar terms to the television/ newspaper cross-media restriction. A person could not have a prescribed interest in both a commercial radio licence and a newspaper that was associated with the service area of the commercial radio licence. This essentially meant that 'the owner of a radio licence could not own more than 15 per cent of a newspaper published 4 days per week and with more than 50 per cent of its circulation in the same area serviced by the radio licence. Similarly, the owner of a television licence was restricted to owning 15 per cent of a radio licence serving substantially the same market, while a newspaper proprietor could own up to 15 per cent of a radio licence.': John Gardiner-Garden and Jonathan Chowns, 'Media Ownership Regulation in Australia' (E-Brief: Online Only, Parliamentary Library, Parliament of Australia, issued 22 October 2001; updated 26 March 2002; updated 16 June 2003; updated 30 May 2006).

37 Julianne Schultz, *Reviving the Fourth Estate: Democracy, Accountability and the Media* (Cambridge University Press, 1998) 83.

emergence of Australia's three regional television networks. Each regional network is affiliated with one of the metropolitan networks and transmits essentially the same programming as their metropolitan counterpart, despite their different ownership, as a result of program supply agreements which are not regarded as conferring control for the purposes of the ownership and control rules.[38] As a result, content diversity within the television industry is low.[39]

When the *Broadcasting Act 1942* (Cth) was replaced by the BSA, the cross-media ownership rules were carried over into that Act, with some alterations.[40] The permissible audience reach was increased to 75% of the Australian population, thereby enabling a media organisation to control commercial television licences in each mainland capital city of Australia. This rule remains in place today.[41] The prohibition on controlling more than one commercial television licence in the same licence area was retained and the number of commercial radio licences that could be controlled within the same licence area was lifted from one to two.[42] Commercial and subscription television were also subject to foreign ownership restrictions.[43] Media mergers remained subject to general competition law, which

---

38 *Broadcasting Services Act 1992* (Cth) Sch 1, cl 2(2). It has been noted that program affiliation agreements tend to distort the picture of media influence. In the context of radio, for example, talkback programs can emanate from Sydney, with audience numbers being captured in Sydney alone, yet the same program might be syndicated throughout regional New South Wales. This increases the program's reach but this is not captured in the statistics: Australian Government, Department of Communications, 'Media Control and Ownership', (Policy Background Paper No 3, 2014) 21. The same can be true of television.

39 Franco Papandrea and Rodney Tiffen, *Media Concentration in Australia* (Paper written for International Media Concentration Research Project, 2011) 11 http://internationalmedia.pbworks.com/w/file/46422518/Draft%20Australian%20Chapter%20%28June2011_Rev%29.docx.

40 *Broadcasting Services Act 1992* (Cth) s 60 (now repealed). The newspaper restriction was lifted from 5% to 15% to match the other restrictions (prior to 1992, newspapers were restricted to owning 5% of a television licence).

41 These restrictions only apply to commercial television and radio broadcasting services that are delivered using the broadcasting services bands, which is that part of the radio frequency spectrum that is designated as being primarily for broadcasting purposes. They do not apply to commercial television and radio broadcasting services delivered by other means, including satellite.

42 Equivalent directorship limits were imposed.

43 Foreign ownership restrictions had also applied to commercial radio and television under the *Broadcasting Act 1942* (Cth).

prohibited mergers that would result, or be likely to result, in a substantial lessening of competition in a market.

C. Current regulation of cross-media ownership

The cross-media ownership rules remained relatively unchanged until 2006, when they were repealed by the Howard Government via the *Broadcasting Services Amendment (Media Ownership) Act 2006* (Cth) and replaced with four less rigid requirements which were ostensibly designed to protect diversity of views.[44] The foreign ownership restrictions imposed on commercial and subscription television were also repealed.[45] However, the statutory control limits that applied within the radio and television industry – that is, the 'one to a market' rule and the audience reach rule imposed on commercial television and the 'two to a market rule' applicable to commercial radio – were retained. The reforms introduced by the *Broadcasting Services Amendment (Media Ownership) Act 2006* (Cth) remain in force today.

The Howard Government's justifications for liberalising the Hawke Government's cross-media ownership rules are articulated in the Explanatory Memorandum to the Broadcasting Services Amendment (Media Ownership) Bill 2006. The Government regarded the restrictions as inhibiting the growth of new services, limiting competition in the media sector, restricting access to capital and foreclosing future developments in the marketplace. The changes in the 2006 package would 'encourage greater competition and allow media companies to achieve economies of scale and scope', which would facilitate the production of quality news and information. It was also anticipated that the new laws would allow media companies to take advantage of the emerging digital media technologies.[46] At the same time, the Government recognised that 'the provision of news and current

---

44 The Howard Government had been in power since 1996 and although it had always been opposed to the cross-media ownership rules, it had been unable to secure enough support in the Senate to repeal them. It was not until its fourth and final term that the Government held a majority in the Senate and was able to secure the passage of its reforms.

45 Newspaper-specific foreign ownership rules made under Australia's foreign investment policy (but not contained in legislation) were revoked at the same time as the passage of the 2006 Act. Foreign ownership of the media is now left to general legislation (the *Foreign Acquisitions and Takeovers Act 1975* (Cth)) and government policy, although the media are treated as a sensitive sector and are subject to more stringent foreign ownership restrictions than other industries.

46 Commonwealth, *Parliamentary Debates*, Senate, 11 October 2006, 115–16 (Helen Coonan).

affairs is still dominated by traditional media organisations', and that 'commercial radio and television and daily newspapers remain the most influential sources of news and information'. Accordingly, it affirmed that diversity in the ownership of these influential media remained a critical objective of Australia's media regulatory framework.[47] Despite the lip service paid to diversity, Papandrea has described the 2006 amendments as based only on economic efficiency considerations and as having paid insufficient attention to the loss of social benefits that would ensue from increased media concentration.[48]

The four new requirements introduced into the BSA in an attempt to protect diversity are: two media diversity rules aimed at ownership and control, known as the '5/4 rule' and the 'unacceptable three way control rule'; a suite of rules requiring minimum levels of local news and information on commercial television and radio in regional areas;[49] and a requirement that entities that form part of a cross-media group must publicly disclose the existence of the common control when the business activities of that cross owned entity are the subject of report or comment, in order to ensure that audiences are made aware of the cross-media ownership and of the possibility that it might affect coverage.[50] The ownership and control restrictions in the BSA continue to operate in tandem with general competition law, which is enshrined in the *Competition and Consumer Act 2010* (Cth) and administered by the ACCC.

The two main media diversity rules require some explanation, as they now constitute the primary restrictions on cross-media ownership and control.

I. 5/4 rule

The 5/4 rule is designed to prohibit an 'unacceptable media diversity situation' from coming into existence. It works on a points system and uses commercial radio licence areas as its basic unit.[51] An 'unacceptable media diversity situation' is deemed to occur in a metropolitan licence area of a commercial radio

---

47 For a critical analysis of the policy goals and justifications underlying the 2006 reforms see: Lesley Hitchens, 'Australian Media Reform – Discerning The Policy' (2007) 30(1) *University of New South Wales Law Journal* 246.

48 Franco Papandrea, 'Media Diversity and Cross-Media Regulation' (2006) 24(3) *Prometheus* 301, 319.

49 *Broadcasting Services Act 1992* (Cth) Part 5, Div 5C. The ACMA had already imposed localism requirements on commercial television. These were now enshrined in legislation.

50 *Broadcasting Services Act 1992* (Cth) Part 5, Div 5B.

51 Television licence areas are much larger than radio licence areas.

broadcasting licence if the number of points in the licence area is less than five, and in relation to a regional licence area of a commercial radio broadcasting licence if the number of points in the licence area is less than four.[52] At present, there are six metropolitan licence areas in Australia[53] and 93 regional licence areas. Basically, one point is accorded to every independently controlled 'media operation' in a commercial radio licence area and one point is accorded to a commonly controlled group of media operations. Only the three traditional forms of media - commercial television, commercial radio and newspapers that are associated with the licence area of a commercial television or radio broadcasting licence[54] - are counted as a media operation. The ACMA maintains a Register of Controlled Media Groups, which provides up to date information about groups of media operations that are under common control.[55] The ACMA also maintains a comprehensive media control database that contains current information about the number of points in each licence area. Transactions that would result in there being less than five independent media voices in a metropolitan licence area or less than four such voices in a regional licence area are prohibited.[56] The onus is on a prospective acquirer to check the registers maintained by the ACMA to ensure that a proposed transaction will not result in a breach of the 5/4 rule. It is a statutory offence or a civil penalty to breach the 5/4 rule, although the ACMA is empowered to give prior approval to a breaches on a temporary basis.[57] The net

52 *Broadcasting Services Act 1992* (Cth) s 61AB.

53 They are the five mainland capital cities of Australia and western Sydney. Although few in number, the metropolitan licence areas serve the majority of the Australian population, which is highly urbanised.

54 The circumstances in which a newspaper is associated with a commercial television or radio licence are discussed below.

55 As its name suggests, this register does not contain information about individual media operations that are not part of a commonly controlled group.

56 The 5/4 rule cannot prevent these numbers dropping below five or four, as the case may be, as a result of the collapse of an owner or a group.

57 *Broadcasting Services Act 1992* (Cth) s 61AJ. Prior approval is likely to be sought by an acquirer where the transaction would result in breaches occurring in some licence areas but not others. In such cases the acquirer will be required to divest itself of interests in licence areas in which it is in breach within the statutory timeframe. The ACMA may accept undertakings from the acquirer to this effect. For an explanation of the intricacies of the operation of the 5/4 rule see: Ian McGill, 'Cross Media Mergers Under the 2006 Amendments to the *Broadcasting Services Act 1992*' (2007) 30(1) *University of New South Wales Law Journal* 280.

effect of the 5/4 rule is that cross-media transactions can occur, provided the minimum number of media voices is maintained. The 5/4 rule is therefore a safety net.[58]

II. Unacceptable three way control rule

To temper the likelihood that the 5/4 rule would constitute a significant threat to diversity, the Government included an 'unacceptable three way control rule' in its reform package, which prohibits an 'unacceptable 3-way control situation' from coming into existence in relation to a commercial radio broadcasting licence area. Such a situation exists if a person is in a position to exercise control of:

- a commercial television broadcasting licence, where more than 50% of the licence area population of the radio licence area is attributable to the licence area of the commercial television broadcasting licence; and
- a commercial radio broadcasting licence, where the licence area of the commercial radio broadcasting licence is, or is the same as, the first radio licence area; and
- a newspaper that is associated with the first radio licence area.[59]

The rule essentially means that no more than two of these media operations can be cross owned in any one market. For this reason it is often referred to as the 'two out of three' rule. Breach of this rule is an offence or a civil penalty, but the ACMA is authorised to give prior approval to a breach in certain circumstances.[60]

III. Associated newspapers

For the purposes of these rules, a newspaper is defined to mean a newspaper in the English language that is published on at least four days in each week, but does not include a publication if less than 50% of its circulation is by way of sale.[61] A newspaper is associated with the licence area of a licence if the newspaper is entered in a Register maintained by the ACMA as being associated with the licence area of a licence. The ACMA must enter the newspaper in the Register as being associated with a commercial television broadcasting licence area if it is satisfied that at

---

58 Senate Standing Committee on Environment, Communications Information Technology and the Arts, Parliament of Australia, *Inquiry into the Broadcasting Services Amendment (Media Ownership) Bill 2006 and Related Bills* (2006) [2.47].

59 *Broadcasting Services Act 1992* (Cth) s 61AEA.

60 The time periods for which an approval can remain in force are stricter that those that apply to the 5/4 rule.

61 *Broadcasting Services Act 1992* (Cth) s 6.

least 50% of the circulation of a newspaper is within that licence area, and must remove it if this figure drops below 50%. The position in relation to commercial radio licences is different. The ACMA must enter a newspaper in the register as being associated with a commercial radio broadcasting licence area only if it is satisfied that at least 50% of the circulation of a newspaper is within that licence area *and* the circulation of the newspaper within that licence area is at least 2% of the licence area population.[62] The newspaper must be removed from the register if these percentages drop below these thresholds.

IV. The effect of the 2006 amendments

Media analysts predicted that the introduction of the 5/4 rule would have little (if any) impact in small regional licence areas. This is because of the 96 separate regional and remote radio markets in Australia which existed at the time the rule was introduced, 57 were already at or below the minimum of four.[63] Accordingly, no mergers could occur in these licence areas unless a new entrant to the market raised the number above four.[64] By contrast, the new rule left scope for significant mergers to occur in the 39 larger regional centres and six metropolitan licence areas,[65] which account for around 83% of the Australian population. Concerns were expressed about the potential reduction in diversity in these areas[66] and it

62 Most small community papers do not meet this threshold: Australian Government, Department of Communications, 'Media Control and Ownership', (Policy Background Paper No 3, 2014) 6.

63 Bob Peters, 'Commercial Implications of the Discussion Paper on Media Reform Options' (Presentation delivered to Network Insight, The Coonan Paper on Media Reform: Information Session, 12 April 2006). http://www.networkinsight.org/verve/_resources/NII_Peters_12April06.pdf. See also: Australian Government, Department of Communications, 'Media Control and Ownership', (Policy Background Paper No 3, 2014) 17.

64 Regional areas in Australia have always had less diversity than their metropolitan counterparts. This is largely due to Australia's enormous land mass and the fact that its population is concentrated in large urban centres, with the result that its regional communities are generally very small.

65 Bob Peters, 'Commercial Implications of the Discussion Paper on Media Reform Options' (Presentation delivered to Network Insight, The Coonan Paper on Media Reform: Information Session, 12 April 2006). http://www.networkinsight.org/verve/_resources/NII_Peters_12April06.pdf.

66 See, for example: Media, Entertainment and Arts Alliance, Submission to the Department Of Communications, Information Technology and The Arts, *Meeting The Digital Challenge – Reforming Australia's Media in the Digital Age* (April 2006).

would appear that these fears have been borne out. Papandrea and Tiffen observed that 'the removal of the cross-media rules has seen the re-emergence of common ownership of radio licences and newspapers … and broadcast radio and broadcast television …'[67] At the time the legislative changes were introduced, Australia's two largest cities, Sydney and Melbourne, which reach approximately 35% of Australia's population, had 12 and 11 media operations respectively. Today, they each have nine. This is a significant degree of consolidation. However, the number of media operations in these larger markets is unlikely to drop to the statutory minimum as a result of the combined operation of the 'one to a licence area' and 'two to a licence area' restrictions on television and radio respectively, the audience reach rule and the unacceptable three way control rule.

D. Observations on the current regulatory regime

The current attempts to secure diversity of ownership and control across different forms of media in Australia suffer from a number of significant shortcomings.

Firstly, the 5/4 rule does not differentiate between media outlets that deal primarily in news and current affairs and media outlets that do not - such as all music radio stations or racing stations - despite the fact that the former exert a relatively high degree of sway over the formation of public opinion, whereas the latter do not engage in public debate on issues and are not, therefore, agenda setters or opinion makers in any direct sense.[68] The rule also lacks balance in so far as it treats as equivalent, a large media conglomerate which owns a daily newspaper and a free-to-air television station in a licence area (or a daily newspaper and two radio stations in the same licence area) and a small, independently owned radio

---

67 Franco Papandrea and Rodney Tiffen, *Media Concentration in Australia* (Paper written for International Media Concentration Research Project, 2011) http://internationalmedia.pbworks.com/w/file/46422518/Draft%20Australian%20Chapter%20%28June2011_Rev%29.docx. The transactions alluded to by Papandrea and Tiffen were: APN News and Media secured common ownership of regional radio and regional newspapers in the same market; the Southern Cross regional television network was acquired by the Macquarie Media Group, which owned a regional radio network of 85 stations with a similar coverage area; and the Seven television network acquired Perth's daily newspaper, the *Western Australian*. See also: Michael Pusey and Marion McCutcheon, 'From the Media Moguls to the Money Men?: Media Concentration in Australia' (2011) 140 *Media Information Australia* 22.

68 Media companies that primarily seek to entertain undoubtedly exert an influence on culture and on public attitudes to social issues, but for the reasons explained below, the focus of regulation should be on securing diversity in news and information.

station with a relatively small listening audience. The fact that each is assigned one point for the purposes of the 5/4 rule means that the rule is no more than a head count of the players in a local market, with no regard to differences in their size or clout.[69] As such, it lacks proportion and sophistication at the analytical level.

Secondly, with the exception of the audience reach rule, the current media ownership and control restrictions all operate within local licence areas, not regionally or nationally. The upshot is that the rules fail to catch national newspapers, such as *The Australian* or *The Financial Review*, or newspapers that publish solely online, since none of these publications has 50% of their circulation within a particular licence area.[70] If the restrictions were extended to other forms of media they would not, in their present form, catch subscription television, which broadcasts nationally, or content delivered online, which knows no geographic boundaries, as they too would be unlikely to have 50% of their end-users located in any one licence area.[71]

Thirdly, the rules must be understood in the context of governments' long standing protectionism towards commercial television. Some kind of moratorium or restriction on the issue of new commercial television licences has been in place for over two decades.[72] In its current iteration, the BSA requires the ACMA to ensure that the number of commercial television broadcasting licences that share the same geographic licence area does not exceed three.[73] Commercial radio broadcasters that provide digital broadcasting services have also enjoyed a six year moratorium on the allocation of new commercial radio broadcasting licences in their respective licence areas. Moreover, artificial restrictions on genre for datacasters limited their ability 'to become alternative sources of information and opinion to the mass market'.[74] These restrictions on new entrants are at odds with

---

69 Communications Law Centre, *Content, Consolidation and Clout* (2006) 22, 25.

70 The original cross-media ownership restrictions suffered from the same flaw.

71 Luke Waterson and Nicholas Dowsley, 'Cold, Dead Hand? Broadcasting Regulation and the Emergence of the National Broadband Network' (2009) 28(1) *Communications Law Bulletin* 1.

72 Franco and Rodney Tiffen, *Media Concentration in Australia* (Paper written for International Media Concentration Research Project, 2011) 2–3 http://internationalmedia.pbworks.com/w/file/46422518/Draft%20Australian%20Chapter%20%28June2011_Rev%29.docx.

73 *Broadcasting Services Act 1992* (Cth) s 37A.

74 Productivity Commission, *Broadcasting Inquiry* (Report No 11, 2000) 315. Although there are no government restrictions on entry in the online realm, there are 'digital intermediaries who are the access route to the internet' and who act as gatekeepers: European Commission, 'A Free and Pluralistic Media to Sustain European Democracy' (The Report

governments' professed commitment to diversity. A reduction in diversity would seem to be an inescapable outcome of a policy which liberalises the ownership and control restrictions without any reduction or elimination of the barriers to entry.

Fourthly, as already noted, the restrictions only apply to the cross ownership of commercial television, commercial radio and associated newspapers. They have never applied to any of the other categories of broadcasting service that are created and regulated by the BSA, namely: community television and radio broadcasters, subscription television and radio broadcasters, subscription television and radio narrowcasters and open television and radio narrowcasters as they are not considered influential. It has already been explained that they do not catch free local newspapers, foreign language newspapers, newspapers that circulate nationally and magazines. Finally, they do not apply to entities that control content delivered over the internet which, in the news and information context, might be standalone news sites, online versions of offline news services, news aggregators or search engines.[75] This means that, subject to compliance with general competition laws, cross ownership of all these other forms of media is permitted, making it possible for one media organisation to control five of the six main sources of information and opinion in markets across Australia.[76] This preoccupation with the traditional media platforms has created a regulatory asymmetry that is becoming increasingly indefensible in view of the fact that the influence of these platforms is waning. Hard-copy newspaper readership is in decline, as is traditional television viewing, particularly by youth and young adults. An increasing number of citizens are accessing their news, information and opinions online and expressing their own opinions through blogs and social media forums. The implications of these shifts are discussed at length below.

Fifthly, there are no restrictions on the cross ownership of media organisations and other industries, yet many of Australia's media magnates have, or have had, significant interests in non-media enterprises, such as brewing, gaming establishments, mining and sport. These combinations create a danger that media coverage of these non-media interests is liable to be skewed. For example, the coverage of issues pertaining to alcohol and gambling advertisements, poker machine licences,

---

of the High Level Group on Media Freedom and Pluralism, 2013) 27 http://ec.europa.eu/digital-agenda/sites/digital-agenda/files/HLG%20Final%20Report.pdf.

75 Australian Government, Department of Communications, 'Media Control and Ownership', (Policy Background Paper No 3, 2014) 7.

76 Rhonda Jolly, 'Media Ownership Deregulation in the United States and Australia: in the Public Interest?' (Research Paper No 1, Parliamentary Library, Parliament of Australia, 2007–8) 43.

taxes on alcohol and the mining industry in media outlets controlled by media magnates with such interests might be influenced by their stake in these non-media interests, and sporting events over which the media organisation owns rights might receive greater coverage. That influence might be real and overt, or journalists working for these media organisations might simply perceive (rightly or wrongly) that sympathetic coverage of these issues is expected if they are to retain their jobs or advance their careers. A highly concentrated media can exacerbate these potential conflicts of interest, since there are fewer voices to counter any coverage that is driven by commercial expediency. This is particularly problematic with newspapers, because apart from Sydney and Melbourne, which have two daily newspapers, every Australian capital city has only one daily newspaper. Similar conflicts of interest can occur on a smaller scale in regional and rural areas where media owners might have local business interests or political associations.

Finally, the current ownership regime was developed in an era when television and radio stations provided passive audiences with a suite of linear programs selected and delivered by the station and newspapers published content selected by the publisher. This traditional model is gradually giving way to vastly different consumption patterns and different types of content.[77] Examples of the changing nature of media consumption include:

- catch up television provided by the free-to-air television broadcasters on their websites;
- the proposed live streaming of all free-to-air programs;[78]
- smart televisions, which are television sets (or set top boxes) that are connected to the internet and which have inbuilt apps that can take advantage of this connection, such as apps for playing videos from Netflix, Presto and Stan,[79] YouTube, a web browser, Facebook, Twitter, LinkedIn, etc;[80]

---

77 See Australian Government, Department of Broadband, Communications and the Digital Economy, *Convergence Review: Background Paper* (2010) http://apo.org.au/research/convergence-review-background-paper.

78 Channels Seven and Nine have announced that they will live stream all content on their free-to-air channels from 2016.

79 Some of these services can also be accessed on computers and smart phones.

80 How to Geek, *Smart TVs are Stupid: Why You Don't Really Want a Smart TV* http://www.howtogeek.com/176392/smart-tvs-are-stupid-why-you-dont-really-want-a-smart-tv/. The take up of smart televisions is expected to increase with the roll out of the open access broadband network (the NBN) across Australia, which will provide high bandwidth internet.

- portable information and entertainment provided over mobile devices;
- social media, which allows people to access and disseminate views and perspectives that may not be aired in the mainstream media. News and information is increasingly shared on social media, especially Twitter; and[81]
- citizens' use of filtering mechanisms to customise their own media, thereby ensuring that they only obtain news and information on topics that interest them and from a perspective with which they identify.[82]

Regulators will need to consider how an ownership and control regime can operate effectively in an era where technology is altering the way in which people access and use media.

E. The future of media ownership regulation in Australia – options for reform

There is a wide consensus of opinion that Australia's current media ownership and control regime has outlived its usefulness and will become increasingly outdated as technology continues to converge and develop. The more difficult question is to determine what should be done about it. A number of options have been canvassed in academic articles and in various reports and reviews that have been conducted independently or at the behest of Australian governments, the most recent being the *Convergence Review*, which reported to the Australian government in 2012 on how it should respond to media convergence. Before identifying and analysing options for reform, it is necessary to consider whether the media landscape in Australian has reached a tipping point whereby technology has now delivered enough

81 Ricardo Bilton, *Facebook's Growing Influence on News Consumption*, Digiday, 15 July 2015 http://digiday.com/publishers/facebooks-growing-influence-news-consumption-5-charts/.

82 European Commission, 'Preparing for a Fully Converged Audiovisual World: Growth, Creation and Values' (Green Paper, 2013) 13. While this enables citizens to navigate the colossal amount of information that is available online, there are risks involved when citizens act as their own censors as it can create 'isolated sub-sets within the overall public sphere' and encapsulate people 'in rigid positions that may hinder consensus-building in society': European Commission, 'A Free and Pluralistic Media to Sustain European Democracy' (The Report of the High Level Group on Media Freedom and Pluralism, 2013) 27 http://ec.europa.eu/digital-agenda/sites/digital-agenda/files/HLG%20Final%20Report.pdf.

new media outlets for news, information and commentary to justify dispensing with media-specific ownership and control restrictions altogether.[83]

I. Has technology delivered diversity?

It is undoubtedly the case that technological developments have provided Australians with significantly more outlets for news, information and commentary. Since the introduction of cross-media rules in 1987, the additions to the media landscape in Australia include: the commencement of subscription television in the mid-1990s;[84] the commencement of multi-channels on commercial television and on the A.B.C. and S.B.S., which came about as a result of the conversion from analogue to digital television transmission; the introduction of digital radio, which has spawned a number of new radio stations; the advent (and now ubiquity) of the internet and mobile devices; the publication of traditional newspapers online; the publication of online only newspapers; and the emergence of internet television, which many regard as the future of television.[85]

Despite the proliferation of new media outlets, the argument is often advanced that specific media ownership and control rules remain necessary. The main reason is that many of these new media platforms are owned or controlled by the same media organisations that own or control commercial television and radio licences and newspapers.[86] Subscription television is a prime example. Foxtel is the sole provider of satellite delivered subscription television in Australia and is 50% owned by Telstra, Australia's largest telecommunications and media company and 50% owned by Murdoch's News Corp, which publishes the majority of capital city daily newspapers in Australia and has a huge share of the market. The multi-channels made possible by the conversion from analogue to digital television

83 For a claim that it has see: Chris Berg, *Turnbull's Weak Media Reform Plans Aren't Fit for the Modern Age*, The Drum, 10 November 2015 http://www.abc.net.au/news/2015-11-10/berg-turnbull's-weak-media-reform-plans/6926066.

84 Foxtel, the main provider of subscription television in Australia, offers a number of news and information channels including: Sky News Local, Sky News Australia, Sky News Business, Sky News Weather Channel, Fox News Channel, Time Warner's CNN International, NBCUniversal's CNBC, A-PAC, BBC World News, Bloomberg Television, Al Jazeera English, CCTV News and NHK World.

85 Internet television is not likely to become pervasive until the national broadband network has been rolled out, since it relies on high speed broadband internet.

86 See, for example, Julian Thomas, 'Media Ownership Rules are Part of a Larger Problem' *Australian Review of Public Affairs* (21 December 2001) http://www.australianreview.net/digest/2001/12/thomas.html.

transmission are another example. As a result of deliberate government policy, all these channels are owned and operated by the same free-to-air television broadcasters that own and operate the primary channel,[87] and the news and current affair programs that are broadcast on these multi-channels (if any) are generally just repeats of programs already broadcast on the primary channel. In similar vein, digital radio stations are for the most part operated by the same enterprises that control the analogue radio stations. Those that specialise in news, current affairs and commentary (and which are not just simulcasts of the analogue stations) are primarily operated by the government-owned broadcasters, the A.B.C. and S.B.S. These examples indicate that new technologies are not intrinsic forces for diversity.

The same cannot be said of the internet. Any citizen with a connection to the internet or a phone network – and most Australians have both – can access an unparalleled volume of news and information from websites all over the world, tune in to streamed radio stations all over the world, subscribe to online newspapers that originate anywhere in the world and read blogs on an infinite variety of topics. Within Australia, there are a myriad of new sources of news and information on the internet including: the new online newspapers and news sites that have broken into the Australian market (such as *Huffington Post Australia*,[88] *The Guardian Australia*, *Daily Mail Online Australia*,[89] *The Saturday Paper*, *Buzzfeed*[90] and *VICE News*); domestic news and information websites and subscription email services run by independent journalists (such as *Crikey* and *New Matilda*); *The Conversation*, which describes itself as 'a collaboration between editors and academics to provide informed news analysis and commentary that's free to read and republish';[91] specialist information bloggers; and social media. The internet not only provides access to a plurality of opinions; it enables citizens to disseminate

87 The primary channel is the term used to describe what was originally the analogue channel.

88 It should be noted, however, that *Huffington Post Australia* is a 50% joint venture between the Huffington Media Group and Fairfax Media.

89 The *Daily Mail Online Australia* is a joint venture between United Kingdom company Daily Mail and General Trust and Australian free-to-air television network Nine Entertainment Company.

90 *Buzzfeed* was originally a social news and entertainment site, but is in the process of branching into political reporting and has recently become a full member of Australia's parliamentary press gallery.

91 http://theconversation.com/au.

their own views,[92] which facilitates freedom of expression and enhances diversity of opinion.[93]

In light of this, it might be thought that the argument that technology has delivered diversity would be unassailable. It might also be argued that the fragmented nature of the market is such that no person can realistically secure a monopoly over content and opinion. However, although the internet has unquestionably facilitated access to a cornucopia of content sources, the fact is that the majority of Australians still rely primarily on television and newspapers for their news, information and political analysis, and the majority of Australians who *do* obtain their news, commentary and opinion from the internet[94] tend to access sites that are operated by traditional media organisations.[95] Since the most popular news and information websites and apps are just new means of accessing the same material provided by these media organisations on their traditional media outlets, information and viewpoint diversity may not be an experienced reality.[96]

Resolution of this issue turns on whether the true measure of diversity is the availability of other sources of information or their actual consumption.[97] That is, is media plurality simply a measure of what is available or is it concerned with influence, which is dependent on what people actually consume?[98] If it is the former, then it is probably safe to dispense with media ownership and control rules,

---

92 European Commission, 'Preparing for a Fully Converged Audiovisual World: Growth, Creation and Values' (Green Paper, 2013) 13.

93 Ibid.

94 In 2012, 34% of Australians nominated the internet as their main source of news: Australian Government, Department of Communications, 'Media Control and Ownership', (Policy Background Paper No 3, 2014) 24 (citing data from a Nielson survey).

95 In 2013, eight of the top ten news websites in Australia (in terms of average unique daily users) were owned by the major media conglomerates: Australian Government, Department of Communications, 'Media Control and Ownership', (Policy Background Paper No 3, 2014) 28.

96 A similar situation prevails in the United Kingdom and the United States: Australian Government, Department of Communications, 'Media Control and Ownership', (Policy Background Paper No 3, 2014) 36; Media Reform Coalition, *The Elephant in the Room: A Survey of Media Ownership and Plurality in the United Kingdom* (2014) 17–19 http://www.mediareform.org.uk/wp-content/uploads/2014/04/Elephantinthe-roomFinalfinal.pdf.

97 This issue has been addressed at length in reviews conducted in the United Kingdom in recent years, but has received a paucity of consideration in Australia.

98 United Kingdom Government, Department for Culture, Media and Sport, *Media Ownership and Plurality*, Consultation (July 2013) 2.

given the abundance of news options accessible online. But if the proper measure is what Australians actually consume, then it seems that the legacy media have just extended their reach and are still setting the agenda and steering the discussion, in which case a tipping point has not been reached. A number of factors combine to suggest that the latter view is preferable. Of the proliferation of voices that are accessible online, 'most have little following and very few have the capacity to challenge the influence of traditional media on public opinion.'[99] Moreover, many online voices do not have the resources to engage in serious journalism and may not have the same commitment to truth and balance as traditional media outlets (in fact they might be overtly partisan). It has been asserted that social media just operates as an 'echo chamber for like-minded people' and 'cannot compete with the sheer collective power of the traditional mass media's one-to-many model'.[100] Furthermore, there is often 'filtering, selecting or hierarchical ordering' of the news and information that end users receive if they access it via a search engine, which means that consumers may be channelled towards certain voices, and denied others, without their realisation.[101]

Since 'diversity of opinion and an informed community are not esoteric concepts but essential components of a democracy',[102] some kind of regulatory controls remain necessary, at least in the short term, to secure an appropriate level of diversity in the Australian media. This gives rise to the question: how are they to be configured and applied and by whom?

II. Options for reform

Any proposals for reform must accommodate changes to the media landscape that have occurred since the cross-media ownership and control rules were first

---

99 Franco Papandrea and Rodney Tiffen, *Media Concentration in Australia* (Paper written for International Media Concentration Research Project, 2011) 31 http://internationalmedia.pbworks.com/w/file/46422518/Draft%20Australian%20Chapter%20%28June2011_Rev%29.docx.

100 Steven Barnett, *Four Reasons Why a Partisan Press Helped Win it for the Tories*, Inforrm, 15 May 2015.

101 European Commission, 'A Free and Pluralistic Media to Sustain European Democracy' (The Report of the High Level Group on Media Freedom and Pluralism, 2013) 5 http://ec.europa.eu/digital-agenda/sites/digital-agenda/files/HLG%20Final%20Report.pdf.

102 Paul Neville, Submission No 21 to Senate Legislation Committee for Environment, Communications, Information Technology and the Arts, Parliament of Australia on *Broadcasting Services Amendment (Media Ownership) Bill* (September 2006) 2.

enacted. In particular, they must account for the fact that the same content is now frequently accessible over numerous platforms, grapple with how online media are best incorporated into the regulatory mix and allow for the increasing capacity of consumers to customise their news and information. Three basic models of reform will be discussed and the feasibility of each option examined in terms of their workability and their effect on diversity.

1. *Option One*

Under the first model, the sector-specific ownership and control limits would be retained, but would be extended beyond commercial television, commercial radio and associated newspapers to embrace media platforms that have emerged since the enactment of the BSA. This has the advantage of eliminating the structural imbalance that characterises the current regime, as well as constituting an acknowledgement that Australians can and do access news, information and commentary over other media platforms. However, this option has three significant downsides.

First, since the same content is now accessible over numerous devices, it seems pointless to persist in regulating separately what technology has already converged.

A further deficiency is that other media platforms may not be amenable to being measured and controlled in the same way as the traditional media. One reason is that they might not operate within small geographic licence areas, which form the basis of the current rules.[103] Subscription television is a prime example. If the current regime was extended to subscription television on the same basis that it applies to newspapers it would fall outside the rules, since it operates nationally not locally, much like *The Australian* and *The Financial Review* newspapers. Thus, it is not simply a matter of adding subscription television to the 5/4 rule and expanding the minimum number of voices accordingly. If the internet is thought of as a single entity then it is not owned or controlled by anyone and so cannot be brought into the cross-media fold as a distinct platform. Any restrictions that target ownership and control must focus on the entities that provide content sources that are accessible over the internet.[104] If regulation is to continue to apply at the local level, it must be possible to identify the end users of news sites in each licence area.

---

103 Luke Waterson and Nicholas Dowsley, 'Cold Dead Hand? Broadcasting Regulation and the Emergence of the National Broadband Network' (2009) 28(1) *Communications Law Bulletin* 1, 4.

104 Decisions would need to be made as to which online entities would be included for the purposes of this rule. This issue is discussed below.

Finally, imposing ownership and control rules on specific platforms is an inflexible approach which will require constant updating if it is to keep pace with advances in the communications sector. Yet changes to media ownership rules are notoriously hard to achieve. The debate over the current rules is a case in point. Governments of both persuasions have acknowledged the need for change but after ten years of discussion, debate, reports and attempts to secure a consensus, the rules remain in their current outdated form. For these reasons, this reform option should not be adopted.

2. *Option Two*

Under this model, the specific ownership and control rules in the BSA would be repealed and media ownership and control regulated solely by the *Competition and Consumer Act 2010* (Cth) (CCA) under the auspices of the ACCC.[105] General competition laws operate in a completely different manner to the ownership and control rules in the BSA. It is necessary to outline these differences and to compare them with media specific ownership and control rules in order to proffer an informed view as to whether they are capable of operating as a reliable safeguard of diversity.

The provision in the CCA that is most likely to impact on ownership and control of the media is s 50, which prohibits the acquisition of shares or assets by a corporation or a person where this would have the effect, or be likely to have the effect, of substantially lessening competition in any market. It is frequently referred to as the merger provision, since it is only triggered by a merger.[106] A market is defined in the CCA to mean a market for goods or services in Australia, a State, a Territory or a region of Australia.[107] Section 50(3) contains a non-exhaustive list of matters which must be taken into account by the ACCC in determining whether an acquisition would have the effect or likely effect of substantially lessening competition in a market. They are: the actual and potential level of import competition in the market; the height of barriers to entry to the market; the level of concentration in the market; the degree of countervailing power in the market; the likelihood that the acquisition would result in the acquirer being

105 This has been the New Zealand approach since 1991: Australian Government, Department of Communications, 'Media Control and Ownership', (Policy Background Paper No 3, 2014) 12–13.

106 The ACCC cannot investigate a situation whereby a company gains market power as a result of its own growth or by the exit of a competitor.

107 *Competition and Consumer Act 2010* (Cth) s 50(6).

able to significantly and sustainably increase prices or profit margins; the extent to which substitutes are or are likely to be available in the market; the dynamic characteristics of the market, including growth, innovation and product differentiation; the likelihood that the acquisition would result in the removal from the market of a vigorous and effective competitor; and the nature and extent of vertical integration in the market.

A party to an impending merger is not obliged to notify the ACCC before the merger takes place. However, the hefty penalties that can be imposed for a breach of s 50 make it advantageous to a party to discover beforehand whether the ACCC is likely to regard a merger as one which would breach the section. There are three mechanisms by which a party can have a proposed merger or acquisition assessed before it occurs: an informal merger review by the ACCC, a formal merger clearance by the ACCC or an authorisation application to the Australian Competition Tribunal.[108]

The primary aim of competition laws is to ensure that markets operate in a competitive manner. The general premise that undergirds such laws is that competition fosters initiative, discovery and economic growth, assists job creation, delivers efficiencies in business and results in lower prices for consumers. Competition laws seek to realise these aims by controlling restrictive trade practices and monopolies and protecting consumers from unfair commercial practices that impact on choice and value for money.[109] Media ownership laws, on the other hand, are primarily concerned with maintaining a diversity of news, information and commentary, not with ensuring that consumers of media products pay reduced prices for media products. Their purposes are therefore quite different.

The media ownership and control rules contained in the BSA are quantitative and operate within licence areas that are known and fixed. As a result, media organisations are aware of what is proscribed and are in a position to know when a transaction must be avoided or a temporary approval from the ACMA obtained.

---

108 For a diagram of these options see: Ian Harper, Peter Anderson, Su McCluskey and Michael O'Bryan, *Competition Policy Review* (Draft Report, 2014) 191. An authorisation application to the Australian Competition Tribunal is of a different character to the other two mechanisms, as the Tribunal can grant an authorisation even if it is of the opinion that the merger would, or might, contravene s 50. The Tribunal can do so only if it is satisfied that the acquisition would result, or be likely to result, in such a benefit to the public that it should be allowed to occur notwithstanding that it would lessen competition.

109 Commonwealth, *Parliamentary Debates*, Senate, 30 July 1974, 540 (Lionel Murphy).

From the perspective of the ACMA, the rules are relatively straightforward to apply.[110]

By contrast, s 50 is expressed in qualitative, not quantitative, terms. The outcome of its application is therefore more speculative and unpredictable. The provision obliges the ACCC to examine mergers on a case by case basis in order to determine whether they would substantially lessen competition in a market. This allows the ACCC to take account of changes in the industry at the time the merger is occurring.[111] Before the ACCC can make an assessment of this issue, it must identify the relevant market. The way in which the market is defined is critical to ascertaining the competitive implications of a proposed merger. Substitutability is typically the main measure: if the price of one product increases, will consumers replace that product with a substitute? This has both a geographic and a product dimension. If there is substitutability, the two products are likely to be treated as being in the same market. The ACCCs assessment of markets can (and does) change over time because markets are dynamic. It used to be the case that the ACCC treated media markets as platform specific. Thus, free-to-air television, subscription television, radio and newspapers were each regarded as separate markets. During this era, cross-media transactions would likely have been allowed to proceed were it not for the presence of specific cross-media ownership restrictions in the BSA.

In August 2006, the ACCC articulated a completely new approach to defining media markets and assessing media mergers.[112] This approach remains current.[113] One of the reasons given by the ACCC for adopting a new framework was the fact that technological convergence and changes in consumer behaviour, media content and the way that media are delivered had collectively altered the nature of competition in media markets. As a concession to the fact that markets can change rapidly, the ACCC stated that when dealing with informal clearance applications it will base its assessment on hard evidence of what a market is likely to look like in the next two or three years. This means that 'media mergers that, based on the

---

110 The rules are straightforward in the sense that what they proscribe is clear. However, in so far as their application requires the ACMA to investigate and make determinations about control, which is not necessarily measured in concrete, numeric terms, it is conceded that the rules do have an element of uncertainty.

111 Australian Government, Department of Communications, 'Media Control and Ownership', (Policy Background Paper No 3, 2014) 7.

112 Australian Competition and Consumer Commission, *Media Mergers* (2006).

113 The paper was updated in 2010 to refer to the *Competition and Consumer Act 2010* (Cth), which had replaced the *Trade Practices Act 1974* (Cth).

best current evidence, are unlikely to substantially lessen competition should not be hindered based on mere speculation of what technology might bring in the future'.[114] Conversely, 'media mergers that, based on the best current evidence, are likely to substantially lessen competition will not be cleared on the basis of mere speculation about future technological developments'.[115]

In recognition of the fact that traditional media boundaries have become blurred, the ACCC has deliberately shifted its attention away from the mode by which information is delivered and refocused it on the actual products offered by media companies. It identified three main product categories that it will consider as part of its assessment: the supply of advertising opportunities to advertisers; the supply of content to consumers; and the acquisition of content from content providers. Other more specific products, 'such as premium content; classified and display advertising; and the delivery of news, information and opinion' may also be critical when considering particular mergers.[116] Merging parties may be significant competitors for advertisers, consumers and/or content even if they are not the same type of media.

The question that must be addressed is whether media mergers that would unacceptably stifle diversity of views and opinion are capable of being identified and prevented by the application of general competition laws in their current form. Notwithstanding the ACCC's revised approach to market definition, there are serious doubts about their capacity to do so. One reason is that general competition laws are not directed at ensuring plurality. The ACCC itself has acknowledged that the key purpose of the CCA is to protect competition in markets in Australia, including media markets, and that media diversity is primarily protected by the restrictions on cross-media mergers in the BSA.[117] The factors listed in s 50(3), which the ACCC must take into account when deciding whether an acquisition would have the effect of substantially lessening competition in a market, are all economic. Although not exhaustive, they demonstrate that the emphasis is on securing outcomes that are economically efficient, not socially beneficial.[118] Moreover, history suggests that concern about the capacity of competition laws to secure diversity is well founded, as reliance on competition law has not prevented

114 Australian Competition and Consumer Commission, *Media Mergers* (2006) 4.
115 Ibid.
116 Ibid.
117 Australian Competition and Consumer Commission, *Media Mergers* (2006) 5.
118 Franco Papandrea 'Media Diversity and Cross-Media Regulation' (2006) 24(3) *Prometheus* 301, 307, 309.

high concentration in the newspaper industry. In fact, Australia has one of the highest concentrations of newspaper ownership in the world.[119]

It is routinely acknowledged that competition and pluralism, though linked,[120] are not the same thing.[121] As Foster explains:

> Society .... may take the view that the outcome of a competitive market does not fully serve the interests of individuals as citizens. For example, markets might provide high quality news to only the most commercially attractive segments of a population, society would prefer all to benefit. Markets might focus only on the most popular types of news; society would like a much deeper and more diverse range of news and views to be widely available, reflecting minority as well as majority viewpoints. Markets might tend towards an oligopolistic structure (with only a few big suppliers) while society would prefer a larger number of different suppliers.[122]

---

119 An International Media Concentration Research Project that analysed media concentration around the world tallied the proportion of daily newspaper circulation controlled by the leading firms in 26 countries. It found that Australia was the only country in which the leading press company accounted for more than half of daily circulation (58%). Australia's top two companies and top four companies also had the highest shares, at 86% and 99% respectively: International Media Concentration Research Project http://internationalmedia.pbworks.com/w/page/20075656/FrontPage. Concentration of ownership in the newspaper industry is particularly concerning, as the press continue to be the primary agenda setters for public debate.

120 They are linked because in so far as competition laws operate to prevent the emergence of monopolies, they will have a positive effect on plurality: Robin Foster, Submission to House of Lords Select Committee on Communications, *Inquiry into Media Plurality* (1 May 2013) [3.5] http://www.parliament.uk/documents/lords-committees/communications/Mediaplurality/MediaPluralityEvidence.pdf.

121 See, for example: Gillian Doyle, 'What's 'New' about the Future of Communications? An Evaluation of Recent Shifts in UK Media Ownership Policy' (2002) 24(5) *Media Culture and Society* 715, 720; United Kingdom Government, Department of Culture, Media and Sport, *Consultation on Media Ownership Rules*, (26 November 2001) [1.10]; European Commission, 'A Free and Pluralistic Media to Sustain European Democracy' (The Report of the High Level Group on Media Freedom and Pluralism, 2013) 23 http://ec.europa.eu/digital-agenda/sites/digital-agenda/files/HLG%20Final%20Report.pdf; House of Lords Select Committee on Communications, United Kingdom Parliament, *Media Plurality*, (1st report of Session 2013–14, 2014) ch 1.

122 Robin Foster, Submission to House of Lords Select Committee on Communications, *Inquiry into Media Plurality,* (1 May 2013) [3.5] http://www.parliament.uk/documents/lords-committees/communications/Mediaplurality/MediaPluralityEvidence.pdf.

In his submission to the House of Lords Select Committee on Communications, Cave explained the difference between competition policy and pluralism policy in the following terms:

> Competition policy (is) … there to ensure that constraints are imposed upon a firm's activities, the constraint arising from other firms competing with them and the constraint arising because their customers can go to those other firms if they wish. That is essentially an individualistic analysis. What we are trying to do is take the customer …. and try to ensure that that customer is able to exercise, without constraint, their own choices as to what they consume. We are not really interested so much in the outcome of what they consume; we are interested more in the ability of the customer to be able to make choices in a way that constrains firms from raising their prices ……
>
> But when somebody is trying to achieve pluralistic objectives …. their interest will be how, in aggregate, people make those consumption decisions. They may observe a situation, for example, in which people make consumption decisions of their own free will and without any presence of market power, but the outcome turns out to be very unpluralistic.
>
> For example, suppose everybody chose to read the same newspaper. That would be, in competition terms, in the absence of market power and in the absence of any kind of abusive behaviour, quite a satisfactory outcome. It is the best newspaper so people buy it. But in terms of achieving the objective of pluralism, which is to ensure that a broad range of opinions are consumed and that no proprietor or owner is in a position to exercise power by virtue of his or her capacity to determine what is in those newspapers, that objective will not be achieved.[123]

A further shortcoming is that the notion of substitutability does not have the same application in this context, as what is sought and celebrated in the ideas market is diversity, which is the antithesis of substitutability.

If the government was committed to regulating media ownership and control solely by means of the CCA, yet wished to address the concerns outlined above, it could insert a media-specific public interest test into the CCA which the ACCC would be required to apply when assessing media mergers. A recommendation to this effect was made by Australia's Productivity Commission in 2000.[124] However,

---

123 Martin Cave, Submission to the House of Lords Select Committee on Communications, *Inquiry into Media Plurality* (15 October 2013) http://www.parliament.uk/documents/lords-committees/communications/Mediaplurality/MediaPluralityEvidence.pdf.

124 The Commission recommended that the competition regulator (now the ACCC) be required to seek input from the media regulator (now the ACMA) on the social, cultural and political dimensions of the public interest. The Commission also recommended the repeal of the cross-media ownership and control rules that were in existence at the time, but only after the inclusion of the media specific public interest test and the

it is questionable whether the ACCC, as a statutory authority whose primary role is to enforce the CCA in order to promote competition and fair trading for Australian consumers, would be a suitable arbiter of media diversity even if empowered and directed to do so. This is particularly concerning in view of the fact that the application of such a test would involve a large element of subjectivity. It is suggested that such judgments are best left to a statutory body that deals exclusively with the Australian media and communications sector.

Media ownership and control should not be left to be regulated by competition law, whether or not it is supplemented by a public interest test.

3. *Option Three*

The third option recognises that media regulation needs root and branch reform if it is to operate effectively in a changed media landscape. Accordingly, this approach would repeal the platform-specific ownership and control restrictions and replace them with a different framework for securing diversity that would operate alongside the CCA. It is suggested that this approach should be adopted by Australian regulators.

Root and branch reform necessitates the resolution of a number of complex issues. Indeed, the proverbial 'devil is in the detail'. They include: determining which media entities, and which genres, should be subject to regulation; developing an appropriate framework for measuring their influence; and deciding what kind of ownership and control restrictions should be imposed on them as a result. Since the regulation will not be technology specific, the restrictions must be capable of being applied fairly and seamlessly across existing platforms and be capable of adapting to new ones. These issues have been investigated in reviews conducted in the United Kingdom in recent years[125] and the following paragraphs draw on some of the possibilities that have been canvassed there.

---

removal of foreign ownership restrictions and regulatory barriers to entry: Productivity Commission, *Broadcasting Inquiry* (Report No 11, 2000).

125 Media plurality has been discussed and analysed in the following reports: Ofcom, *Measuring Media Plurality: Ofcom's Advice to the Secretary of State for Culture, Olympics, Media and Sport* (June 2012); Right Hon Lord Justice Leveson, *An Inquiry into the Culture, Practices and Ethics of the Press* (2012); House of Lords Select Committee on Communications, United Kingdom Parliament, *Media Plurality*, (1st report of Session 2013–14, 2014). See also: the European Commission, 'A Free and Pluralistic Media to Sustain European Democracy' (The Report of the High Level Group on Media Freedom and Pluralism, 2013) <http://ec.europa.eu/digital-agenda/sites/digital-agenda/files/HLG%20Final%20Report.pdf>.

III. Implementing the Third Option

1. *Genres*

While all genres have an impact on citizens, news and current affairs are the most relevant genres for the delivery of public policy goals.[126] Accordingly, it is the most important genre to consider when implementing policies on diversity.[127] An Australian government considering reform will have to decide whether it will target this genre alone when formulating new media policies or whether it will take into account all forms of media when assessing diversity. It is suggested that a focus on the news media is preferable.

2. *Which media entities should be subject to ownership and control restrictions?*

The threshold for regulation should be determined in such a way that it excludes from regulation entities that do not provide professional content and (perhaps) special interest news media outlets that do not attract large audiences.[128] At least three other issues must be addressed: should subscription services be included? Should the public broadcasters be included? Should online entities be incorporated and if so, which ones?

When the BSA was first enacted, the ownership and control rules were not applied to most subscription television and radio services because they provided 'a discretionary service that consumers must pay to receive' and arguments about their ability to influence were not regarded as persuasive.[129] If this view were applied across the board in a new regulatory framework, entities that publish hard-copy newspapers that are not free issue or that make news available online behind a paywall would be excluded from regulation. Given that the press generally sets

---

126 This is explained at length in Ofcom, *Measuring Media Plurality: Ofcom's Advice to the Secretary of State for Culture, Olympics, Media and Sport* (June 2012) [3.11]–[3.16].

127 This is not to deny that the coverage of issues such as race, gender and terrorism in drama programs can affect public opinion and attitudes on these matters. See Rachael Craufurd Smith, 'Reviewing Media Ownership Rules in the UK and Europe: Competing or Complementary Investigations?' (2013) 5(2) *Journal of Media Law* 332, 337.

128 Australian Government, Department of Communications, 'Media Control and Ownership', (Policy Background Paper No 3, 2014) 42.

129 Explanatory Memorandum to the Broadcasting Services Bill 1992 (Cth). Ownership and control restrictions were initially imposed on subscription television services, but these were repealed some years later.

the narrative agenda for most other media outlets,[130] this is not a feasible approach. Media services should not be excluded from regulation on the basis that a fee is charged for their provision to the consumer.

Decisions will also need to be made about the public broadcasters. In the United Kingdom, the House of Lords Select Committee on Communications recommended that the BBC should be included in any assessment of media plurality,[131] but should not be subject to any control measures as a result of that assessment, 'at least from outwith its own regulatory framework',[132] since it is already subject to internal controls that are designed to provide diversity, including impartiality and right of reply requirements and control by the BBC Trust.

As statutory corporations, the A.B.C. and S.B.S. are not subject to changes in ownership and control and are likewise not amenable to being included in the regulatory regime in terms of being subject to its requirements. However, like the BBC, they might be included in any framework that is used to measure contribution to diversity. The ABC, in particular, ranks highly in the list of Australia's most visited news sites and enjoys strong ratings for its television and radio news and information services, although it is less dominant than its commercial counterparts.

The internet presents particular difficulties when it comes to deciding who should be included in an assessment of diversity. Online audio-visual and text news services that originate content (both websites and applications) are obvious candidates, but a reliable measure of news traffic on the internet is needed in order to ascertain which ones are large enough to meet the threshold for regulation. News aggregators, such as Google News, and search engines pose particular challenges. News aggregators do not create content and are therefore not news organisations as such. They collect news and information from a variety of news sources (usually by pulling news from RSS feeds provided by a news publisher via an automated process using a complex algorithm designed by computer engineers), sort that

---

130 Pew Research Centre Project for Excellence in Journalism, *How News Happens: a Study of the News Ecosystem of One American City* (2010) http://www.journalism.org/analysis_report/how_news_happens. There is no reason to think that the position in Australia is any different: Rob Harding-Smith, *Media Ownership and Regulation in Australia*, Centre for Policy Development Issue Brief (2011) https://cpd.org.au/wp-content/uploads/2011/11/Centre_for_Policy_Development_Issue_Brief.pdf.

131 The BBC is the dominant news provider in the United Kingdom so it was regarded as particularly important that its impact on plurality be included in any assessment of the market.

132 House of Lords Select Committee on Communications, United Kingdom Parliament, *Media Plurality*, (1st report of Session 2013–14, 2014) 17.

information into different news categories and assemble it in the one place.[133] In so doing, they 'connect audiences with content'.[134]

The extent to which these internet intermediaries have a bearing on diversity is a contested point. A news aggregator that does nothing more than pull news from sites using an automatic algorithm arguably has little impact on diversity. The position may be otherwise if the news aggregator is in a position to make active editorial decisions and/or is involved in 'commercial arrangements that could distort its mode of operation' and prevent content providers from gaining 'access to key distribution networks'.[135] For example, the factors used in an aggregator's algorithm might include a reputational element and consumer usage, which arguably 'tend to favour online versions of traditional media outlets over online-only news producers'.[136] Citizens may not be aware that they are being channelled towards certain media offerings and deprived of others.[137] News aggregators might argue that news algorithms that are configured to take account of a user's location and news search history are 'facilitating open plurality of news by allowing users to construct their own bottom-up editorial machines through 'friending', 'liking', past searches and a range of online behaviours'.[138] However, editorial control and mediation, whether a result of human agency or based on navigation tools that direct computers how to select among multiple items is problematic, because they control the news and views to which citizens are exposed. It is a gate keeping power that is susceptible to abuse.

The way in which these intermediaries might be meaningfully factored in to the diversity framework is a difficult question. Moreover, any attempt to regulate entities that operate online sites and intermediaries is likely to encounter jurisdictional challenges and enforcement problems if they are not Australian companies.

---

133 *What is a News Aggregator?* http://www.buildanewsaggregator.com/what-is-a-news-aggregator/.

134 Rachael Craufurd Smith, 'Reviewing Media Ownership Rules in the UK and Europe: Competing or Complementary Investigations?' (2013) 5(2) *Journal of Media Law* 332, 338.

135 Ibid.

136 Australian Government, Department of Communications, 'Media Control and Ownership', (Policy Background Paper No 3, 2014) 32.

137 European Commission, 'Preparing for a Fully Converged Audiovisual World: Growth, Creation and Values' (Green Paper, 2013) 13.

138 Damian Tambini, *Media Plurality Dialogue: What Have We Learned, and Where Next?* Inforrm, 18 January 2015.

3. *How should influence be measured across platforms?*

A government seeking to implement root and branch reform will need to determine what instruments for measuring diversity are best able to work across platforms and whether diversity should be measured by just one metric or by a combination of metrics. This will in part depend on which media entities are included in the mix. Ofcom, the United Kingdom's communications regulator, has identified three broad categories of metrics: availability, consumption and impact.[139] It regarded consumption as the most important measure of diversity.

Availability metrics capture the number of providers of news sources that are available at the point of consumption.[140] In this online era, where news sources from all around the globe can be accessed, the number is indeterminate. It has already been explained that actual usage is a better measure of diversity than availability, since the latter only measures the potential for diversity of viewpoints.[141]

Consumption metrics measure how many people actually use a news media source, with what frequency and for how long. As discussed earlier in this chapter, the issue of 'availability versus consumption' as the most appropriate diversity measure has been the subject of recent debate in the United Kingdom. The House of Lords Select Committee on Communications preferred consumption to availability as the measure, but was at pains to explain that a plurality policy must not seek to actively stimulate consumption, as it is not the proper role of such a policy to intervene in consumer behaviour and dictate to citizens which news sources they should or should not access. Rather, consumption is simply a means of discovering which media entities have actual power and influence. The Committee stated:

> We recognise the importance of ensuring that no content provider has an unreasonably high level of consumption and recommend that a media plurality policy should take into account both the supply and consumption of content, albeit that any interventions available will have to be limited in application to the supply side.[142]

---

139 Ofcom, *Measuring Media Plurality: Ofcom's Advice to the Secretary of State for Culture, Olympics, Media and Sport* (June 2012) [5.3].

140 Ibid, [5.5]; House of Lords Select Committee on Communications, United Kingdom Parliament, *Media Plurality*, (1st report of Session 2013–14, 2014) 44.

141 Ofcom, *Measurement Framework for Media Plurality: Ofcom's Advice to the Secretary of State for Culture, Olympics, Media and Sport* (March 2015) [4.10].

142 House of Lords Select Committee on Communications, United Kingdom Parliament, *Media Plurality*, (1st report of Session 2013–14, 2014) 20.

Audience share is one type of consumption metric.[143] However, to be capable of operating as a successful diversity measure, the available data sets must be capable of comparing a consumer's 'consumption' experiences across different media.[144] This means finding an appropriate basis for comparing the viewing of a television news program with readership of a newspaper and visits to a news website etc. Does an online 'view' equate to readership of a newspaper? Is reading a newspaper equivalent to watching a 30 minute news program?[145] Should the Twitter followings of major journalists be factored in? Do the different platforms provide different types of news? For example, hard-copy newspapers might engage in deeper analysis of issues but do not break news. Television provides a visual immediacy, but, unlike talkback radio, has less scope for citizen interaction and reflection. The internet permits citizens to curate their news. It has been suggested that if audience share is measured in terms of time, it is likely to have a bias towards television because citizens tend to spend more time per day watching television than they do reading newspapers.[146] Audience share would be difficult to monitor when it comes to free internet news and information services, as consumers are able to change their preferences rapidly.

Another consumption metric that might be used to measure diversity is that of revenue or turnover. To be successfully employed it must be possible to isolate revenue generated by news and current affairs programs from revenue derived from other genres (assuming that the regulatory focus is confined to the former). Decisions would need to be made regarding what sort of revenue would be included: revenue from subscriptions? Advertising revenue? All revenue? And is there a feasible method of 'tracing revenues from multiple platforms back to

143 Audience share can be measured by a reputable market research company. See, for example, recent results on newspaper readership: http://www.roymorgan.com/findings/6228-roy-morgan-research-newspaper-readership-results-march-2015-201505070329. However, if calculated by survey, it poses the potential unreliability of limited samples: Media Reform Coalition, *The Elephant in the Room: A Survey of Media Ownership and Plurality in the United Kingdom* (2014) 24. It also relies heavily on claimed use: Ofcom, *Measuring Media Plurality: Ofcom's Advice to the Secretary of State for Culture, Olympics, Media and Sport* (June 2012) [1.9].

144 Sector specific measures have long been used for television, radio and newspapers. These might continue to be used, but as Ofcom points out, it is essential to develop an indication of consumption across all platforms.

145 Australian Government, Department of Communications, 'Media Control and Ownership', (Policy Background Paper No 3, 2014) 43.

146 This is likely to be true if overall television viewing is the measure, but may not be the case if the measure is confined to news and current affairs programs.

the originating media provider'?[147] What if a media entity bundles its products? Ofcom suggested that revenue is a good measure of an entity's economic power but not necessarily of its ability to influence.[148]

Impact metrics aim to 'capture the influence of news content consumption on how people's opinions are formed'.[149] It is the most difficult metric to implement as it is inherently subjective and consumers may not even be able to articulate how they are influenced. For example, is there a difference between how people discover the news and what influences them? A person might learn of a news item via social media, but their reaction to it might not be formed until they have read and digested newspaper analysis.[150] A trust quotient has been suggested as another form of impact metric,[151] but it is open to manipulation in terms of who is surveyed and how the questions are framed. Accordingly, impact would seem to be an unreliable and intangible measure of influence upon which to base a diversity policy.

4. *The nature of restrictions*

Having selected a metric or combination of metrics that can be employed to measure influence, it is then necessary to determine what outcomes should follow as a consequence of their application. One possibility is to impose fixed, bright line rules, such as a prohibited share or a statutory cap. For example, if availability was the sole metric, the simplest approach would be to impose a numerical minimum along the lines of the current 5/4 rule, although the floor would need to be higher if diversity is to be secured (since more media entities would be part of the mix). If audience share is a metric, a limit might be imposed on the audience share that

147 Australian Government, Department of Communications, 'Media Control and Ownership', (Policy Background Paper No 3, 2014) 43.

148 Ofcom, *Measuring Media Plurality: Ofcom's Advice to the Secretary of State for Culture, Olympics, Media and Sport* (June 2012) [5.12]. The same conclusion was reached by Rachael Craufurd Smith and Damian Tambini, 'Measuring Media Plurality in the United Kingdom: Policy Choices and Regulatory Challenges' (2012) 4 *Journal of Media Law* 35, 51.

149 Ofcom, *Measuring Media Plurality: Ofcom's Advice to the Secretary of State for Culture, Olympics, Media and Sport* (June 2012) [5.22].

150 Media Reform Coalition, *The Elephant in the Room: A Survey of Media Ownership and Plurality in the United Kingdom* (2014) 17–19 http://www.mediareform.org.uk/wp-content/uploads/2014/04/ElephantintheroomFinalfinal.pdf.

151 Essential Media, Report, *Trust in Newspapers* http://www.essentialvision.com.au/trust-in-newspapers-4; Andrew Catsaras, *Which Newspapers Most Influence Public Opinion?*, The Drum, 29 July 2015 http://www.abc.net.au/news/2015-07-29/catsaras-which-newspapers-most-influence-public-opinion/6653778.

a news voice is permitted to have. If revenue is a metric, the rules could impose a cap across the media market at a particular percentage. If a cap of 15% of revenue was imposed, it would ensure the presence of at least 6–7 players in a market.

While fixed rules have the advantage of certainty, there are at least two other options, both of which have been extensively investigated in the United Kingdom. The first is to conduct a statutory review of media diversity at set time intervals. Such a review would presumably be conducted by a statutory regulator[152] who would be tasked to investigate and report on the current diversity situation by employing a number of metrics, highlight any concerns (thereby putting media entities on notice about future transactions that might increase their dominance) and refer issues that require immediate redress to the relevant Minister.[153] The advantage of this approach is that it enables the ownership and control regime to keep pace with organic growth and changes in consumption trends. The disadvantage is that it reposes a large measure of discretion in the regulator. If Australia was to adopt this approach, the relevant Minister should be required by legislation to respond publicly to the report of the statutory regulator within a certain timeframe in order to prevent it from being 'swept under the carpet'.

The other alternative is transactional review, which would be triggered by specific merger activity. Unlike the periodic review process, transactional review

---

152 In the United Kingdom, the House of Lords Select Committee on Communications recommended that reviews be conducted by Ofcom at four- to five-year intervals. It recommended that Parliament provide overarching legislative guidance to Ofcom, but that Ofcom should design the assessment framework and select the appropriate metrics according to the circumstances at the time of the review in a way most likely to balance the twin objectives of delivering certainty to the market and sufficient flexibility for a proper assessment of plurality at the time: House of Lords Select Committee on Communications, United Kingdom Parliament, *Media Plurality*, (1st report of Session 2013–14, 2014) [200], [203]. The plurality review report 'should contain both a narrative assessment of the sufficiency of plurality in specific media markets and across media; and a clear indication of where plurality may be under threat, which will guide the decisions over intervention in the event of any transaction': [205].

153 The House of Lords Select Committee on Communications recommended that where immediate and pressing concerns resulting from organic change come to light in a periodic review, Ofcom should be able to require a media enterprise to divest but only in extreme circumstances, namely: where there is a real and immediate problem, divestment is the only way to remedy the problem and the proposed divestment will be effective in doing so: House of Lords Select Committee on Communications, United Kingdom Parliament, *Media Plurality*, (1st report of Session 2013–14, 2014) [211]. Even in such circumstances, the Secretary of State should be able to overrule Ofcom's direction, but would be obliged to publish reasons for doing so.

is not competent to deal with organic change. A transaction may also trigger a review by the ACCC on competition grounds, so if a proposed merger was to be independently reviewed for its effect on diversity there would need to be a clarification as to how the two regimes would operate in tandem.[154]

As explained above, Australian ownership and control regulation applies solely within local markets, with the exception of the audience reach rule. Should a new regime continue to focus on local markets or should it operate at the level of a national news market or both? If the focus is to remain on individual service areas, it would have to be possible to calculate the number of end users of news content in each area, such as the number of pay television subscribers or the number of persons in that licence area who view particular news websites in order to catch entities that operate on a national level. Given that internet television is the expected future of television, rules that operate on a national level would seem desirable. However, citizens in regional areas are experiencing a serious decline in local news and information and this needs to be captured by the metrics and addressed in some capacity. If consolidation is to be permitted at the local level at the expense of diversity in order to secure the commercial survival of local outlets, then it may be necessary to maintain or increase local content obligations.

Finally, there are other measures that could be brought into the mix. They might include behavioural obligations, such as a requirement that editorial boards within a media organisation be independent so that they are not subject to direction from the owner, a requirement to invest in original news content and an obligation to publish alternative viewpoints or offer rights of reply.[155] Governments might also consider creating and fostering new entrants through public money.[156]

---

154 The House of Lords Select Committee on Communications proposed that Ofcom conduct a plurality assessment of a transaction and make a recommendation as to whether it should proceed. If Ofcom concludes that a specific transaction is expected to result in a material and unacceptable lessening of plurality, it should recommend that the transaction not proceed. The plurality review and any competition review conducted in respect of the same transaction should then be submitted to the Ofcom Board, which would reconcile and implement them as a single public interest decision: House of Lords Select Committee on Communications, United Kingdom Parliament, *Media Plurality*, (1st report of Session 2013–14, 2014) [234].

155 Rachael Craufurd Smith, 'Reviewing Media Ownership Rules in the UK and Europe: Competing or Complementary Investigations?' (2013) 5(2) *Journal of Media Law* 332, 340.

156 The House of Lords suggested a hybrid model. If a media organisation meets a minimum threshold it becomes subject to certain behavioural obligations. If it reaches

F. Implementing the third option in Australia: the Convergence Review

The Convergence Review Expert Committee was commissioned by the Labor government to advise on the appropriate policy framework for the production and delivery of media content and communications services in a converged environment. The Committee reported in April 2012.[157] While the general approach of the Review is one of de-regulation, three areas were identified as requiring continued government intervention in the public interest, one being media ownership and control because it is vital to ensuring the maintenance of a diversity of news and commentary.[158] Although the Committee's recommendations have not been acted upon by the Australian Government, they are outlined in the following paragraphs because they provide an example of how the third option could be implemented in the Australian context.

As proposed in this chapter, the Review recommended that media ownership regulation cease targeting the delivery platform on which the content is accessed, and focus instead on the media enterprises that provide the content, with an emphasis on principles rather than fixed rules. However, the Review proposed that only large media enterprises – called 'content service enterprises' or CSEs – should be subject to ownership regulation. These CSEs would be identified by three essential criteria: they have control of the professional content they deliver;[159] they meet a threshold of a large number of Australian users of that professional content;

---

a maximum threshold, then it becomes subject to structural obligations, including the possibility of divestment.

157 Convergence Review Expert Committee, *Convergence Review: Final Report* (2012).

158 The other two areas concerned content standards and Australian content.

159 Content from social media, including bloggers, and user generated content was not within the purview of the regulation because, typically, the only control open to the platform provider is the ability to take down the content. Nevertheless, the Review contemplated that enterprises which host user-generated content could become CSEs under certain circumstances: '(p)latforms that host user-generated content are increasingly entering into arrangements with professional content providers. Content owners can establish and manage their own channels on a service like YouTube under a revenue-share advertising arrangement between content owner and platform. In that role, the platform operator is acting like a channel aggregator, much like the subscription television service Foxtel. The platform operator has a financial interest in offering the content covered by that arrangement. Even if it cannot exercise direct editorial control over particular programs, the enterprise's financial agreement with the channel provider gives it significant control over the content': Convergence Review Expert Committee, *Convergence Review: Final Report* (2012) 11.

and they meet a threshold of a high level of revenue derived from supplying that professional content to Australians. The precise thresholds for users and revenue would be determined and periodically reviewed by a new communications regulator which would replace the ACMA. The thresholds would be set at a high level so that only the most substantial and influential entities are counted as CSEs. As an indicative starting point, the Review suggested that to qualify as a CSE and be subject to the regulatory regime, a media content provider must earn revenue of $50 million per annum from professional content sourced in Australia and have 50,000 audience/ users per month.[160] Modelling conducted for the Review indicated that, at the time, only 15 media operators would have been classified as CSEs.[161] Interestingly, all were broadcasters and newspaper companies; no internet media would have met these thresholds, including Telstra, Apple and Google. While the application of this threshold might undermine the regulatory parity espoused in the report, it is likely that new media would be included over time with the anticipated growth in online news consumption. It is unclear how the regime would deal with entities at the margins, which might move in and out of the regulatory scheme due to fluctuations in revenue and users.[162] Nevertheless, the thresholds would be arbitrary and prospective CSE's would expect the regulator to explain the basis on which they are determined.[163]

The Committee recommended that the regime should promote a diverse range of owners at both a local and national level but should do so in a different manner. At the local level, the Review proposed that a quantitative 'minimum number of owners' rule be imposed on all CSEs that provide news and commentary services

---

160 The Independent Inquiry into the Media and Media Regulation (the Finkelstein Report), which was also commissioned by the Australian Government, was tasked with recommending news media standards. Interestingly, and by way of contrast, it set a very low level at which a news outlet would be treated as sufficiently 'influential' to be subject to regulatory news media standards that would be set by a News Media Council. The Inquiry recommended that these standards be applied to a publisher that distributes more than 3000 copies of print per issue or a news internet site with a minimum of 15,000 hits per year.

161 Convergence Review Expert Committee, *Convergence Review: Final Report* (2012) 12.

162 Thomas Jones and Jennifer Dean, 'The Convergence Review - Did ISPs and Carriers Get Off Lightly?' (2012) 31(2) *Communications Law Bulletin* 6.

163 The significant discretion that the Review would vest in the regulator, both in relation to the entities to which the regulation would apply and the scope of the regulation, has been identified as creating significant uncertainty: Kon Stellios and Catherine Bembrick 'Competition and Convergence Regulation: Too Much of a Good Thing?'(2012) 31(2) *Communications Law Bulletin* 16.

in a local market 'to ensure that no media operator has a dominant influence'.[164] It recommended that different quantitative limits continue to be set for metropolitan and regional markets. The Review recommended abandoning radio licence areas as the basis for regulation;[165] accordingly, the new regulator would be tasked with defining what would constitute a 'local market for news and commentary' for the purposes of applying the 'minimum number of owners rule'. The Review took the view that within these local markets for news and commentary there should be scope for media operators that do not meet the thresholds for CSEs to be made subject to the 'minimum number of owners' rule. In view of the fact that influential news and commentary services might be provided by media operators that are not CSEs, the new communications regulator should have the power to declare that the rule applies to a specified media operator in a particular local market if:

- the media operator has editorial control over its news and commentary service; and
- the number of users for that service reaches a minimum percentage of the population or reaches a minimum number of users in that market on an annual basis. This threshold would be deliberately set high by the regulator to ensure that only influential media are captured.[166]

The Review recommended that the new regulator be empowered to provide for exemptions from the minimum numbers rule in extraordinary circumstances if a proposed merger would breach the rule but would provide a public benefit in a specific local market. For example, a merger may ensure that a local radio station continues to operate if its owner goes bankrupt or if it might lead to a substantial increase in the volume of local news and information, advertising, current affairs that is specifically relevant to the local market.[167]

In recognition of the fact that media convergence has made content readily available on a national basis, the Review recommended that a public interest test

---

164 Convergence Review Expert Committee, *Convergence Review: Final Report* (2012) 21. The new regulator should be empowered to exempt CSEs from the rule in particular markets where it does not provide a news and commentary service or does not provide a service that reaches the user threshold in that market: Convergence Review Expert Committee, *Convergence Review: Final Report* (2012) 22.

165 For further explanation see: Bernard Keane, *The Regulation Revolution of the Convergence Review*, Crikey, 1 May 2012, http://www.crikey.com.au/2012/05/01/keane-regulation-revolution-of-the-convergence-review/.

166 Convergence Review Expert Committee, *Convergence Review: Final Report* (2012) 21.

167 Ibid, 22.

should be applied to changes in control of CSEs of national significance in order to maintain the diversity of content services at a national level.[168] The Review envisaged that the regulator would delineate the criteria for national significance and maintain and publish a register of CSEs that meet the criteria. At a minimum, it considered that, to be classified as such, an entity must provide a content service in multiple markets and in more than one state or territory.[169] The new communications regulator would administer this test and would be empowered to block a proposed transaction if satisfied - having regard to diversity considerations - that the proposal is not in the public interest.[170] Factors relevant to assessing the public interest should include:

- whether the outcome of the transaction would diminish the diversity of unique owners providing general content services as well as news and commentary at a national level;
- whether the outcome of the transaction would diminish the range of content services at a national level; and
- whether the person(s) taking control of a CSE would represent a significant risk that the CSE would not comply with its obligations.

Because the public interest is a nebulous concept, it has been suggested that the criteria be specified with precision so that there is a degree of predictability about its application. For example, Selvaduri suggests that it might be specifically expressed to take into account matters such as the potential effect of an acquisition on editorial independence, the free expression of ideas and on the fair and accurate representation of news.[171]

The Review envisaged that this national public interest test should operate independently of the 'minimum number of owners' rule and should 'complement, not duplicate', the ACCC's mergers and acquisitions powers.[172]

---

168 The Review noted that a public interest test had been advocated by the Productivity Commission in its report in 2000.

169 Convergence Review Expert Committee, *Convergence Review: Final Report* (2012) 24.

170 The onus of proof should be on the regulator to demonstrate that 'the outcome of the proposed transaction is not in the public interest': Convergence Review Expert Committee, *Convergence Review: Final Report* (2012) 24.

171 Niloufer Selvadurai, 'Convergence and Media Ownership: the Merits of Repealing the '2 Out of 3 Rule' and Adopting a National Public Interest Test' (2012) 62(3) *Telecommunications Journal of Australia* 1, 10.

172 It has been suggested that overlap between the two regimes is inevitable: Kon Stellios and Catherine Bembrick 'Competition and Convergence Regulation: Too Much of a Good Thing?' (2012) 31(2) *Communications Law Bulletin* 16.

Finally the Committee proposed that implementation of its recommendations should be accompanied by the abolition of the 'one to a market' rule, the 'two to a market rule', the 75% audience reach rule and the 'two out of three' rule.

G. Where to from here?

The Labor Government responded to the Convergence Review by issuing a media release in which it outlined its intention to introduce a package of legislation that would enact a number of reforms.[173] As far as media ownership is concerned, these reforms would take the form of a public interest test 'to ensure diversity considerations are taken into account for nationally significant media mergers and acquisitions' and the appointment of a Public Interest Media Advocate (PIMA) to decide whether a media merger of national significance can proceed. The Government also committed to establishing a parliamentary committee to inquire into (inter alia) the repeal of the 75% audience reach rule.

In 2013 the Government introduced a package of six bills into Parliament.[174] However, limited time for debate was permitted and most of the Bills failed to pass, including the two that would have implemented the aforementioned media ownership reforms.[175]

---

173 Stephen Conroy, Minister for Broadband, Communications and the Digital Economy, *Government Response to Convergence Review and Finkelstein Inquiry* (Media Release, 12 March 2013).

174 The Broadcasting Legislation Amendment (News Media Diversity) Bill 2013 would have prohibited transactions that resulted in a person becoming the controller of a registered 'news media voice' unless the change of control was approved by the PIMA, which was an independent statutory office that would have been created by the Public Interest Media Advocate Bill 2013 (Cth). The PIMA would not have been able to approve a change of control unless it would not result in a substantial lessening of diversity of control of registered news media voices or, if it would have this result, the change of control would be likely to result in a net benefit to the public which outweighs the detriment to the public constituted by the lessening of diversity. No definition of diversity was included in the bill; it would be left to the PIMA to apply its own definition with no legislative guidance. The Bill did not contain a provision permitting a review of the PIMA's decision.

175 For a full account of the introduction and fate of the failed 2013 media reforms see: Rhonda Jolly, 'Media Reform: In Shallows and Miseries' (Research Paper 2013–14, Parliamentary Library, Parliament of Australia, 13 October 2013).

As promised, the 75% audience reach rule imposed on commercial television was subsequently investigated by a joint select parliamentary committee.[176] The Committee issued a report in June 2013. It concluded that the reach rule was 'becoming redundant with the advent of the internet and converging media' and recommended its repeal.[177] However, due to concerns as to whether local regional news would continue if the reach rule was abolished, the Committee's support for the repeal was contingent on there 'being legislation or legally enforceable undertakings to support local content in regional Australia'.[178] While the economic benefits of removing the rule are evident, its removal would not assist in providing diversity.[179] The big picture of media ownership in a converged environment was not considered by the joint select committee.

Following its election to government in September 2013, the Liberal Government indicated that it was amenable to considering the repeal of the 75% reach rule, but only if it could secure wide media consensus. When this failed to eventuate,[180] reforms were put on hold. However, since the change of Prime Minister in September 2015, there has been a renewed effort to introduce change.[181]

---

176 House of Representatives Joint Select Committee on Broadcasting Legislation, Parliament of Australia, *Three Broadcasting Reform Proposals* (June 2013). The Committee was not asked to investigate and report on media ownership in general, just the audience reach rule.

177 House of Representatives Joint Select Committee on Broadcasting Legislation, Parliament of Australia, *Three Broadcasting Reform Proposals* (June 2013) Foreword.

178 Ibid.

179 The same can be said of the repeal of the 'two out of three' rule. Indeed, repeal of these rules without any other adjustments would have a detrimental impact on diversity.

180 Media organisations that favour change argued that repealing the audience reach rule will enable metropolitan television networks to merge with their regional counterparts, which will assist struggling rural and regional television broadcasters to survive and continue to provide a service to regional audiences, including regional news services. Media organisations that oppose the repeal of the audience reach rule contended that regional newsrooms will be at risk if the rule is scrapped. They maintain that regional news is unprofitable and will therefore be a likely casualty of any mergers that take place after the repeal of the rule unless stringent local content requirements are imposed.

181 It is reported that 'Communications Minister Mitch Fifield has instructed his department to draft options for an overhaul of media ownership laws he can present to cabinet before Christmas, signalling the government will move quickly to deregulate the sector': Matthew Knott and James Massola, 'Turnbull Government Moves Quickly on Media Ownership Laws' Sydney Morning Herald (online), 30 October 2015

Yet the discussion is still centred on the repeal of the reach rule[182] and (possibly) the two out of three rule, not on root-and-branch reform.[183]

While it seems unlikely that a comprehensive media reform package of the kind discussed in this chapter will be introduced in the near future, it is inevitable that at some stage governments will have to confront the fact that the media ownership laws no longer reflect the realities of Australia's media landscape. This chapter has sought to outline the broad possibilities for change.

---

http://www.smh.com.au/federal-politics/political-news/turnbull-government-moves-quickly-on-media-ownership-20151030-gkn2d0.html.

182 In the meantime, the announcement by Channels 7 and 9 that they will live stream all their free-to-air commercial television programs in 2016 (presumably the other commercial television broadcasters will follow suit) has essentially sounded the death knell for the audience reach rule, as regional broadcasters are unlikely to be willing to purchase programs for broadcast on their free-to-air channels if the same programs are being streamed straight into regional areas. Debate is likely to centre on how local content can be maintained if the rule is repealed: Loiuse Yaxley, 'Regional TV Ownership Shake-up on Cards as Backbenchers Push to Scrap 'Reach Rule', ABC (online), 28 October 2015 http://www.abc.net.au/news/2015-10-28/regional-tv-ownership-shakeup-on-cards/6890766.

183 For a scathing criticism of the modest nature of the mooted reforms see: Chris Berg, *Turnbull's Weak Media Reform Plans Aren't Fit for the Modern Age*, The Drum, 10 November 2015 http://www.abc.net.au/news/2015-11-10/berg-turnbull's-weak-media-reform-plans/6926066.

Eric Windholz*

Regulating for Broadcasting Diversity: Balancing Economic and Social Values in the Public Interest

Abstract: This paper examines the public interest underpinning Australian and German media diversity regulation. It finds that notwithstanding different historical and constitutional origins, both countries regulation today espouses similar public interest rationales but increasingly is shaped by the power of private broadcasters and the role of politics.

1. Introduction

Watching television in Marburg, Germany and Melbourne, Australia, one is struck by the similarities of the viewing experience. Both countries have a dual broadcasting system with a mix of public and private broadcasters producing programs catering for a variety of different interests and tastes. These programs include: news and current affairs; local and personal interest stories; games shows; documentaries; drama; comedy; sport; and culture and art. At the same time, however, there are important differences. Some are obvious such as the language differences and the reception in Germany of programs from other countries. Others are more subtle such as the significantly greater number of German public broadcasting channels producing state based programming focusing on local culture. This contrasts with Australia where private broadcasters with a focus on programs with mass appeal attractive to advertisers dominate.

Underlying these similarities and differences in the viewing experience are similarities and differences in the manner with which, and the institutions through

* Senior Lecturer and Associate, Monash Centre for Commercial Law and Regulatory Studies, Faculty of Law, Monash University.

which, the two countries have sought to balance the social and economic values underpinning broadcasting regulation. Each country's broadcasting regulation was forged under very different circumstances and in the face of very different challenges: Germany in the shadow of the abuses of National Socialism with a promise of 'never again'; Australia in a period of relative prosperity with economy-of-scale challenges. German broadcasting regulation is primarily the responsibility of the *Länder* (states); in Australia, it is the responsibility of the federal (national) government. In Germany, the Constitutional Court plays a central role in defining the guiding principles of broadcasting regulation to be followed by *Länder* parliaments; in Australia, the Federal Parliament has a much freer hand. But against these differences are two important similarities, the power of private broadcasters and the role of politics. In both Germany and Australia, broadcasting regulation is, and always has been, a political issue and media interests powerful political players.

The purpose of this chapter is to examine the impact these similarities and differences have had on German and Australian regulation for broadcasting diversity, with a focus on over-the-air television broadcasting. Notwithstanding the presence and growth of other media, over-the-air television remains the predominant form of media in both Germany and Australia, and the medium that has attracted the most regulatory attention in both countries. Its regulatory experience holds lessons and insights for the regulation of other media.

The chapter focuses on broad themes and avoids becoming mired in the detail and complexity of each country's regulatory system. Other chapters cover this detail well. Focusing on the broad themes enables us to better understand the influence of social and economic values in forging the public interest underpinning each country's broadcasting diversity regulation, and the manner with which each country's different constitutional and regulatory institutions have responded to the challenges presented by these sometimes competing values. From this examination important insights can be drawn to inform future reforms.

2. The Public Interest and Broadcasting Diversity Regulation

The public interest is ubiquitous in modern legal, regulatory and public policy discourse. It goes to the heart of why we regulate, what we regulate, and the manner with which we regulate. At the same time, however, the 'public interest' is a term that defies precise definition; its meaning is inflexible and indeterminate outside the particular context in which it is used. The public interest also is a heavily contested concept. Different people can hold different and sometimes clashing images of the public interest and how best to achieve it.[1]

'Diversity' also is a term with different meanings. Hitchens, for example, notes that 'diversity' used in the context of broadcasting can have one of four meanings: (1) diversity of media outlets; (2) diversity of ownership and control; (3) diversity of opinion and ideas; and (4) diversity of programming. Hitchens points out that in Australia, the term 'diversity' is used loosely to refer to all four meanings; whereas in the US, 'diversity' is used mainly to refer to ownership (meaning 2), and in the UK 'diversity' is used to refer to content (meanings 3 and 4).[2] Consistently with this chapter's focus on broad themes, diversity is used here in a general sense that refers to all four meanings.

A review of the literature reveals numerous arguments advanced in support of government regulation for broadcasting diversity. One set of arguments focuses on the airwaves on which broadcasts are transmitted. For example, the public resource argument posits that the airwaves are a public resource, and governments have an interest in ensuring their effective and efficient use. Thus, according to this argument, government regulation is justified to allocate frequencies in a manner that avoids broadcasters using frequencies that interfere with one another. This is not an especially persuasive basis for regulation for diversity, however.[3] Moreover, as Barendt notes, it confuses opportunity to regulate with whether one should regulate.[4]

A stronger and more persuasive argument focuses on the scarcity of the public resource. Broadcasting spectrum is limited. Therefore, by definition, there are limits to the number of broadcasters. According to adherents of this view, governments therefore have an interest in ensuring this scarce resource is used not only effectively and efficiently, but also equitably and in a manner that ensures diversity of information, opinions and ideas. Historically, this has been a much stronger basis for broadcasting diversity regulation, at least until satellite, cable and digital technologies created numerous new broadcasting channels.

Another set of arguments focuses on broadcasting's power of influence. According to adherents of this view, airwaves are not simply assets to be allocated

---

1 R Baldwin, M Cave and M Lodge, *Understanding Regulation: Theory, Strategy, and Practice* (Oxford University Press, 2nd ed., 2012) 42 who describe regulation often taking place 'amidst a clashing of images of the public interest'.

2 Lesley Hitchens, *Broadcasting Pluralism and Diversity: A Comparative Study of Policy and Regulation* (Hart Publishing, 2006) 8–9.

3 Ibid 60.

4 E M Barendt, *Broadcasting Law: A Comparative Study* (Clarendon Press, 1995) 4.

and utilised. Rather, they form the space in which information and ideas central to the functioning of a liberal Western democracy and capitalist system are exchanged and debated. Moreover, they are not a neutral conduit of information and ideas. Broadcasting exerts significant influence over viewers and listeners. Neither governments nor the private sector can be trusted with this important medium. As a result, regulation is needed to protect against the potential misuse of the medium by governments and private entities seeking to advance their sectorial interests, and to ensure diversity of information, opinion and ideas in support of our social, cultural and democratic values and norms. A related argument is the public trust theory. It states that given '[t]elevision stations are in a position to exercise a constant and cumulative effect on public taste and standards of conduct, and, because of the influence they can bring to bear on the community, … possession of a licence [to broadcast] is … a public trust for the benefit of all members of our society.'[5]

This second set of arguments place great weight on the inherent value attaching to a diversity of information, opinions and ideas in the public sphere. But what is this value? Barendt identifies three arguments in support of free speech, each of which also operates as an affirmation of the value of, and a justification for, diversity of information, opinion and ideas.[6] The first is the 'arguments from citizen participation' justification. According to Barendt, television's ability to influence citizen's democratic choices cannot be overemphasized. Therefore, there is a public interest in ensuring that this power is not abused or misused, and that citizens have access to a variety of information and opinions upon which to inform themselves about political issues and base their democratic decision making. This, according to Feintuck and Varney, serves as the '*prima facie* justification for regulation within a democratic society.'[7] Barendt's other two justifications are the 'argument from truth' justification and the 'argument from self-fulfilment' justification which respectively posit that open discussion and a pluralistic exchange of information and opinions are essential to: the discovery of truth and

5 Commonwealth, *Parliamentary Debates*, House of Representatives, 19 April 1956, p. 1536 (Mr Davidson, Postmaster General).

6 E Barendt, *Freedom of Speech* (Clarendon Press, 1985) 8–23. In the second edition, Barendt adds a fourth argument – suspicion of government. However, as Barendt himself acknowledges, this is not so much an argument extolling the virtues of free speech as it is a negative argument highlighting the evils of regulation (E Barendt, *Freedom of Speech* (Oxford University Press, 2nd ed., 2005) 21–23).

7 Mike Feintuck and Mike Varney, *Media Regulation, Public Interest and the Law* (Edinburgh University Press, 2nd ed., 2006) 5.

the formation of accurate judgements; and individual growth and the formulation of personal beliefs and attitudes.

Barendt's analysis views the broadcasting audience primarily as citizens and focuses on democratic and social values. However, the broadcasting audience also is made up of consumers with individual preferences. In this regard, a number of commentators identify two contrasting schools of thought.[8] The first school takes an economic, market orientated, libertarian view that emphasises the rights of individuals and envisions broadcasting diversity being delivered through broadcasters satisfying individual preferences expressed in the marketplace. This view adopts a utilitarian approach and assumes that the public interest is the aggregation of individual preferences revealed by market behaviours, and that regulation only is justified to correct for market failures such as efficiency or competition reducing monopolies and oligopolies and public good, collective action and other coordination problems. The second school of thought takes a social-democratic view of the world. It defines the public interest in terms of attaining socially desirable outcomes such as justice, equity and fairness. This school of thought views markets with suspicion that, if left unchecked, produce results that are inconsistent with a just, fair and equitable society. According to this view, 'there are social objectives which the market cannot and should not, as a matter of principle, be allowed to deliver.'[9] For this school, strong public broadcasters and government regulation of private broadcasters are essential to providing the diversity of information, ideas and opinions needed to meet citizens' social and democratic needs.

The problem with viewing the public interest in this two dimensional manner is that neither school conveys a complete picture of what occurs in practice: television viewers are both citizens and consumers. Moreover, the two schools risk polarising debate with one view being advanced to the exclusion of the other. As Lunt and Livingstone observe when referring to the 'tension between regulating according to market logic and regulating to promote … social democratic values' in media regulatory debates, 'there is scant agreement on whether market

8 See for example: Christopher Witteman, 'Constitutionalizing Communications: The German Constitutional Court's Jurisprudence of Communications Freedom' (2010) 33 *Hastings International and Comparative Law Review* 95–201, 124; Peter Lunt and Sonia Livingstone, *Media Regulation: Governance and the interests of citizens and consumers* (Sage, 2012); Eric Windholz and Graeme Hodge, 'Conceptualising Social and Economic Regulation: Implications for Modern Regulators and Regulatory Activity' (2012) 38 *Monash University Law Review* 212–237.

9 Windholz and Hodge, above n 8, 224.

failure should itself be defined in purely market terms or also include social and cultural values.'[10]

Windholz and Hodge posit an alternative model of conceptualising the public interest underpinning modern regulatory practice. According to Windholz and Hodge, regulation rarely, if ever, is framed by reference to one set of values (image of the public interest) in isolation. Rather, they argue that regulation is underpinned by a mix of interconnected and interdependent economic and social values and that while one set of values may be given primacy at any point of time, the stability and legitimacy of the regulatory regime often can depend upon governments and regulators acknowledging and substantively addressing other competing values.[11] This is consistent with the views of other commentators for whom media regulation is as much (if not more) a product of political compromise and accommodation, as it is the result of 'policy considerations devised at arms' length in the public interest'.[12]

With this overview of the different ways the public interest underpinning broadcasting diversity regulation can and have been conceptualised, let us examine their influence in shaping Germany's and Australia's broadcasting diversity regulation.

3. Very Different Constitutional Starting Points

The starting point of each country's broadcasting regulation could not have been more different.

Germany

Modern Germany rose like a phoenix out of the ashes of World War II and its constitution, known as the Basic Law, is strongly influenced by a desire to prevent a repeat of the excesses of National Socialism. The National Socialists understood and exploited the power of the new broadcasting medium, often with the support of German industry. As Josef Goebbels, Hitler's Minister of Propaganda, observed in a speech to German broadcasters in 1933:

> 'You [broadcasters] have in your possession the most modern instrument in existence for influencing the masses. By means of this instrument you are the creators of public

---

10 Lunt and Livingstone, above n 8, 15.

11 Windholz and Hodge, above n 8.

12 Des Butler and Sharon Rodrick, *Australian Media Law* (Lawbook Co, 4th ed, 2012) 865. See also Lunt and Livingstone, above n 8, 22; and more generally Baldwin, Cave and Lodge, above n 1, 42.

> opinion … As the piano is to the pianist, so the transmitter is to you, the instrument on which you play as sovereign masters of public opinion.'[13]

As a result, the victorious allies were concerned to ensure post war Germany's media was free from both state influence, and the influence of any particular group of individuals. The key mechanisms though which the allies sought to achieve these goals were constitutional provisions designed to ensure decentralisation and democratic pluralism.[14] Articles 30 and 70 of the Basic Law combine to make cultural issues (which includes television content) the responsibility of the *Länder* (states);[15] and Article 5(1) of the Basic Law contains what have come to be known as the 'communication freedoms'. Given its importance to the design of German broadcasting regulation, it is worth quoting Article 5(1) in full:

> 'Every person has the right freely to express and disseminate his opinions in speech, writing and pictures, and to inform himself without hindrance from generally accessible sources. Freedom of the press and freedom of reporting by means of broadcast and films shall be guaranteed. There shall be no censorship.'

The first communication freedom is the 'broadcasting freedom'. It refers to the constitutional guarantee of 'freedom of reporting by means of broadcast'. The second communication freedom is the 'information freedom'. It refers to the constitutional right of every citizen 'to inform himself without hindrance from generally accessible sources'. As such, the Basic Law's protections apply to both the speaker and the recipient, protecting the rights of each to disseminate and receive a diversity of information and opinion. The impact of these complementary guarantees on German broadcasting regulation has been significant, as discussed below.

---

13 Josef Goebbels, Speech to German Radio Management, 23 March 1933, quoted in Witteman, above n 8, 111.

14 Witteman, above n 8, 111–112; Peter Humphreys and Matthias Lang, 'Regulating for media pluralism and the pitfalls of standortpolitik: the reregulation of German broadcasting ownership' (1998) *German Politics* 176–201, 181–182.

15 Article 30 states: 'Except as otherwise provided or permitted by this Basic Law, the exercise of state powers and the discharge of state functions is a matter for the *Länder*'; Article 70(1) states: 'The *Länder* shall have the right to legislate insofar as this Basic Law does not confer legislative power on the Federation'. Cultural issues are not listed as within the Federal government's jurisdiction. Translations of Articles of the Basic Law come from the translation available on the Deutscher Bundestag (Federal Republic of Germany National Parliament) website - <https://www.btg-bestellservice.de/pdf/80201000.pdf>.

Australia

Australia, on the other hand, was created by a desire of the then British colonies to secure the economic and security benefits that would flow from greater integration and nationhood. At this time (1890s), broadcasting was not yet invented and as a result was not mentioned in the new nation's constitution. However, the Australian Constitution's reference to '[p]ostal, telegraphic, telephonic, and other like services' over which the national government has power, subsequently has been interpreted to include radio and television broadcasting.[16] This makes the national government the predominant site of broadcasting regulation, with inconsistent state and territory regulation invalidated by clause 109 of the Constitution.

The Australian Constitution also does not contain a guarantee of broadcasting and information freedom as in Germany's Basic law, or a First Amendment guarantee of freedom of speech such as found in the United States Constitution. Freedom of speech protection in the Australian Constitution lay dormant until 1992 when the Australian High Court discovered an implied freedom protecting political speech in the Constitution's prescription of a system of representative government.[17] While in some early cases, a number of justices left open the possibility that some regulation might be justified 'to ensure some balance in the presentation of different points of view',[18] later High Court cases significantly narrowed the scope of the implied freedom. In the pivotal case of *Lange v Australian Broadcasting Corporation*, the High Court unanimously held that the constitutional guarantee of political free speech operates as shield and not a sword, and that the constitutional provisions from which it is implied 'do not confer personal rights on individuals. Rather they preclude the curtailment of the protected freedom by the exercise of legislative or executive power.'[19]

---

16 Australian Constitution, s 51(v). *R v Brislan; Ex parte Williams* (1935) 54 CLR 262 confirmed its application to radio; and *Jones v Commonwealth (No. 2)* (1965) 112 CLR 206 confirmed its application to television.

17 An implied freedom of political communication was first recognised by the High Court in *Nationwide News Pty Ltd v Wills* (1992) 177 CLR 1 and *Australian Capital Television Pty Ltd v Commonwealth of Australia (No 2)* (1992) 177 CLR 106.

18 *Australian Capital Television Pty Ltd v Commonwealth of Australia (No 2)* (1992) 177 CLR 106, 175 per Deane and Toohey JJ. See also McHugh J in the same case at 239; and Mason CJ, Toohey and Gaudron JJ in *Theophanous v Herald & Weekly Times* (1994) 182 CLR 104 who held the freedom operated to protect 'all speech relevant to the development of public opinion on the whole range of issues which an intelligent citizen should think about' (124).

19 (1977) 189 CLR 520, 560. Recently, in *Tajjour* v. *New South Wales* (2014) 88 ALJR 860, the Court rejected the idea of implying a guarantee of freedom of association from the

4. Pluralistic and Independent Public Broadcasting

In addition to the constitutional differences discussed above, the birth of television broadcasting in Germany and Australia was accompanied by important practical and commercial differences.

Germany

World War II severely weakened German industrial and commercial capacity. Private interests with the resources necessary to make the significant investments required to start a broadcasting service were non-existent. As a result, German broadcasting initially was solely a public sector responsibility. Individual *Länder* established public broadcasters, and some were set up by *Länder* jointly. The *Länder* also cooperated to establish nationwide public broadcasters: the first, *Arbeitsgemeinschaft der öffentlich-rechtlichen Rundfunkanstalten der Bundesrepublik Deutschland* or ARD, was established in 1954; the second, *Zweites Deutsches Fernsehen* or ZDF, was established in 1963.

To guard against state control or undue influence of these new public broadcasters, and to ensure broadcast programming reflecting societal diversity, a number of safeguards were implemented. Most important of these are the concepts of 'internal control' (requiring German public broadcasters to have a broadcasting or television council to monitor the diversity and independence of its programming) and 'internal pluralism' (requiring directors of the broadcasting or television council to be drawn from diverse 'socially relevant groups'.[20] These groups include labour and business groups, religious institutions, political parties, and cultural and social organizations). Also important was guaranteeing public broadcasters a revenue source largely independent of political interference. In Germany, public broadcasting is funded by a user-pays system pursuant to which every television owner pays a periodic broadcast fee.[21] The new public broadcasters also looked to the British Broadcasting Corporation (B.B.C.) as a role model for how a

text, further underlining the generally restrictive attitude it has taken over the last two decades or so.

20 This is the translation employed by Witteman, above n 8, 106, footnote 24. Humphreys and Lang, above n 14, 182 use 'socially significant groups'. See also Greg Taylor's essay in this volume at fn 29.

21 Only a small part of public broadcasters' revenue is derived from advertising.

'non-market, non-state' broadcaster should operate – impartially, independently and with a commitment to the public good.[22]

The importance of these features was reinforced by the German Constitutional Court in 1961 in what has become known as the first broadcasting decision.[23] This case concerned a constitutional challenge by *Länder* to a federal government proposal to introduce a national television service.[24] In upholding the challenge, the Constitutional Court laid down a number of guidelines or principles that have left an inedible mark on the shape of German broadcasting regulation. First, the Court affirmed broadcasting to be a 'cultural phenomenon' within the jurisdiction of the *Länder*.[25] Second, the Court upheld the monopoly of public sector broadcasters primarily on the grounds of spectrum scarcity. Third, the Court emphasised 'that broadcasting was not simply a "medium" but also a key "factor" for the functioning of democracy with the power to influence and shape opinion,'[26] and for this reason must offer a diversity of information and opinion. Importantly, the Court held this diversity should apply not only to news coverage and the expression of political opinions, but to all forms of information and opinion including entertainment, culture and the arts. Finally, and critically, the Court held this was not a subjective right, but an objective guarantee obliging lawmakers proactively to ensure a pluralistic broadcasting system while at the same time ensuring broadcasting remained state-free.[27]

---

22 Witteman, above n 8, 182. See also: Wolfgang Hoffmann-Riem, *Regulating Media: The Licensing and Supervision of Broadcasting in Six Countries* (The Guilford Press, 1996) 115.

23 BVerfGE 12, 205. This was the first of a series of important broadcasting decisions rendered by the German Constitutional Court. For a detailed discussion of the 'broadcasting decisions' and of the constitutional principles that underpin them, see Witteman, above n 8, on whose description of the decisions this chapter's examination and analysis relies heavily.

24 The federal government also sought to create two internationally focused broadcasters. The establishment of these broadcasters was not challenged by the *Länder*.

25 The Court distinguished broadcasting from management of the technical transmission facilities that it held was within the federal government's jurisdiction over telecommunications (Article 73(7)).

26 Humphreys and Lang, above n 14, 183.

27 Witteman points out there are inherent paradoxes in these requirements: that the state must at once both ensure a diversity of opinion, and do so in manner that does not control or censor the media (above n 8, 116). See also Hoffmann-Riem, 'Regulating Media', above n 22, 119, and Wolfgang Schulz, Uwe Jurgens, Thorsten Held and Stephen Dreyer, *Regulation of Broadcasting and Internet Services in Germany: A Brief Overview* (Working Papers of the Hans Bredow Institute No. 13, October 2002) 6.

The decision reflects a number of aspects of the public interest discussed above. While the Court recognised a key economic rationale for broadcasting regulation – spectrum scarcity – it is clear economic values played a secondary role to social values. Moreover, those social values extended beyond protecting the functioning of democracy (the citizen participation justification) to protect an individual's ability to access all forms of information and opinion important to all areas of life (the self-fulfilment justification).

Australia

In contrast with Germany, television broadcasting commenced in Australia in 1956 with a dual system of public and private sector broadcasters. The 1953 Royal Commission on Television informed the initial regulatory regime.[28] No attempt was made by the Commission to articulate a coherent conception of the public interest underpinning broadcasting diversity regulation. Rather, the Commission's recommendations reflect a pragmatic balancing of economic and social considerations. (This is most evident in the Commission's recommendations with respect to the regulation of private broadcasters discussed in Section 5 below.)

Unlike in Germany, the birth of television in Australia saw a number of private sector interests (mainly newspaper proprietors) willing to invest in the new medium on its commencement, and the Commission accepted almost without question private sector ownership of commercial television broadcasting stations. However, the private sector's interest generally was limited to the major metropolitan cities where high population densities held out the greatest promise of a profitable market. Rural and regional markets did not attract comparable interest, thus necessitating a public broadcaster, as was the case in Germany. The Royal Commission recommended that the public radio broadcaster, the Australian Broadcasting Commission (A.B.C.), should become the first public television broadcaster.[29]

Like its German counterparts, the A.B.C. is based on the B.B.C. model with a commitment to the public good, independence and impartiality. The A.B.C.'s Charter makes clear the strong social role it is to perform.[30] Its functions include: contributing to a sense of national identity; providing broadcasting programs

---

28 Commonwealth, Royal Commission on Television, *Report of the Royal Commission on Television* (1954).

29 The A.B.C.'s name was changed to the Australian Broadcasting Corporation in 1983, but the abbreviation A.B.C. still applies. A second public broadcaster, the Special Broadcasting Service (S.B.S.), commenced in 1979.

30 The current A.B.C. Charter is set out in s 6 of its enabling legislation, the *Australian Broadcasting Corporation Act 1983* (Cth).

that reflect the cultural diversity of the Australian community; encouraging and promoting musical, dramatic and other performing arts in Australia; and encouraging awareness of Australia and an international understanding of Australian attitudes on world affairs.

Importantly, the A.B.C. is to discharge this role independently and impartially. The A.B.C.'s enabling legislation provides for it to be overseen by a Board of Directors responsible for ensuring its functions are performed efficiently and with the maximum benefit to the people of Australia.[31] The legislation also imposes on the Board a duty to maintain the A.B.C.'s independence and integrity and to ensure the gathering and presentation by the A.B.C. of news and information is accurate and impartial according to the recognised standards of objective journalism.[32]

The extent to which the A.B.C. is, in fact, independent is a matter of some controversy. It appears more susceptible to political influence than its German counterparts. Appointments to the board of the A.B.C. (and the other Australian public service broadcaster) are effectively made by the government of the day and are therefore, by definition, political decisions. While rules designed to guard against overtly political appointments exist, the rigour which they and their spirit are adhered to can vary, as discussed by Taylor in his chapter. The A.B.C. also is funded by an annual central budget appropriation, and is thus more susceptible to the vagaries and politics of the annual budget process than its German counterparts. Some suggest its reliance on government funding can make it hesitant to criticise incumbent governments.[33] Quentin Dempster, for example, refers to the A.B.C.'s 'pre-emptive buckl[ing]' and 'practice of making changes in response to the perception of coming political pressure from the government'.[34]

As can be seen, social values have predominately shaped public broadcasting in both Germany and Australia. In the case of commercial broadcasting though, economic values and the interests that hold them always were destined to play a more meaningful role, as the discussion in the next section demonstrates.

---

31 *Australian Broadcasting Corporation Act 1983* (Cth), s 8(1)(a).

32 *Australian Broadcasting Corporation Act 1983* (Cth), s 8(1)(b) and (c).

33 David Rolph, Matt Vitens and Judith Bannister, *Media Law: Cases, Materials and Commentary* (Oxford University Press, 2010) 10–11 (and references cited therein).

34 Quentin Dempster, 'The Slow Destruction of the A.B.C.' in R Manne (ed), *Do Not Disturb: Is the Media Failing Australia?* (Black Inc, 2005) 101, 107–108.

5. The Rise and Regulation of Private Broadcasters

Germany

As noted above, the first broadcasting decision of the German Constitutional Court upheld the monopoly of public sector broadcasters primarily on the grounds of spectrum scarcity. However, this monopoly came under increasing pressure in the late 1970s and early 1980s from commercial broadcasters who argued that technological developments in over the air, cable and satellite broadcasting meant public broadcasters' monopoly could no longer be justified on spectrum scarcity grounds.

These arguments were accepted by the German Constitutional Court in 1981 in its third broadcasting decision that lay down the ground rules for the introduction of private broadcasting in Germany.[35] While acknowledging the inevitability of private broadcasting, the Court was conscious of the need to protect diversity of information and opinion from being dominated by private interests with the financial resources to establish a broadcasting service, and of the inability of market forces to prevent the accumulation and abuse of power in the broadcasting sector. According to the Court, regulation is required to produce socially desirable outcomes in preference to those produced by an efficiently operating market.[36]

In response to this decision, individual *Länder* began to license private broadcasters. Whereas public broadcasters were governed by rules of 'internal control' and 'internal pluralism', private broadcasters would be governed by rules of 'external control' and 'external pluralism'. External control involved oversight of private broadcasters by external independent *Länder* media authorities;[37] and external pluralism required an overall balance of diverse programming across all channels. However, the regulatory regimes were not consistent and their constitutionality uncertain.

Greater certainty was provided by the Constitutional Court's fourth broadcasting decision in 1986 that provided the framework for the dual public private system that still characterises German television broadcasting.[38] That case laid down two critical principles; first, that the provision of adequate public broadcasting services

35 BVerfGE 57, 295.

36 BVerfGE 57, 295. See also Hoffmann-Riem, 'Regulating Media', above n 22, 119.

37 The independence of the new media authorities (*Landesmedienanstalten*) was assured by them having pluralistic internal supervisory boards in the same manner as public broadcasters, and being financed primarily by the broadcasting fee levied on television and radio owners.

38 BVerfGE, 73, 188.

was an indispensable and essential condition for the introduction of private broadcasting and that reduced legal requirements for private broadcasters only are acceptable if public broadcasters are fulfilling their role of providing the public with a basic pluralistic service (Grundversorgung);[39] and second, that while the nature of private broadcasting and its reliance on advertising revenue means it ought not be subject to the same standards as public broadcasters, private broadcasters nevertheless should contribute to the plurality of information and opinion and be regulated to prevent undue concentration of influence over information and opinion.

The Constitutional Court also made two other important observations: that general competition laws alone are insufficient protection against the accumulation of power in the broadcasting sector;[40] and that broadcasting is an area that only can be regulated effectively by the *Länder* acting in common or by a central authority for the entire country. As the latter was prohibited by the Constitution, the 'Constitutional Court called for common action in the field of broadcasting and encouraged the *Länder* to harmonize their regulation.'[41]

The *Länder* quickly acted on the Court's exhortations. The principles of the fourth broadcasting decision formed the foundation for two inter-state agreements on broadcasting. The first inter-state agreement was entered into in March 1987 by the *Länder* of the former West Germany. The second inter-state agreement, known as the Interstate Agreement on Broadcasting, was entered into in August 1991 to accommodate unification with the *Länder* of the former East Germany. This second agreement – which has been amended fifteen times – continues to provide the framework for broadcasting regulation in Germany today.[42] It deals with a broad

---

39 This principle was reinforced by the Constitutional Court's fifth broadcasting decision delivered in 1987 that struck down prohibitions on local public broadcasting designed to protect private broadcasters on the ground they violated the basic principle of free opinion-building (BVerfGE 74, 297); and the Court's 2007 broadcasting decision that struck down *Länder* attempts to reduce the broadcasting fee on the grounds that it was a political attempt to limit the activities of public broadcasters rather than the product of independent and objective economic analysis (BVerfGE 119, 181).

40 Hoffmann-Riem, 'Regulating Media', above n 22, 135. See also Jessica Sanger, 'Media and Power – How to guarantee pluralism and diversity? (Presentation given to the German Israeli Lawyer's Association, 8 January 2014, available at http://www.dijv.de/media-and-power-how-to-guarantee-pluralism-and-diversity).

41 Jan Erk, 'Federalism and Mass Media Policy in Germany' (2003) 13(2) *Regional and Federal Studies* 107–127, 121.

42 The most recent version commnced on 1 January 2013. The original German version and an English translation is available on the website of the *Länder* media authorities - http://www.die-medienanstalten.de/en/legal-basis.html.

range of topics including the financing of public broadcasters and the licensing of private broadcasters, advertising principles, the protection of minors, access to major public events, and the rules governing product placement and teleshopping, for example. Importantly from our perspective, it also includes provisions addressing diversity requirements and ownership and media concentration limits.

Initially, the Agreement imposed four sets of ownership rules to guard against excessive concentration and to ensure the pluralism of German broadcasting. First, the Agreement defined external pluralism to be the national availability of three national private channels. Until this threshold was reached, each private broadcaster had to provide for internal pluralism in the manner required of public broadcasters. Second, the number of licences a national private broadcaster could hold was limited to two radio and two television channels, with only one of each being a news and current affairs channel. Third, strict limitations were placed on individual shareholdings. An individual shareholder was restricted to a single holding of 50% in one channel, or two holdings of less than 25% in two channels. These were designed to ensure 'broadcasting operations were "pluralistic" associations of different enterprises.'[43] Fourth, there were rules regulating the vertical integration of broadcasting and program supply. The Agreement also envisioned individual *Länder* establishing independent media regulatory authorities (*Landesmedienanstalten*) to administer and enforce the rules.

This approach to pluralism strongly reflected the social values underpinning broadcasting regulation. However, it was not long before economic values, and political acquiescence to the holders of those values, came to the fore. Indeed, the absence from the initial Interstate Broadcasting Agreement of rules regarding cross-media ownership is an example on point. By the time the 1987 agreement was designed, major press interests were already principal investors in private television broadcasters. The agreement reflects the decision of the *Länder* not to incur the anger of these powerful interests by compelling them to divest some of their existing interests.[44]

Another example of the ascendency of economic values and interests can be seen in the failure of the new media regulatory authorities 'to prevent the emergence of a powerful oligopoly, indeed a quasi-duopoly, of private broadcasting interests.'[45] According to Humphreys and Lang, the main reason for this failure was unhealthy deregulatory competition amongst the *Länder*. Referred to

43 Humphreys and Lang, above n 14, 185.
44 Ibid 186–187.
45 Ibid 185.

as *Standortpolitik* in German, this 'locational policy' saw *Länder* lower regulatory standards to incentivise private broadcasters to locate their operations there, bringing much needed investment, jobs and tax revenue to the *Länder*. The result, as Humphreys and Lang observe, was that 'individual Land broadcasting laws bore the stamp of the legislators' concern to promote the economic development of their respective *Länder* … as well as the concern to safeguard pluralism.'[46]

But probably the most glaring example was the replacement in 1996 of the system of strict limitations on individual shareholdings with an audience share model placing a ceiling on the national audience share attributable to an individual investor. Under the audience share model, there are no prescribed limits on the number of channels an individual or company may own, or programs they may broadcast. However, if the audience share of channels and programs attributable to an individual or company reaches 30% or more, then that individual or company is presumed to be able to exercise predominant power over public opinion. An individual or company also is presumed to be able to exercise predominant power over public opinion if the audience share reaches 25% and they hold a dominant position in other media markets, or if an overall assessment of its activities in television and other media markets suggest its influence is equivalent to that of a company with an audience share of 30%.[47]

The audience share model was initially proposed by the *Länder* to overcome complex ownership structures being employed to circumvent the individual shareholding rules. It also was initially proposed with lower thresholds and a greater emphasis on cross-media ownership. However, concerted lobbying by the major broadcasters resulted in a system with such high thresholds that it has been criticised not only for leaving the broadcasting interests of the 'quasi-duopoly' largely untouched, but also for giving them generous room to grow into new media technologies.[48]

---

46 Ibid 186.

47 Interstate Agreement on Broadcasting and Telemedia, Articles 25–34. The formulae for calculating audience share are complex. There exist, for example, 'bonus rules' and 'regional windows' whereby private broadcasters can increase the thresholds by including independent and regional programs on their channels. For an overview of how audience shares are determined, see Sanger, above n 40.

48 Humphreys and Lang (1998) 188–195 (and the references cited therein). The *quid pro quo* for this liberalisation of media ownership rules was a moderate increase in the broadcasting licence fee for public broadcasters (giving effect to the Constitutional requirement that public broadcasting be supported as a condition for the expansion of private broadcasting), new investigative powers for the *Länder* independent regulators,

Australia

The initial challenge for Australia was not a shortage of private sector interests as in Germany, but how to allocate television broadcasting rights among those private interests. The Royal Commission on Television, on whose recommendations the original regulatory regime was modelled, identified a number of familiar public interest justifications for regulating ownership of the new medium. For example, the Commission makes reference to spectrum scarcity,[49] the influence of television stations on the community,[50] the dangers associated with 'monopoly control' of such an influential communication vehicle,[51] and the public trust associated with possession of a television broadcasting licence,[52] as grounds for some ownership restrictions. On the other hand, the Commission acknowledged the economic challenge of providing a television service to the whole of Australia,[53] and the 'advantages to be derived from the common ownership or control of stations' such as enabling broadcasting stations 'in districts which may not be in a position to provide the necessary financial support to justify a station operating as an independent unit.'[54] Relevantly, there is no express discussion about the value of diversity of information, ideas and opinions, although it is arguably implicit in the discussion of the dangers of monopoly control – the underlying assumption being that concentration of broadcasting ownership leads to a lessening of diversity of broadcasting content.

The Royal Commission distilled the regulatory challenge before it to designing a regulatory regime that 'would be sufficient to prevent such a degree of concentration of ownership as would be contrary to the public interest, and at the same time would enable advantage to be taken of the economies of operation which the ownership of a number of stations would permit.'[55] To meet this challenge, the Commission pragmatically recommended that similar limitations then applying to the ownership of commercial radio stations also should apply to the

---

and the establishment of a national Commission on Concentration in the Media (in German *Kommission zur Ermittlung der Konzentration im Medienbereich*, or KEK) to ensure the media concentration rules are applied uniformly nationwide.

49 Royal Commission on Television, above n 30, paras 93–106.

50 Ibid paras 121–166.

51 Ibid para 363.

52 Ibid paras 375.

53 Ibid paras 107–108, Chapter V.

54 Ibid para 365.

55 Ibid para 366.

ownership of commercial television stations, with any residual concerns about the concentration of ownership being dealt with through the licensing process.[56]

The recommendations of the Royal Commission led to the *Broadcasting and Television Act 1956* (Cth). Section 53A of the Act introduced two prohibitions. The first prohibited a person from owning or controlling more than one commercial television station in an Australian capital city (or the Australian Capital Territory). This has since become known as the 'one to a licence area' restriction after the provision was amended to make the prohibition referable to a 'licence area' rather than a city. The second prohibited a person from owning or controlling more than two commercial television stations in Australia. This subsequently became known as the 'two station' rule. Section 45(1) of the Act conferred on the relevant Minister the power to grant a licence for a commercial television station upon such conditions as the Minister determined. The Minister was, however, required to request and consider the recommendations of the newly established Australian Broadcasting Control Board with respect to the grant of a licence.[57]

The first grant of commercial television licences related to Australia's two largest metropolitan markets, Melbourne and Sydney. Two licences were granted in each city to applicants with existing media interests. The implications of granting television broadcasting licences to existing media interests did not receive extensive consideration by the Australian Broadcasting Control Board in its report to the Minister. While the Board noted the public interest required 'the widest possible diffusion of ownership of television stations',[58] it concluded the new stations would benefit from being able draw on the experience of other media sectors.[59]

It was with respect to the second grant of television licences for Brisbane and Adelaide that the issue of media and broadcasting diversity came to the fore. The Australian Broadcasting Control Board rejected applications from persons associated with Sydney's and Melbourne's licence holders and recommended to the Minister that new applications be called from interests independent of them. The Board not only expressed concern about one person controlling licences in multiple capital cities, it also expressed concern about the influence of newspaper

---

56 Ibid.

57 *Broadcasting and Television Act 1956* (Cth), ss 47(1) and 69A.

58 Australian Broadcasting Control Board, *Report and recommendations to the Postmaster-General pursuant to the Television Act 1953 and the Television Regulations on Applications for Commercial Licences for the Sydney and Melbourne areas*, Parl Paper No 37 (1959), para 42, cited and discussed in Hitchens, above n 2, 121. The date of the report is misleading. The Board completed its inquiry in 1955.

59 Ibid.

interests holding television licences.[60] These recommendations were rejected by the Minister, however, who required the Board to recommend licences be granted from among the existing applicants. This the Board did, but not without first reiterating its concerns about cross-media ownership.[61] As Hitchens observes, these initial decisions established a tolerance for media ownership concentration that has come to be a hallmark of Australian media law.[62] They also demonstrate the political nature of broadcasting decision making, and the amenability of Australian politicians to the interests of established media proprietors.

Licensing decisions remained with the relevant Minister until 1977 when they were transferred to the Australian Broadcasting Tribunal, which replaced the Australian Broadcasting Control Board as the independent statutory regulator of broadcasting in Australia.[63] The regulator has since gone through a number of changes in name and form.[64] These changes have reinforced the independence of the regulator's licensing role. For example, under the initial 1977 transfer of licensing responsibilities, the Minister retained the power to determine the nature, purpose and area of the licence.[65] This power has since been removed, and today the Minister can only issue directions 'of a general nature' in relation to the regulator's broadcasting functions.[66] Of course, this has not removed politics from the regulatory process. Governments retain the ultimate power of being able to change both the functions and independence of the regulator and the rules according to which the regulator discharges its licensing functions which, as we shall see, they have done on a number of occasions.

---

60 Australian Broadcasting Control Board, *Report and Recommendations to the Postmaster-General on Applications for Commercial Television Licences for the Brisbane and Adelaide areas*, Parl Paper No 38 (1958), discussed in Hitchens, above n 2, 121–122.

61 Australian Broadcasting Control Board, *Supplementary Report and Recommendations to the Postmaster-General on Applications for Commercial Television Licences for the Brisbane and Adelaide areas*, Parl Paper No 39 (1958), discussed in Hitchens, above n 2, 121–122.

62 Hitchens, above n 2, 122.

63 The Australian Broadcasting Tribunal was created by the *Broadcasting and Television Amendment (No. 2) Act 1976* (Cth). Licensing decisions were transferred to it by the *Broadcasting and Television Amendment Act 1977* (Cth).

64 The Australian Broadcasting Tribunal was replaced by the Australian Broadcasting Authority which, in turn, was replaced by the current regulator, the Australian Communications and Media Authority.

65 *Broadcasting and Television Act 1942 (Cth)*, s 84(1).

66 *Australian Communications and Media Authority Act 2005* (Cth), s 14.

One such occasion was the passage of the *Broadcasting (Ownership and Control) Act 1987* (Cth). This Act replaced the two-station rule with an audience each rule limiting a person to controlling interests in broadcasting licences serving a maximum of 60 per cent of the population. The Act also introduced cross-media restrictions designed to prevent a person from controlling a commercial television and a commercial radio broadcasting licence with the same licence area, or a newspaper having more than 50 per cent of its circulation in the same area served by a commercial television or radio broadcasting licence.[67] According to the then Minister for Communications, the new regulatory regime would support a more balanced and competitive media market, encourage greater investment in the television industry, discourage concentration of media ownership in regional markets, and enhance 'public access to a diversity of opinion, information, news and commentary.'[68]

The 60% maximum audience reach in the *Broadcasting (Ownership and Control) Act* reflected a compromise negotiated to ensure passage of the Bill, the government originally having proposed a 75% limit. The 75% limit did, however, eventually find its way into legislation with the passage of the *Broadcasting Services Act 1992* (Cth). The primary objective of the *Broadcasting Services Act* was to provide a more flexible regulatory regime that would accelerate the introduction in Australia of new subscription and 'niche' broadcasting services.[69] Although it has been amended several times, the *Broadcasting Services Act* continues to be the primary regulatory instrument governing commercial broadcasting in Australia.

The *Broadcasting Services Act* expressly adopts a 'degree of influence' approach. The Act prescribes different regulatory regimes for different categories of broadcasting services, with commercial broadcasting services being the most heavily regulated and in respect of which diversity of control is most encouraged. Section 4(1) – which is headed 'Regulatory Policy' – explains the rationale for this approach:

---

67 The *Broadcasting (Ownership and Control) Act 1987* also grandfathered interests existing at the time the policy was announced (27 November 1986) thereby avoiding the need for any divesture.

68 Second reading speech for the Broadcasting (Ownership and Control) Bill 1987 (Cth). Commonwealth, *Parliamentary Debates*, House of Representatives, 29 April 1987, 2191–2196, 2193 (Michael Duffy, Minister for Communications).

69 Explanatory Memorandum, Broadcasting Services Bill 1992, available at <https://www.comlaw.gov.au/Details/C2004B01820/Explanatory%20Memorandum/Text>.

> 'The Parliament intends that different levels of regulatory control be applied across the range of broadcasting services according to the degree of influence that different types of broadcasting services are able to exert in shaping community views in Australia.'[70]

The Act also seeks to balance social and economic values. Section 4(2) states that it is Parliament's intent that broadcasting services in Australia be regulated in a manner that encourages the development of broadcasting technologies and the provision of broadcasting services made practicable by those technologies, and that public interest considerations be addressed in a way that does not impose unnecessary financial and administrative burdens on providers of those broadcasting services.

'Public interest considerations' is not defined in the Act. Guidance to its meaning is found in the Act's objects in section 3. Several objects promote social values in language that bears a strong resemblance to the charter of the A.B.C. They include promoting diverse entertainment, education and information programs; encouraging diversity of control of the more influential broadcasting services; and reflecting Australia's identity, character and cultural diversity. Others promote economic values, most notably providing a regulatory environment that will facilitate the development of a broadcasting industry in Australia that is efficient, competitive and responsive to audience needs.

The 75% audience reach and one to a licence area restriction continue to be cornerstones of Australia's television broadcasting diversity regulation.[71] The cross-media ownership rules, however, underwent significant change in 2006. The *Broadcasting Services Amendment (Media Ownership) Act 2006* (Cth) introduced a more liberal regime that permits cross-media ownership unless it results in an 'unacceptable media diversity situation' or an 'unacceptable three-way control situation'. An unacceptable media diversity situation is determined by the application of a complex point system the detail of which is beyond the scope of this chapter (but which is explained in the chapter by Rodrick). The practical effect of the system is to require at least five separate media groups to operate commercial television licences, commercial radio broadcasting licences, and newspapers in a metropolitan commercial radio broadcasting licence area, and at least four in a regional commercial radio broadcasting licence area (known as the '5/4 rule').[72]

70 This is the original wording in the Act as passed in 1992. The section (and Act) has since been amended also to apply to 'datacasting services and internet services'.

71 These rules are now referred to as 'statutory control rules' (*Broadcasting Services Act 1992* (Cth), s 61AD).

72 *Broadcasting Services Act 1992* (Cth), Division 5A – Media Diversity (especially ss 61AB-61AC). A radio broadcasting licence area was chosen as the point of reference as it is smaller and assumed to more accurately reflect the influence of radio stations and

An unacceptable three-way control situation is more straightforward and exists if, within the licence area of a commercial radio broadcasting licence, a person is in a position to exercise control of: a commercial radio broadcasting licence; a commercial television broadcasting licence whose licence area overlaps with the radio broadcasting licence area by more than 50%; and a newspaper with 50% of its circulation within either the commercial television or radio licences area.[73]

Like the *Broadcasting Services Act 1992* which it amends, the *Broadcasting Services Amendment (Media Ownership) Act 2006* was designed to modernise Australia's media ownership laws to provide for emerging new technologies in a manner that balanced both economic and social interests. The Act's explanatory memorandum explains that the proposed changes will encourage greater competition, allow media companies to achieve economies of scale and scope, increase access to capital, expertise and opportunities for growth, while protecting the public interest in a diverse and vibrant media sector.[74]

Rapid technological change continues to challenge the concepts and paradigms that traditionally have shaped broadcasting regulation. As the Australian Government's Convergence Review Committee recently concluded: 'Convergence of media content and communications technologies has outstripped the existing media policy framework. Many elements of the current regulatory regime are outdated or unnecessary and other rules are becoming ineffective'.[75]

Recent government commissioned reviews have recommended replacing and/or supplementing existing media ownership laws.[76] For example, the Convergence Review Committee recommended that existing media ownership rules be replaced by a 'minimum number of owners' rule and a media specific public interest test. The minimum number of owners rule would in effect be the existing 5/4 rule updated to take into account all entities that provide a news and commentary service that has a significant effect in a local market. The public interest test would focus on

newspapers in a community than larger and more geographically diverse commercial television licence areas.

73 *Broadcasting Services Act 1992* (Cth), s 61AEA.

74 Explanatory Memorandum, Broadcasting Services Amendment (Media Ownership) Bill 2006, 2.

75 Convergence Review Committee, *Convergence Review: Final Report* (Department of Broadband, Communications and the Digital Economy, 2012) 1.

76 See for example: Convergence Review Committee, above n 75; Report of the Independent Inquiry into the Media and Media Regulation, Report to the Minister for Broadband, Communications and the Digital Economy (Australian Government, February 2012); Productivity Commission, *Broadcasting*, Report No. 11 (AusInfo, 2000).

maintaining diversity of content providers at the national level. It would authorise the media regulator to block a proposed change in control of content providers of national significance if 'satisfied – having regard to diversity considerations – that the proposal is not in the public interest.'[77] According to the Committee, factors the regulator could be required to consider when making the assessment include whether the change in control would diminish the diversity of unique owners of content providers or the range of content services at the national level.[78]

Instructively for our purposes, the Convergence Review Committee recommended that its media specific public interest test apply in addition to existing general competition laws which, in the Committee's opinion, 'are insufficient to address media ownership concerns. A pure competition analysis is likely to overlook important non-economic criteria when assessing media mergers.'[79] As such, the recommendations were designed to strike a more appropriate balance between the economic values underpinning general competition law, and the social, cultural and democratic values served by a diverse broadcasting sector. Government attempts to act on these recommendations failed, however. Legislation implementing the reforms was withdrawn in the face of significant opposition from established media interests concerned that the public interest test's subjectivity could pave the way for political interference in licensing decisions.[80]

Thus, as anticipated, unlike the case with public broadcasting, economic values generally have played a greater role than social values in shaping Germany's and Australia's diversity regulation of commercial broadcasters. However, in both cases, politics arguably has played a greater role than both. In both Germany and Australia regulatory attempts to reinforce social values underpinning broadcasting diversity regulation have been undermined by the political influence of vested economic interests with the result that some reforms arguably strengthened the position of existing broadcasting interests and reinforced existing media oligopolies.

6. Conclusion

So what have we learned about the public interest underpinning German and Australian broadcasting diversity regulation? What insights can we draw? First, we have learned that no one public interest theory or set of values alone explains

77 Convergence Review Committee, above n 75, 18.

78 Ibid 24.

79 Ibid 23, citing the submission to it of the Communications Law Centre.

80 Rhonda Jolly, 'Media reform: in shallows and miseries' (Research Paper, Parliamentary Library, Parliament of Australia, 2013–2014).

the evolution or nature of broadcasting diversity regulation in Germany and Australia. Regulating for broadcasting diversity has involved striking a balance between competing conceptions of the public interest (economic and social), and between the public interest and legitimate private interests. This is consistent with Windholz's and Hodge's conceptualisation of regulation as a mix of interconnected and interdependent economic and social values, and with the political view of regulation as the product of compromise and accommodation, rather than coherent theory.

We also have learned that the balance struck between social and economic values is content and context specific – with different balances being struck with respect to public and private broadcasting, and at different points of time in light of changing economic, social and political circumstances. Initially the German and Australian approaches to broadcasting diversity reflected very different political and economic circumstances, and very different conceptions of the role of public broadcasting and market forces in democratic governance. Over time, however, Germany and Australia evolved similar approaches - strong public broadcasters and private broadcasters subject to rules designed to promote diversity of information, opinion and ideas, enforced by independent media regulatory authorities - in response to similar forces - most notably globalisation, technological progress and the increasing role of the market.

Another lesson is that one cannot fully understand a country's broadcasting regulation without understanding the constitutional arrangements that support it. As Feintuck and Varney observe: 'awareness of the constitutional context is crucial'.[81] A key difference between German and Australian broadcasting regulation has been the different constitutional and institutional arrangements through which the public interest has been forged, and economic and social values weighed and balanced. Most important here are the German constitutionally guaranteed broadcasting and information freedoms. Australia has no such constitutional guarantees, and the prospect of a constitutional amendment to create them is remote. Nor can the Australian High Court be expected to discover in the present constitutional text such broad guarantees in the future, having already rejected opportunities to imply a more expansive positive right to political speech.

Also important is the role played by the German Constitutional Court in giving the constitutional freedoms shape and force. As we have seen, the German Constitutional Court effectively laid down the guiding principles for a diverse and pluralistic broadcasting environment for German legislatures to follow. Hoffmann-Riem

81 Feintuck and Varney, above n 7, 8.

describes the Court acting 'much like a legislature' with respect to the development of German broadcasting regulation,[82] and refers to its 'heroic battle … to preserve the orientation of broadcasting around the common good'.[83] Witteman similarly describes the Court acting as a counter balance to political and economic forces that sought to advance the interest of private broadcasters at the expense of public broadcasting.[84] Yet both commentators also concede the limitations associated with the Court's role, noting that regulatory outcomes beneficial to politically powerful commercial interests generally have prevailed.

Indeed, the role played by these politically powerful commercial interests should not be underestimated. As this chapter's examination of the evolution of German and Australian broadcasting diversity regulation has demonstrated, many reforms served to strengthen and reinforce their positions in the market. And while Rolph, Vitens and Bannister may be correct that it might be going too far (as some do) to talk of conspiratorial trading of favourable media policy for favourable media coverage, it is hard to resist the conclusion that in several instances, media policy has been designed to ensure powerful media interests are not too disappointed or angered.[85]

One important question not yet answered by this chapter's analysis is: has the German and Australian public interest been served by their respective country's broadcasting diversity regulation? As we have seen, the public interest underpinning broadcasting diversity regulation has been a fluid and pragmatic balancing of competing social and economic values undertaken in a politically responsive environment. This makes evaluating the success or failure of that regulation very difficult. Moreover, that difficulty is compounded by defining the public interest in terms of diversity. What does diversity look like? What proportion should be public broadcasting and what proportion should be private broadcasting? As Lunt and Livingstone ask: 'if a government wants to encourage diversity of content, how is an appropriate level of diversity to be judged?'[86] A central concern of governments in both Germany and Australia has been to ensure the broadcasting medium produces programming providing a diversity of information, ideas

---

82 Hoffmann-Riem, 'Regulating Media', above n 22, 119.

83 Wolfgang Hoffmann-Riem, 'Rundfunkverfassung als Richterrecht [Broadcasting Constitution as Judge-Made Law]', in Peter Glotz and Reinhold Kopp (eds), *Das Ringen um den Medienstaatsvertrag der Länder* (1987) 37, cited and translated in Witteman, above n 8, 123–124 (footnote 83).

84 Witteman, above n 8, 121–123.

85 Rolph, Vitens and Bannister, above n 32, 122 (and references cited therein).

86 Lunt and Livingstone, above n 8, 24.

and opinion. On these measures, the report card is mixed. My initial impression watching television in Germany and Australia was of a mix of public and private broadcasters producing programs catering for a variety of diverse interests and tastes. However, that is off-set by the degree to which ownership and management of those broadcasters is concentrated in the hands of a relative few.

In conclusion, there are a number of important lessons and insights to be drawn from this chapter's examination of the public interest underpinning broadcasting diversity regulation in Germany and Australia. These lessons are not limited to the regulation of broadcasting, however. They also apply to the regulation of new and converging media technologies where governments also face the significant challenge of how to create a sustainable economic environment whilst simultaneously protecting and promoting social, cultural and democratic values and norms.

Romy Nicole Fleischer*

Antitrust Regulation, Innovation and Dynamic Competition in the Internet sector with particular focus on unilateral market behaviour of online platforms

---

* Dr Fleischer works as a corporate lawyer for Noerr LLP, a leading European law firm. Previously, she worked as a law tutor and research fellow at Philipps University Marburg, focussing on European antitrust law.

Abstract: Social-political concerns regarding online platform rivalry in Europe can be faced best with the current provision against an abuse of market power (art. 102 TFEU), if applied in line with its purpose plus slightly modified evaluation standards to preserve and boost the beneficial innovative forces of online markets, whose structure is in constant flux.

A. Introduction

The digitalisation of information and modern methods of data transmission in the 21st century have caused various concerns regarding the formation of people's opinion. Apart from the ongoing 'convergence of the media'[1] and the opportunity to offer a wide range of internet services by single providers that bundle technology with supply and communication processes, some large companies, operating within a (legal) desire to boost their revenue, are increasingly seen as a risk for society and media diversity. The debate gets heated up by court decisions related

1 This is a process of transformation in which the differentiation between the traditional types of media press, television broadcast, radio, and direct distribution fades away due to an overlapping distribution of information and approximation of content and thus a convergence of supply and use.

to data protection law[2], privacy or copyrights,[3] as well as numerous press reports,[4] speeches by politicians,[5] open letters of competitors[6] or other political measures, like the resolution of the European Parliament in late November 2014 calling for the unbundling of huge media companies. They emphasise social-political dangers and the lack of transparency of large online players like *Google* – the 'top dog' among internet search engines in Europe. These concerns have led to ever-louder calls for a stricter antitrust enforcement policy, especially with respect to controls on the abuse of market power, at the European level,[7] or even sharper media regulation against a predominant media power in diverging media markets. However, simply 'being pioneering, thriving and eventually big' is not automatically a sign of an abuse of market power. On the contrary, it can be an indication of a flourishing, innovative and quality competition from which consumers benefit, although it is not always seen this way at first glance. The following analysis will show that there is currently no need for new, harsher antitrust measures or additional regulation against unilateral abusive media market behaviour. Far more essential is a thorough enforcement policy that remembers fundamental antitrust principles and modifies certain evaluation standards if needed to meet the new challenges in the digital economy. Hence, the study starts with a brief assessment of the divergent 'players' involved, since a lot of public misconception about online media platforms comes from the lack of knowledge about their role in society, their functionality, and the behaviour patterns of their customers. It continues with a glimpse at the current guiding principles in media and antitrust law and focuses afterwards on the structural framework and limits in competition law,

---

2 ECJ, decision from the 13th of May 2014, case no. C-131/12, [2014] ECR 317 – Google Spain SL & Google Inc. versus Agencia Española de Protección de Datos (AEPD) & Mario Costeja González.

3 ECJ, decision, 11th of Sept. 2014, case o. C-117/13 – Technische Universität Darmstadt v Eugen Ulmer KG.

4 Cf. an article published in the German ‚Frankfurter Allgemeine Zeitung', 16 September 2014, available at http://www.faz.net/googles-transparenz-wir-kuemmern-uns-13156824.html (28 September 2014).

5 See *Sigmar Gabriel* of the German Social Democratic Party and current minister of Economic Affairs and Energy, May 2014, available at http://www.bmwi.de/DE/Presse/reden,did=638890.html (March 2016).

6 See BBC News regarding an open letter of Mathias Dophner, chief executive of the German media company Axel Springer SE, 17 April 2014, available at http://bbc.com/news/technology-27063372 (March 2016).

7 Other regulations are not discussed such as the law against unfair competition, civil law (contractual terms and conditions), broadcasting law and telecommunications law.

apart from the implications for the market process and the formation of an opinion. It concludes by discussing potential solutions and the necessity to preserve the innovative competitive conditions in online media markets.

B. Selected aspects from a media and behavioural point of view

I. Challenges, concerns and contrasts for the formation of opinion

1. Social importance of free access to data

a. Reasonable way to cope with a vast amount of digital content

The rivalry of online platforms is a cornerstone of the new digital economy, the formation of public opinion and consumer welfare. However, like every pioneering achievement in society that raises concerns and doubts at first, it challenges traditional ways of living and, in particular, gathering information and ways of usage for the formation of a public opinion. The internet, being a constantly changing virtual realm and the digital counterpart of the real world, is no exception. In particular, online platforms like *Facebook* have led to a veritable explosion of data accessible online, especially personal data. Such data do not necessarily involve only written scientific and informational news, but also come in the form of pictures and blogs. For example, the web blog of tumblr.com reflects a digital diary or journal by which users can publish divergent texts, images, quotes, links, chat logs, videos and audio data. A reasonable way to cope with the vast amount of digital content is practically impossible without the use of such a platform, which is why they possess a key position in this area.[8] They represent economic networks that allow access to the 'Word Wide Web' and the distribution of mass data and information and - from a technical point of view - digital computer programs that search through a collection of online documents for specific content. They help users to find and retrieve specific, pre-evaluated information from the World Wide Web (as long as no login is requested) within the shortest time. Hence, online platform providers serve as intermediaries[9] of data in an information society and at the same time, as distributers of journalistic products and services, and as private entities in an economic market system. In connection with this

8 Cf. *Pasquale*, Frank, Beyond Innovation and Competition: The need for qualified transparency in internet intermediaries, (2010) 104 Northwestern University Law Review, 105, 110.

9 *Thèpot*, Florence (2013), Market Power in Online Search and Social Networking: A Matter of Two-Sided Markets, p. 196.

special social-political responsibility that is shared by many others in the media industry,[10] there exists a public responsibility. Particularly for the formation of public opinion, the value of collecting, processing and using data by and from the World Wide Web increases constantly. Digital search engines play an important role in spreading such data and, since they are the most significant research tool on the internet which is characterised by a high freedom of choice and decision, are both suppliers and consumers.

b. *Dangers of a restricted internet structure*

The debate that has arisen about the dangers of online platforms for the formation of public opinion, such as in the case of *Google* in 2014 and other single huge market participants, resulted in a rather short sighted tendency in society for regulation that was, in particular, nurtured by sensational reporting by the national press and online media. The discussion often neglects the risks for the formation of opinion that results from a stricter regulation in the internet sector. It strengthens governmental control in this field and may contribute to a hidden censorship of digital data. Derision, parody, satire, caricature, irony and mockery, just like 'the postillion' (www.der-postillion.de) are especially popular forms to express an opinion about social grievances[11] but also often seen as an unwanted side effect of the freedom of opinion. The questionable outcome of a strictly regulated internet structure in the long run can be seen, for example, in China where often information which is connected to internal political interests is either suppressed or manipulated within the media, including the strongly regulated internet structure.[12]

---

10 Cf. BVerfGE 12, 205, 246.

11 For instance, in mid 2015 people across Germany expressed their incomprehension at the lack of enthusiasm of the Department of Public Prosecution in Limburg (state of Hesse) for prosecuting Bishop Tebartz-van Elst on an allegation of embezzlement (such as in online video montages on Youtube).

12 The following example is based on a personal experience of the author who visited China in 2013 (Wuhan City) and worked at Nanjing University as a visiting scholar for a couple of months. Certain stereotypes and allegations have been seeded in the media, mainly controlled by central government, towards some ethnicities like the Uighurs. The members of this Muslim minority are often considered to be criminal, dangerous, even unintelligent which - furthermore – is supposed to be their own fault because they do not send their children to school. However, there is nothing in the media about the political suppression in their home province, nothing about their traditional way of raising and educating their children on their own and nothing about the many limits in pursuing certain careers and professions in society, but only news on television or

2. *Divergent interests and rights of providers and consumers*

Public concerns about the use of large online platforms like *Google* or *Facebook* often concentrate on the aspect of manipulation of people's opinions which is in turn shaped by the information provided and by this being open to influence. Their right to form an opinion free from any influences is an important aspect of the fundamental right of the freedom of information. It underpins the public interest in media and information diversity. On the other hand, online search engines providers commercial interests and, generally, are entitled to exercise fundamental rights without state intervention, such as the right of freedom of action, the freedom of opinion and information, since they produce their own content to some extent, i.e. select and prioritise search results and therefore assist in the process of the formation of public opinion. Nonetheless, in consideration of the responsibility of the state to secure the genuine supply of information by these mostly private entities, the promotion of media variety and freedom of information are crucial but require at the same time a notable regard towards the technical possibilities and the specific characteristics of the internet.

3. *Behavioural patterns of consumers*

It is important to remember that many worries in society[13] about potential influences of powerful online media companies on people's opinion are initiated by behavioural patterns of consumers. For instance, people still use certain websites although they are annoyed about their tracking cookies, such as *Facebook* with its 'Facebook Cookie', that save websites in which users have shown curiosity to analyse, through a backdoor, their interests and affinities and in turn use this gathered information to adopt advertising on their own website once the user enters it again. More striking is the loudly expressed concern in Europe about *Google* that is often called a 'data leech'. Its once existing crystal clean image seems to have faded away, especially with respect to data protection and copyright law, and despite the US internet giant's growing media market power, many Europeans use the platform anyway. They too often take internet products and services which they have got used to for granted. Especially in case of social networks, it is striking

---

online of the crimes some individuals have committed. Hence, the government practically has shaped the public opinion about an entire populace.

13 There are negative side effects, especially of social media, such as new possibilities to find people without leaving the house and live a fantasy instead of a real life, or a gambling addiction, or, in general, people's dependency on the internet, since the latter offers a profile for every purpose and intention.

how many tend to share a massive amount of personal data. They provide thoughts and private information willingly and freely, although it can be used to manipulate people's opinions and to ruin someone's career or reputation. One reason for such behaviour may be that people like routine and normally lack time and interest to change habits, which, by the way, is characteristic and accepted in a 'performance society' (Leistungsgesellschaft) that is driven by the idea of efficiency and output, such as in Germany. People usually stick to a digital service or product that meets and satisfies their needs and interests quickly and sufficiently. For instance, in case of *Google*, its popularity as a search engine for private users may come from its relatively clear design and the high quality of search results. If settled with one provider, users normally stay with it[14] (the 'single homing phenomenon') and barely switch to others or use more than one ('lock-in effect'). Despite the lack of empirical data, it is safe to assume, additionally, that search engine users typically consider the first four or five results and click on them, either believing these are the most relevant results or lacking time and interest to read 10 to 15 pages, since the purpose of a search machine is after all to find information as fast as possible, in contrast, to the use of social networks, e-commerce websites or e-mail services where users usually spend much more time.

II. Application of online search engines

From a social point of view, the operating system of online platforms, such as digital search engines (algorithms), being highly complex, is difficult for general members of society to grasp. Moreover, many private users[15] have little or no knowledge about the actual functionality and business model of their preferred provider, in general, although the basic information is available online. Despite the lack of empirical data, some people who frequently use search engines still seem to believe that highlighted hits on top of the search results list means 'important',

---

14 Different *Thèpot*, Florence (2013), Market Power in Online Search and Social Networking: A Matter of Two-Sided Markets, p. 219 who states that multi-homing is typical in the field of social networking, which is, for instance, barely the case any more in Germany and even less the case within online search engines.

15 In particular, children (approx. between six and twelve years) who use the internet to meet friends and gather information that is entertaining or interesting, lack basic knowledge about its operation. To protect them from certain content that is unsuitable for their age and to provide them free use of the internet at the same time, some search engines are especially designed for children, such as the German platform *fragfinn.de* that was introduced in 2007. It is based on a 'white list' surf, i.e. only websites that are editorially reviewed by media educators will be displayed.

even though these are paid ads. It is safe to assume, that a lot of misconception about an online media company's core service and behaviour is not caused by general intransparency but rather a lack of knowledge about the business itself. Thus, a closer look helps to understand their behavioural motives, patterns and certain forms of market conduct which is important for every antitrust analysis.

1. Functionality of indexed based search engines

In Europe, most popular search engines are 'index based'.[16] This means that the information that is required by a searcher is stored on a computer system, meaning data banks of computer servers. For instance in case of *Google,* the vast amount of data is stored on several huge servers located in one distant place to prevent their loss (Cloud Computing), making it, however, vulnerable for spy attacks by hackers and interesting for governmental institutions regarding personal data with whose demands online providers like *Google* often tend to comply. The provided information is constantly updated by real time search engines, such as 'web spiders' or 'web crawlers', which are sent on to the World Wide Web automatically to retrieve new data. It is safe to assume that in the future online search engines will use more and more artificial intelligence (e.g. software agents) to improve the efficiency of the business concept. From a technical point of view, the computer server registers the received information in the shape of an index, which is why the actual search does not take place on the web itself (which would take more than a few moments) but in the indexed content of the search engine servers. For instance, the data banks of *Google* include a constantly updated copy of the entire internet.[17] A search enquiry is basically target-orientated in terms of person, place and season. The search engine's banks will be accessed with the help of a search algorithm which is an automatic computer program that operates by certain parameters determining the order of the displayed search results (hyperlinks) including a brief description of their content. The order of results in case of *Google* depends on the 'PageRank' algorithm that evaluates mathematically different websites that include the searched information. A value is assigned to every webpage and it can

---

16 They are also so-called 'web spider search engines'. Other search engines are web directories (index based, editorial search engines) and 'meta search engines', see more *Eberwein*, Helgo, Wettbewerbsrechtliche Aspekte von Domains und Suchmaschinen, 2012, p. 133.

17 *Ehmann*, Timo, Wettbewerbsfreiheit und Institutionenschutz von Datenbanken, 2011, p. 9.

be transferred on to others and received by links on them; hence, the higher the cumulated value, the higher the page rank in the search results.

2. *Financing and advertising*

a. Online search engines are profit orientated private entities, constantly seeking to boost their revenue. While very few are financed by paid searches, most of them, in particular large entities like *Google*, *Microsoft Bing* or *Baidu* offer a free search service for consumers that is financed by advertising. *Google* presumably makes more money by advertising than any other online company. In order to sell advertising space, the aforementioned digital search machines operate on an auction-based system (see *Google Adwords* or *Bing Ads*). It involves two customer groups, i.e. the 'demand dispatcher' (user or searcher) and a non-identical person who provides a service in return (advertiser).[18] The latter normally pinpoints advertising to certain search keywords ('keyword advertising'[19]) and bid for priority placement which in turn depends on both the score of the quality of an ad (which is based on the relevance that is mainly determined by an analysis of past searches and click-through results)[20] *and* the price for the link the advertiser has agreed to pay ('bidding fee').[21] They are not being charged by the number of times a searcher visits and sees a website with the displayed advertisement but instead for each click by a customer on the advertiser's link in the search page ('pay per click method'). Additionally, advertisers can buy a placement in the index of the search machines ('paid inclusion') without any preference or even buy a specific rank position of their links ('paid placement').

b. Google Adwords and Facebook Ads, among others, have become a part of everyday life in the last years and are widely accepted advertising tools, although sponsored links, i.e. paid search results, still trigger less likely customer confidence than natural search results (organic hits). It also increases the risk of deception

18 *Körber*, Thorsten, Google im Fokus des Kartellrechts, WRP 2012, 761–772 (p. 763) with further reference.

19 See *Eberwein*, Helgo, Wettbewerbsrechtliche Aspekte von Domains und Suchmaschinen, 2012, p. 129, fn 975.

20 Other factors are geographic proximity, landing page quality and landing page loading time, see Justus *Haucap*/Christiane *Kehder*, Suchmaschinen zwischen Wettbewerb und Monopol: Der Fall Google, Ordnungspolitische Perspektiven, 2013, p. 9.

21 *Zhang*, Angela Huyue, Using a Sledgehammer to Crack a Nut: Why China's Anti-Monopoly Law was Inappropriate for Renren v. Baidu, Competition Policy International Journal, Vol. 7, No. 1 (Spring 2011), p. 277 (280) regarding *Google*.

about a website's reputation and relevance by means of its rank in the search results list. Despite the missing empirical data on the actual amount of information on the internet and the lack of transparency regarding the search algorithm[22] of large search engines like *Google*, private users have no effective means to control the relevance and factual origin of the search results or the operation and methods in context of delivering bits and ranking websites.[23] In order to reduce antitrust concerns and to avoid any disguise about the hyperlink's reputation, ad-sponsored links that serve online platform providers economically ought to be identified clearly. Colour markings alone with respect to the wording or background often are not sufficient and therefore should be combined with a sufficiently large and clear 'advertisement', revealing its purpose so that even users with little or no search experience are able to identify it immediately.

3. *Interaction of free and fee-based services*

Online search engine providers are characterised by different functions. While they provide private users a service that allows a quick and easy search to receive vast information without paying for it in monetary terms, they offer advertisers an efficient medium to distribute their online advertisements broadly and in a target-orientated fashion. Despite the different services, indications suggest that the diverse functions are twisted, i.e. interact in a way where the free search service influences the fee-based advertising service and vice versa, from which the two types of customers benefit.[24] Accordingly, (historic) data that are collected from the searches optimise the quality of a search algorithm, leading to better results for consumers and supposedly an increase of purchases in favour of advertisers instead of just a non-profitable click on the ad.[25] However, the rise of *Google* itself and its success against the older *Yahoo* search engine reveals that it is not entirely clear whether these indirect network effects are characteristic for online

---

22 *Körber*, Thorsten, Google im Fokus des Kartellrechts, Wettbewerb in Recht und Praxis (WRP) 2012, 761–772 (p. 771 f).

23 *Pasquale*, Frank, Beyond Innovation and competition: The need for qualified transparency in internet intermediaries, (2010) 104 Northwestern University Law Review 105, 106.

24 These are called asymmetrical indirect network effects, since the revenue of a search engine provider on the advertising market depends on the amount of users and content while the opposite link is not mandatory.

25 Justus *Haucap*/Christiane *Kehder*, Suchmaschinen zwischen Wettbewerb und Monopol: Der Fall Google, Ordnungspolitische Perspektiven, 2013, p. 23, with further reference.

search machines, i.e. whether solely the size of a platform results necessarily in better search quality for consumers who click *and* buy, since no empirical data or detailed analyses exist.[26]

III. Neutrality as a guiding principle

The social-political discussion about online platform providers, their market behaviour, especially of large search engines, and competition is often couched in terms of 'neutrality'. It is a significant guiding principle within online media regulation, in general. However, the popular expression of 'net neutrality' differs from 'search engine neutrality'. The first refers to the transmission of data over the internet that is free from discrimination. Data should be treated equally, independent of their source, the addressee or content.[27] From a technical point of view, the data are split into packages and transmitted equally over all available distribution channels (such as cable, satellite, radio) according to the 'best efforts principle' and independent of their content or format (text, music, video, calls, etc.), as long as capacity is available.[28] In contrast, 'search engine neutrality' refers to transmitted data and describes the need for a search that is free from illegitimate influences on the search results,[29] since consumers do not seek an advertising medium for special products and services. Such influences appear in various forms, such as potential external influences in form of spamming, or internal search manipulations with regard to the algorithm. However, not every difference between the results of a certain search machine like Google and those of competitors such as Microsoft Bing is based on manipulation, since the pre-evaluation of the mass data is based on different search algorithms that determine the quality of the online platform. The purpose is to display the most relevant results first without skewing them by influences on the order of results, any exclusion or favouring certain results due to search bias or payment. Hence, 'search neutrality' cannot mean an absolutely

---

26 *Manne*, Geoffrey/*Wright*, Joshua D., Google and the Limits of Antitrust: The case against the antitrust case against Google, (2011) 34 Harvard Journal of Law and Public Policy 171, 206f.

27 *Redeker*, Helmut, IT-Recht, 5th edition, NJW Praxis, München 2012, Rn. 1069.

28 See *Ufer*, Frederic, Kampf um die Netzneutralität, Kommunikation und Recht (K&R) 2010, 383–389 (p. 384 f).

29 Cf. *Schulz*, Wolfgang, Von der Medienfreiheit zum Grundrechtsschutz für Intermediäre?, Überlegungen zur Entwicklung der Gewährleistungsgehalte von Art. 5 Abs. 1 GG am Beispiel von Suchmaschinen, Computer und Recht (CR) 2008, 470–476 (p. 470 ff).

'neutral search' in consideration of the factual and technical reasons,[30] since this would mean a search without any filtering of the most significant websites and sub-pages,[31] which is hardly in the interest of consumers. It neglects the core function of a search engine which marks its quality, i.e. to pre-evaluate information in an impartial, comprehensive way that is solely based on relevance (so-called 'organic searches'). Although public search engines may meet the 'neutral search' requirement and be less economic orientated, there are other obstacles apart from the disadvantages of a non-pre-evaluated search, such as the openness to public interest and influences, high transparency demands and administration costs, as well as technological and innovative efforts to prevail against private search engines.[32]

C. Selected aspects from an antitrust point of view

The protection of information and media diversity cannot be found directly as a goal in European antitrust law or, in particular, the abuse control regulation. Nonetheless, a tight connection with competition, being the overall aim of the law, can be made out. One of its social-political functions is to control market power and to promote freedom and the justice of performance equally[33] that, in turn helps to prevent a decrease of information variety and the development of a predominant power of opinion. The abuse control in its current shape, embedded in article 102 of the '**Treaty on the Functioning of the European Union**' (TFEU), is an effective tool in this matter, if enforced in light of the challenging circumstances of digital markets. This, in turn, includes some detailed modifications to traditional evaluation standards, but without ignoring fundamental guiding principles of the law and the special nature of the new economy. To what extent adjustments are possible, plausible and reasonable will be discussed in the following antitrust analysis.

30 *Paal*, Boris P., Suchmaschinen, Marktmacht und Meinungsbildung, Rechtsstudie, Mai 2012, p. 10, available at: http://i-comp.org/wp-content/uploads/2013/07/PAAL-Suchmaschinen-Marktmacht-und-Meinungsbildung-2012-final.pdf (March 2016).

31 *Körber*, Thorsten, Google im Fokus des Kartellrechts, WRP 2012, 761–772 (p. 770).

32 See *Ott*, Stefan, Marktbeherrschende und öffentlich-rechtliche Suchmaschinen, K&R 2007, 375–380 (p. 379 f).

33 See generally *Schmidt*, Ingo/*Haucap*, Justus, Wettbewerbspolitik und Kartellrecht: Eine interdisziplinäre Einführung, 10th edition, 2013, p. 36.

I. Information variety by effective competition

1. *Normative principle guidelines*

The core of modern antitrust law is the protection of the – indefinable, complex and unpredictable – phenomenon of economic competition[34], although it is not easy for general members of society to grasp. It is not just a means to another end but the eventual goal. On the European level, it is normally viewed in light of the 'ordoliberal tradition'.[35] The maintenance and promotion of the rivalry process requires a market structure that allows all participants to compete freely without state interventions and private restrictions from which consumers eventually benefit.[36] Although high evaluation standards have been developed by the European courts that support the effectiveness of the structural approach, the EU Commission favours a 'more economic approach'[37] within the application of article 102 TFEU which suggests the promotion of efficiencies and thereby the optimisation of consumer welfare,[38] despite various difficulties. For instance, such economic aspects cannot be found as direct goals within European antitrust law, i.e. neither in the TFEU nor in its protocols. It is the same with 'media diversity'. Although principles outside the law text such as economic aspects can be integrated in the law in case of an obvious statutory gap, such unification has to be plausible to avoid a system discontinuity. The Commission's economic approach cannot fulfil such requirement, in its current shape leading to doubts in terms of legal systems[39] and a lack of clarity on how to measure long-term dynamic efficiencies precisely such as innovation, in contrast to the "ordoliberal approach" by the protection of effectiive competition as the primary goal that, in turn, results in consumer benefits such as media and information variety.

---

34 Cf. *Von Hayek*, Friedrich August, Der Wettbewerb als Entdeckungsverfahren (1968), Kiel 1968.

35 See more *Fleischer*, Romy, Die Dynamik des Wettbewerbsschutzes, 2013, p. 38.

36 An additional key objective on the European level is the promotion of the integration of the EU common market, see ECJ, decision, 6th of Oct. 2009, case no. C-501/06 P, [2009] ECR I-9291 (note 61) – *GlaxoSmithKline (Spain)*.

37 The term is from the 1990s and therefore outdated, since the European courts have implemented various economic aspects in their decisions over the last few years, such as an efficiency defence.

38 EU Commission, decision from the 4th of July 2007, case no. COMP/38.784 (note 280 and 543) – *Telefónica*.

39 See more *Fleischer*, Romy, Die Dynamik des Wettbewerbsschutzes, 2013, p. 119 f.

2. Limits to a paradigm shift

A normative re-evaluation of the antitrust key objective in favour of 'non-competition related' goals like media and information variety seems reasonable, at least from a practical point of view. Like economic aspects in terms of efficiencies they are more comprehensible by society at large than 'the protection of competition'. However, their implementation into the provision against an abuse of market power is difficult. It remains questionable whether social and political objectives can be plausibly integrated into the purely normative abuse control regulation. German and (most) European antitrust law is generally based on a codified system of principle, despite some case law tendencies.[40] New aims of any sort cannot be squeezed in by force without breaching it. Such a result-oriented approach requires a more open and simpler shaped provision, such as like that of section 2 of the US Sherman Act. In the U.S., case law is traditional, principle-orientated and rather multifaceted and hardly supports a purely normative standard for the application of law,[41] making it easier to switch to a different approach with new goals like the diversity of media, information and opinion.

II. Efficiency of the European abuse control

1. Scope and structure of article 102 TFEU

a. Online platform hosts, such as search engines, provide a wide range of digital information which they can manipulate, since the possibility to access online data and the actual transmission of requested information depends on their will. However, the correct distinction between legitimate and unlawful influences on the indexing process or search ranking, for instance, is difficult. It can refer to discrimination, if it differs from the normal market competition of products and services. On the European level, such anti-competitive market behaviour can be pursued effectively by the provision against an abuse of market power[42] embedded in article 102 TFEU. Within the context of online media platforms, the European

40 See ECJ, decision from the 6th of March. 1974, case no. 6/73, [1974] ECR 223 – Commercial Solvents.

41 *Lepsius*, Oliver, Der Einfluss des ökonomischen Denkens auf die Rechtsvergleichung, ZVglRWiss 109 (2010) 327 (329 ff) with further references and additional reasons.

42 The European and German provision is not limited by the sector-specific telecommunication regulation. German broadcasting regulation against media concentration requires a link to broadcasting (See § 2 paragraph 1st and 2nd sentence of the German Interstate Broadcasting Treaty). Within the meaning of the law online search engines cannot be qualified as such, see *Danckert*, Burkhard/*Mayer*, Frank Joachim, Die vorherrschende

abuse control will mostly be applicable,[43] since within the context of 'online players' or the internet, in general, normally international facts and therefore cross-border markets are affected. Therefore, the focus lies on unilateral market behaviour which influences trade between the member states of the EU.

b. From a structural point of view, the abuse control provision includes a general clause in sentence 1 that leaves room for evaluations and interpretation and contains in sentence 2 a non-conclusive set of examples of abuses that represent typical forms of unilateral unlawful behaviour. This means that it prohibits concluded individual or collective abusive conduct of powerful market participants. Covered are all forms of business behaviour (such as conducted by merchants, sales representatives or freelancers,[44] in contrast to pure state activities, or conduct by private consumers or workers, including the entire labour market), as long as it constitutes an independent economic activity in the widest sense, while the legal status of the actor plays no role.[45] Hence, article 102 TFEU allows to pursue online platform providers like "Google & Co." without difficulties.

2. *Market media power of online platforms*

A number of implementation and application issues occur within the precise determination of a dominant market position – a concept that in turn depends on the scope of the relevant market whose definition is difficult and even more multifaceted within online platform rivalry. It is safe to assume that this, for instance, will be one major issue in the initiated investigation of the German Federal Cartel Office against Facebook on March 3 2016 which is the first antitrust investigation that examines whether, by collecting and using vast amounts of personal data, a single company may obtain competetive advantages that were not attainable with

---

Meinungsmacht von Google, Bedrohung durch einen Informationsmonopolisten?, MMR 2010, 219–222 (p. 220).

43 European antitrust provisions are superior to national norms and a special regulation according art. 3 paragraph 1 and 2 VO (EC) No. 1/2003, although national provisions can be stricter within the framework of unilateral market behavior. An example is §§ 18 ff of the German Restriction of Competition Act, in German: 'Gesetz zum Schutz gegen Wettbewerbsbeschränkungen' [GWB], as most recently amended on 1 August 2014.

44 ECJ, decision from the 12th of Sept. 2000, case no. C-180/98 [2000] ECR I-6451 – *Pavel Pavlov;* Commission, decision from the 30th of June 1993, OJ 1993, L 203 S. 27 (note 40) – *CNSD; de Bronett.*

45 ECJ, decision from the 28th of June 2005, case no. C-189/02 P [2005] ECR I-5425 (Tz. 113) – *Dansk Rørindustri.*

functioning competition, because it is not easily or swiftly that operating a social network may qualify as a "market" in the meaning of antitrust law.

a. *Analysis of the product market – principles and problems*

(1) Generally, in 'classic markets' the product and geographic scope of the market is to be determined first. The product market contains all goods and/or services that are easily substitutable from the perspective of consumers. As long as products and services are functionally interchangeable due to their characteristics, they belong to the same relevant market.[46] This may be indicated by several facts, like the intended use in consideration of quality, features and function, price differences, preferences of consumers and occasionally costs and risks hindering consumers to switch to other goods. However, in more complex cases an additional hypothetical 'monopolist test' (SSNIP - 'Small but Significant and Non-Transitory Increase in Price') has proven to be a helpful tool. A separate market is to be assumed if the monopolist hypothetically increases its prices generally by a small amount (between 5 %–10 %) within one year and still profits, while in contrast one market is to be assumed if its revenue shrinks due to a switch by the consumers to other goods.

(2) On the other hand, the law has to adapt to changing circumstances in a particular market. In the online media sector, a steady development of technology and advances is typical and goes hand in hand with a change of the traditional market structure (and consumer behaviour), which is why the meaning of 'What is effective competition in that area?' has to be re-evaluated accordingly – and suggests a different approach from traditional market assessment standards. Within internet platform rivalry mainstream antitrust analysis criteria have to be modified. Online media markets are normally contestable and rivalry often comes from different media platforms.[47] Despite the lack of empirical data on the amount of indirect network effects between the sides of the market, these externalities are characteristic for online platforms like search engines or social networks.[48] Hence,

---

46 Regarding Australian law, see section 4E *Competition and Consumer Act* 2010 (Clth) ("CCA") and *Boral Besser Masonry Ltd. v. ACCC* (2003) 215 CLR 374, 394, and with respect to European Law, see ECJ, Decision, 9 November 1983, Case No. 322/81, ECR [1983] p. 3461 (at 7) – *Michelin I;* ECJ, Decision, 15 February 1979, Case No. 85/76, ECR [1979] p. 461 (at 28) – *Hoffmann-LaRoche* or Alison *Jones/Brenda Sufrin*, EU Competition Law, 2012, p. 294.

47 *Zingales*, Nikolas, Product Market Definition in Online Search and Advertising, (2013) 9(1) CompLRev, p. 29 (38) with further reference.

48 *Thèpot*, Florence (2013), Market Power in Online Search and Social Networking: A Matter of Two-Sided Markets, p. 197.

the relevant horizontal market for search engines is often qualified as a 'two- or more-sided' market,[49] having an advertising and retail market side.[50]

b. *Complexity of functional inter-changeability in online markets*

In case of a complex online product like a search engine, a broad market definition would considerably reduce antitrust concerns but also neglect a specific function that is twisted to other functional features and for which a consumer demand exists. Hence, a market consisting of the platform for the purpose of the transmission of people's intentions would be too broad a definition. More based on reason in consideration of the diverse functional services of a digital search machine is the presumption of separated markets for (1) the use of the search machine, (2) the indexing process and (3) the advertising service.[51]

aa. Identification of a business exchange relation in case of 'free services'

With regards to the definition of the relevant product market, traditional evaluation standards based on a price in monetary terms or in consideration of the SSNIP tests fail in the case of a 'free service', since no direct monetary advantage exists. A direct business relationship between the parties involved cannot be justified simply on the fact of an overlap between the use of the search engines and the advertising service or the presumed indirect network effects between the different market sides, since they cannot be sufficiently backed up by empirical data. However, the provider receives, through the search requests of users, potentially valuable data in form of personal information (e.g. affinities, interests, search behaviour patterns) which shows that the search service is not entirely free[52] and the assumption of a business exchange relation between consumers and platform providers of a separate product market for the use of a search engine possible.[53]

---

49 *Evans*, David, (2003) 20 Yale Journal of Regulation 325, 325 ff.

50 Cf. EU Commission, Decision, 17th of February, case no. COMP/M.5727 (note 86) – Microsoft/Yahoo Search Business; EU Commission, Decision, 7th of October 2011, case no. COMP/M.6281 (note 10 ff) – Microsoft/Skype.

51 *Paal*, Boris P., Suchmaschinen, Marktmacht und Meinungsbildung, Rechtsstudie, Mai 2012, p. 25, with further references, available at: http://.i-comp.org/wp-content/uploads/2013/07/PAAL-Suchmaschinen-Marktmacht-und-Meinungsbildung-2012-final.pdf (March 2016).

52 *Körber*, Thorsten, Google im Fokus des Kartellrechts, Wettbewerb in Recht und Praxis (WRP) 2012, 761–772 (p. 762).

53 *Paal*, Boris P., Suchmaschinen, Marktmacht und Meinungsbildung, Rechtsstudie, Mai 2012, p. 26, with further references, available at: http://i-comp.org/wp-content/uploads/

In this context, the SSNIP test could be modified, i.e. instead of the price, the amount of advertising that is hypothetically placed or the differentiation of media platforms and the amount of indirect network effects.[54] The situation is similar for the determination of a separated product market for the indexing process and following ranking. While some advertisers pay for the sole inclusion in the index, most will be included without payment. However, the previous search of websites by real time search engines of the platform provider represents a duplication which relevant to copyright and therefore sufficient for a business exchange relation[55]. That suggests a separated product market.

bb. Competition between online platform providers selling 'advertising space'?

(1) With respect to the search advertising service for which advertisers pay, a market price exists as well and so the traditional SSNIP test can apply. In this context, an 'online advertising market' can be determined, if a hypothetical monopolist raises its prices for advertising space so that advertisers switch to other less expensive providers with cheaper replacement products which decreases the amount of advertising and therefore minimises the value of the online platform. Whether competition with other media platforms providing advertising space exists depends on the functional inter-changeability from the perspective of consumers.

(2) Doubts remain regarding traditional offline advertising services (e.g. radio broadcasting and TV), despite the lack of empirical data. There are various reasons that support the existence of separated markets. First, online advertisers are not just interested in advertising space and presumably do not simply view the internet as another media channel among many. From their perspective, online and offline services differ in terms of business techniques and the calculation system: they receive only with the internet a medium that allows a target-orientated usage by an efficient evaluation of collected data, and are not being charged for the sole

2013/07/PAAL-Suchmaschinen-Marktmacht-und-Meinungsbildung-2012-final.pdf (March 2016).

54 Justus *Haucap*/Christiane *Kehder*, Suchmaschinen zwischen Wettbewerb und Monopol: Der Fall Google, Ordnungspolitische Perspektiven, Juni 2013, p. 20.

55 *Paal*, Boris P., Suchmaschinen, Marktmacht und Meinungsbildung, Rechtsstudie, Mai 2012, p. 26, with further references, available at: http://i-comp.org/wp-content/uploads/2013/07/PAAL-Suchmaschinen-Marktmacht-und-Meinungsbildung-2012-final.pdf (March 2016).

possibility of perception, but for the actual perception by users who have to click on the advertising link displaced on the online platform.[56]

(3) The identification of a lack of competitive pressure between online search engines providing advertising space towards other online services is more difficult, although the progressing digitalisation of the media and increasing shift from an analogue to a digital media application indicates competition between them. A lack of interchangeability with other online platforms like news broadcasting, E-mail account providers (Web mail, etc.), real-time data transmission (e.g. *Skype, Twitter, Facebook, MSN*), e-commerce providers (as Amazon or Alibaba) or other services (like Ebay or Apple) cannot be assumed simply by reason of intended use, since they also sell advertising space in a similar fashion. For instance, search engine based ads are used by *Google* and *Facebook* (cooperating with *Microsoft Bing*), display advertising by *Amazon, Google, Facebook*, and mobile advertising by *Google, Apple*[57] and *Facebook*.

(4) The rapidly developing contestable online media markets suggests that a final definition may not be possible due to the usual lack of empirical data on the cross-elasticity of substitution.[58] Hence, other indicators than the intended use have to be considered in addition, such as product quality which is defined by the usage of consumers and, in particular, the dynamics of the internet industry, especially innovation in form of developments, improvements and redesigns. Therefore, a focus may lie on the competitive constraints that result from the dynamics of innovation competition such as the ease with which consumers can switch to other products and/or services or the ease with which competitors can enter the web-based businesses.[59] A sufficient scope of the relevant media market and its structure could be drawn, since special product characteristics and functional

---

56 Justus *Haucap*/Christiane *Kehder*, Suchmaschinen zwischen Wettbewerb und Monopol: Der Fall Google, Ordnungspolitische Perspektiven, 2013, p. 7 f.

57 *Medien Nordrhein-Westfalen*, Digitalkompakt 05, October 2012, Apple, Google, Facebook, Amazon, Strategien und Geschäftsmodelle einfach auf den Punkt gebracht, p. 32–33.

58 So *Zingales* Nikolas, Product Market Definition in Online Search and Advertising, (2013) 9(1) CompLRev, p. 29 (38).

59 Cf. EU Commission, decision, case no. Comp/M.6281 (at 121 f) – Microsoft/Skype (merger case).

substitution are significant parameters of (feature) competition and crucial for the market definition.[60]

(5) For instance, *Google's* business design and its revenue sources still differ to some extent from that of social networks like *Facebook*, e-commerce providers like *Amazon* or intelligent end device producers like *Apple*.[61] Internet telephone services (like *Skype*), communication services (such as Twitter or business and social networks, for example Linkedin or Facebook), do not work on the basis of indirect network effects, in contrast to auction-based online services[62] as *Google or Ebay*. However, the latter differ again with respect to the dissimilar functions and users. The search function is still the company's core,[63] although it presents itself in TV commercials often as the assistant in every situation in life. Despite *Google's* other specialised commercial services for instance, Youtube, Google Mail, Google Street View, Google Games, Google Books, Google News or Google Shopping, its basic purpose lies not in real time data transmission or other consumer communication services, although it is making an ongoing attempt to compete *for* a market rather than on its own[64] which includes an increasing convergence of online goods. Certain functional differences remain and cannot be neglected in defining the relevant product market.

c. Geographic market dimension

aa. The legal assessment of the relevant geographic market depends on economic aspects as well as actual market circumstances including structure and limitations. Generally, it refers the area in which consumers can acquire products and/or

---

60 In favour of the concept of a functional substitution, see ECJ, decision, 9th of Nov. 1983, case no. 322/81 [1983] ECR 3461 (at 7) – *Michelin I;* ECJ, decision, 15th of Feb. 1979, case no. 85/76 [1979] ECR 461 (at 28) – *Hoffmann-LaRoche*; similar *Queensland Wire Industries Pty Ltd. v. Broken Hill Pty Co. Ltd.* (1989) 167 CLR 177, 188, 201 citing the *Hoffmann-LaRoche* case.

61 For more, see Landesamt für Medien Nordrhein-Westfalen, Digitalkompakt 05, October 2012, Apple, Google, Facebook, Amazon, Strategien und Geschäftsmodelle einfach auf den Punkt gebracht, p. 6–31.

62 Justus *Haucap*/Christiane *Kehder*, Suchmaschinen zwischen Wettbewerb und Monopol: Der Fall Google, Ordnungspolitische Perspektiven, Juni 2013, p. 3 and 6.

63 *Landesamt für Medien Nordrhein-Westfalen*, Digitalkompakt 05, October 2012, Apple, Google, Facebook, Amazon, Strategien und Geschäftsmodelle einfach auf den Punkt gebracht, p. 7.

64 For instance, *Facebook* introduced in fall 2015 an online shopping function that allows users to sell products just like on *Ebay*.

services under sufficiently homogenous competition conditions or a level playing field from a competition perspective. Important aspects to be considered are conduct patterns of consumers in case of price changes, access barriers or distribution channels, in contrast to the production site and headquarters of the company, next to the supply side if competitive pressure emerges from there.

bb. Regarding online products and services the assumption of a global product market can be supported by the fact that online search engines are available worldwide. However, linguistic specialisations play a major role in determining the interchangeability of online products and services, suggesting a narrower market definition, sometimes even on a national level. Normally, search engines operate with a specific language, depending on user preferences. Providers like *Google, Yahoo* or *Microsoft Bing* offer their services in English, being the dominant and preferred language in Europe, Australia or North America, in contrast to other parts of the world, like China or Russia. The Chinese counterpart *Baidu* or the Russian equivalent *Yandex* are other large online search machines (especially because of the huge population and thus the large number of users) that offer their services in the native language that meets the needs of their customers. Just like *Baidu* that is designed for the Chinese people (and often limited to Chinese websites that occasionally include single English words), *Google* and other English online search machines are developed for English speakers that suggests different competition conditions towards non-English providers. However, it is safe to assume that language barriers will be reduced in the future by the introduction of improved translation programs, in contrast to governmental limitations and regulations of the internet which is outside the sphere of platform providers.

d. *Analysis of market media power of online platforms*

aa. Standards and problems

(1) To establish a violation of article 102 TFEU a considerable *market position* must be proven. However, a huge size alone is not prohibited under current antitrust law[65] but rather reflects internal growth that is the result of a desirable workable competition, innovation, know-how and outstanding performance. Rather, it is forbidden to exercise a dominant position[66] in a way where an undertaking possesses the power to behave to an appreciable extent independently of its competitors, its

65 ECJ, decision from the 9th of Nov. 1983, case no. 322/81, [1983] ECR 3461 (at 10) – *Michelin I.* Commonwealth of Australia, Senate, 14th of Aug. 8. 1974, p. 923 (*Senator Murphy*, New South Wales, Attorney General).

66 Cf. legal definition in § 18 of the GWB.

customers and ultimately of the consumers.[67] The presumed monopolist must be able to exclude competitors or control market prices.

(2) On the other hand, it cannot be denied either that a company's size is crucial in the context of an internet search machine, especially in case of *Google* where past searches or click-through results improve its value on the market. It is to be considered and viewed with caution that important providers receive each day more and more data that help to improve customer profiles and can be used independently from consumers' interests, such as privacy rights, distribution and evaluation, and which allow an existing market power to expand.

bb. Limited use of market shares

(1) Typical for online media markets are high market shares of single entities. Some of them even hold over 90%, such as *Google* in the market for classic online search services[68] in Europe.[69] It is similar in other digital industries, e.g. *Amazon* is the leading e-commerce provider and *Facebook* (still) dominates the social network sector, while *Apple* grows faster than its competitors in the field of intelligent end devices such as iPhone, iPod, iPad.[70] Although percentages of market shares are fragmentary substitutes and determined by economic data which are often incomplete,[71] they are considered to be an important economic indicator to determine market power on the European level,[72] among others such as competition

---

67 ECJ, decision from the 2nd of April 2009, case no. C-202/07 P, [2009] I-2369 (note 103) – *France Télécom SA*; ECJ, decision from the 15th of Feb. 1979, case no. 85/76, [1979] 461 (fn 38) – *Hoffmann-LaRoche*; cf. section 46 (3) CCA and *ACCC v. Cabcharge Australia Ltd.* [2010] FCA 1261 (at 11).

68 Searches which links are provided that lead to websites with various possible topics, see further Justus Haucap/Christiane Kehder, Suchmaschinen zwischen Wettbewerb und Monopol: Der Fall Google, Ordnungspolitische Perspektiven, Juni 2013, p. 5.

69 European Parliament, Think Tank, Google antitrust proceedings: Digital business and competition, available online at: http://www.europal.europa.eu/thinktank/en/search.html?word=Google+antitrust+proceedings%3A+Digital+business+and+competition (March 2016).

70 Landesamt für Medien Nordrhein-Westfalen, Digitalkompakt 05, October 2012, Apple, Google, Facebook, Amazon, Strategien und Geschäftsmodelle einfach auf den Punkt gebracht, p. 3.

71 *Hovenkamp*, Federal Antitrust Policy, § 6.2b (S. 274).

72 Cf. ECJ, decision, 13th of Feb. 1979, case no. 85/76 [1979] ECR 461 ff (at 39) – *Hoffmann-LaRochee* The ECJ affirms a dominant position by a market share of more than 75% and disputably presumes it at the threshold of 50% to approx. 45%. A similar approach is defined in § 18 (4) GWB that presumes a market position at a threshold of at

conditions, control of commodity and sales markets, financial power, technical features or the dependence of competitors, and especially entry barriers[73] including high costs and investments, know-how for the development, running and progress of a search machine algorithm, historical data,[74] soft- and hardware, marketing,[75] range of product differentiation[76], the existence of intellectual property rights[77] or the degree and nature of vertical interconnections on the market.[78]

(2) The difficulty of establishing an abuse case is considerable, since 'market power' is a core element of the abuse control regulation. Sufficient substantiated information must be provided, as was highlighted in the Chinese *Baidu* decision[79] in 2009, which referred to a blockage of an advertiser's website and the reduction of hits on the search engines ranking.[80] Such high quality requirements are not met simply by providing media reports or superficial calculations but rather by special economic statistics based on scientific, factual and comprehensive analysis. However, market shares are not easy to prove, especially in civil proceedings, since most of the relevant data originate from the defendant's sphere that is why

---

least 40%. Below 40% to 25% the ECJ requires additional reasons referring to important market and business structure such as the distance and number of competitors or an economic and technical dominance. A market share beneath 25 % is hardly considered critical and below 10 % market dominance is practically impossible. See references in *Fleischer*, Romy Die Dynamik des Wettbewerbsschutzes, 2013, p. 76.

73 ECJ, Decision, 29 April 2004, case no. 418/01, [2004] ECR I-5039 (at 25) – *IMS Health*; *Boral Besser Masonry Ltd. v. ACCC* (2003) 215 CLR 374, 419 (at 121); *ACCC v. Cabcharge Australia Ltd.* [2010] FCA 1261 (at 11).

74 Questioned by Justus *Haucap*/Christiane *Kehder*, Suchmaschinen zwischen Wettbewerb und Monopol: Der Fall Google, Ordnungspolitische Perspektiven, 2013, p. 14 with further references.

75 *Körber*, Thorsten, Google im Fokus des Kartellrechts, WRP 2012, 761–772 (p. 762) regarding online search engines.

76 *Boral Besser Masonry Ltd. v. ACCC* (2003) 215 CLR 374, 398 (at 29).

77 *NT Power Generation Pty Ltd. v. Power and Water Authority* (2004) 219 CLR 90 (at 85 und 125).

78 *Boral Besser Masonry Ltd. v. ACCC* (2003) 215 CLR 374, 423 (at 137), 493 (at 365 f).

79 Chinese Supreme Court, Decision, 9th of July 2010, Case No. 489 [2010] Gao Min Zhong Zi (高民终字), *Tangshan Renren Information Services Co., Ltd. versus Beijing Baidu Network Technology Co.* (唐山市人人信息服务有限公司与北京百度网讯科技有限公司垄断纠纷), Ltd., available at: www.bjgy.chinacourt.org/paper/detail/2011/08/id/542054.shtml.

80 Angela Huyue Zhang, Using a Sledgehammer to Crack a Nut: Why China's Anti-Monopoly Law was Inappropriate for *Renren* v. *Baidu*, (2011) 7 Competition Policy International Journal 277, 285, 290.

its procurement is often impossible or at least linked to high and disproportionate costs for the claimant. Against this background, problems in satisfying the burden of proof are considerable. Hence, a reversal of the onus of proof seems appropriate in the context of the determination of a 'substantial market position' that is presumed while the defendant is granted the chance to exculpate itself.

(3) Moreover market share within the digital industry is a short-term phenomenon.[81] Large online media companies can be under significant competitive pressure if new entities are able to take over a leading position despite their high market shares.[82] In addition, in exceptional cases, market dominance might *not* even be mandatorily found at a threshold of even 100 % market share[83] if the market is open and contestable. In the field of horizontal search engines *Google* possesses a quasi-monopoly position and therefore does not qualify necessarily as an essential facility[84], since other providers (e.g. *Microsoft Bing, Yahoo!, Ecosia, Startpage*) exist, in spite of their current minor role.

(4) On the other hand, market shares are static indicators unlike the internet industry which is highly dynamic and characterised by potential (innovation) competition.[85] To assess more efficiently whether a single entity in the field of online media is able to behave independently from its competitors, consumers and customers, its actual nature has to be considered accordingly which means dynamic competitive conditions[86] such as 'likely future competition' or potential investments in research and development, etc.

---

81 *Queensland Wire Industries Pty Ltd. v. Broken Hill Pty Co. Ltd.* (1989) 167 CLR 177, 189. However, the relevance of the criterion of market share gained an additional meaning by the *Birdsville Amendment* in 2007 and following the introduction of section 46 (1AA) CCA (former section 46 (1AA) TPA). In contrast to section 46 (1) CCA which demands a *substantial degree of power in a market*, section 46 (1AA) CCA requires a *substantial degree of market share* which is usually easier to determine.

82 Inge Graef, Sneak Preview of the future application of European competition law on the internet: Cisco and Messagenet, (2014) 51 Common Law Market Review 1263, 1274.

83 *Kling/Thomas*, Kartellrecht, 2007, § 5 Rn. 46; *Fleischer*, Die Dynamik des Wettbewerbsschutzes, 2013, p. 76.

84 *Körber*, Thorsten, Google im Fokus des Kartellrechts, WRP 2012, 761–772 (p. 762 and 764) with further reference.

85 Cf. European Court of first Instance, decision, 17th of Sept. 2007, case no. T-201/04, [2007] ECR II-3601 – *Microsoft*.

86 See *Katz*, Michael L./*Shelanski*, Howard A., Schumpeterian competition and antitrust policy in high tech markets, Vol. 14, Competition (2005), p. 47 (57).

cc. Flux tendencies in online media markets

(1) The internet market landscape is in constant flux, meaning characterised by short-term stability of online media market players. For instance, with respect to the horizontal market for the use of internet search engines, the once rising *Gopher* search machine is almost forgotten, while the *Altavista* service shut its doors entirely in 2010. Also in the field of social networks, platforms come and go more often than society realises. Even the presumably almighty *Facebook* that succeeded a couple years earlier against the German counterparts *studiVZ* and *meinVZ*, lost a significant number of young users in 2014.[87] The same happened to *Orkut*, a social network owned by Google that was very popular in Iran, Brazil and India but was outpaced by other platforms and services and therefore closed in 2014 after 10 years of running. Social networks rise and fall equally fast, especially when they cannot keep up with changing consumer behaviour. Such providers eventually disappear from the market, like the German platform *schülerVZ* that was established in 2007 for German-speaking school pupils in Europe and closed in 2013 due to a drastic drop of active users. Young consumers in particular change behavioural patterns rather quickly, especially if they are suddenly being charged for the use of a once free service. Such behavioural patterns are not limited to social networks, but appear in all market segments related to digital technology. For example, in Germany the once popular instant messaging program *ICQ* had been practically replaced by the trendy messaging instant app for smartphones called *WhatsApp*.[88] Similarly, in the midst of 2013 the largest online carpooling company in Europe (*Mitfahrgelegenheit.de*) introduced a rather complicated and cumbersome charging system that upset many users who started to look for free alternatives. Hence, newcomers like *Blablacar.de* or *Bessermitfahren.de*, offering free services, entered the market and established themselves within a few months, although the once dominant rival has still a significant number of users. A similar development took place with the auction platform *Auxion.de* that was a well-known competitor of *Ebay*, when it introduced a membership fee in early 2013; it abandoned its operation in early 2015.[89] In conclusion, it is safe to say that online media companies usually come and rise quickly but also fall faster than undertakings operating on conventional, traditionally one-sided markets.

---

87 Cf. http://de.statista.com/infografik/2806/diese-social-networks-nutzen-us-teenager/ (March 2016).

88 WhatsApp Inc. was acquired in 2014 for 19 billion US Dollar by *Facebook* that has tried to interlock the messenger with its social network since early 2015 with a *Facebook App*.

89 *Auxion's* pages were taken over by *Filmmundo.de* at the end of Feb. 2015.

(2) Tendencies of concentration in online media markets are characteristic but not necessarily permanent. The observable fact of 'come, rise and fall' of online platforms is a distinctive feature in the digital economy and takes place, in spite of an undertaking's size that qualifies as an entry barrier. It reflects abundantly and clearly one of competitions's greatest functions, namely to reduce market power (*Entmachtungsinstrument*[90]). For instance, *Microsoft* used to be quasi-dominant (in Europe) on the market for web browsers with its 'Internet Explorer' but lost its general relevance eventually because newcomers entered the market with more preferable featured browsers in light of design, clarity, easy use and smaller programs, like '*Mozilla Firefox*' in 2002, *Safari* in 2003 or '*Google Chrome*' in 2008. As long as other competitors exist and enter, the market cannot be closed and incontestable.

3. *Anti-competitive behaviour of online platform providers*

At the European level, single powerful undertakings have a special responsibility in the market, which is why their conduct must not restrict residual competition.[91] Its regulation against abusive market strategies is conduct-orientated and excludes the possibility of an exemption. It covers various forms[92] like an unjustified discrimination that is the most relevant in context of online platform rivalry.[93] Discrimination of an actual or potential business partner can only be assumed if the monopolist imposes different prices or other business conditions in case of equal services without an objective reason to justify it.[94]

---

90 *Böhm*, Franz, in: Institut für ausländisches und internationales Wirtschaftsrecht, Kartelle und Monopole im modernen Recht, S. 22.

91 ECJ, decision from the 16th of March 2000, case no. C-395/96 P among others, [2000] ECR I-1365 (note 37) – *Compagnie Maritime Belge*; ECJ, decision from the 9th of Nov. 1983, case no. 322/81,[1983] ECR 3461 (note 57) – *Michelin I*; European Court of first Instance, decision from the 23th of Oct. 2003, case no. T-65/98, [2003] ECR II-4653 (note 158) – *Van den Bergh Foods*.

92 See 'abuse of market power' in article 102 TFEU and § 19 GWB and 'taking advantage of' in section 46 CCA.

93 See the well-known *Microsoft* investigation (EU Commission - MEMO/09/15 17/01/2009, available at: http://europa.eu/rapid/press-release_MEMO-09-15_en.htm?locale=en (March 2016) where a similar investigation of the EU Commission took place; the company's conduct was finally sanctioned in 2013 with a 561 Million Euro fine because it bundled its 'Internet Explorer' with its operating systems from *Windows* without offering alternative (competitive) products to consumers as it had promised in 2009.

94 See article 102 (2) lit c TFEU; § 19 (2) lit. 3 GWB.

a. Indications of illegitimate conduct and discrimination

In consideration of the important social-political position of *Google*, one major issue is its use of external content that originates from competitors in vertical markets. The search engine displays a thumbnail of it on its own website without permission or payment. In case of complaints and state regulations, since the company group restricts the information supply by deleting the snippets from its index or the entire competitor's website[95] or even shuts down the entire substitutionary service.[96] Further concerns refer to *Google's* supply of consumers with a wide range of own content in second and third markets which is often placed above the actual results list such as music videos on *Youtube* and in a notable size where other providers seemingly get crowded out from the monitor which, in turn, likely leads to less content and economic variety in the long run. For vertically integrated companies, there exists a strong economic incentive to create a search algorithm that prefers specialised services and its own content on second and third markets in their ranking.[97] The problem emerges from the conflict of interests, since such companies are both a provider of a search engine service *and* a supplier of their own commercial content and services. However, any internal manipulation of the search algorithm that places rivals and non-competitive providers at a worse spot in the search results list while favouring their own online goods or a total disregard of competitive products is unlawful, since the search is not based on relevance but rather on commercial or other interests without justification. Although *Google* responded to the antitrust concerns expressed by the European Commission and proposed in 2014 to stop favouring its own specialised search services like Google Shopping, Google Maps or Youtube whenever it promotes

95 See *Paal*, Boris P., Suchmaschinen, Marktmacht und Meinungsbildung, Rechtsstudie, Mai 2012, p. 20, with further references, available at: http://i-comp.org/wp-content/uploads/2013/07/PAAL-Suchmaschinen-Marktmacht-und-Meinungsbildung-2012-final.pdf (March 2016).

96 On 11th of Dec. 2014 Google announced that it would shut down *Google News* in Spain which is a response to a new publishing law that requires that aggregators pay publishers a fee for linking to their content.

97 See *Paal*, Boris P., Suchmaschinen, Marktmacht und Meinungsbildung, Rechtsstudie, Mai 2012, p. 14, with further references, available at: http://i-comp.org/wp-content/uploads/2013/07/PAAL-Suchmaschinen-Marktmacht-und-Meinungsbildung-2012-final.pdf (March 2016).

them,[98] indications of anti-competitive behaviour remain and lead to a sneaking politicisation of antitrust problems[99] which is clearly questionable.

b. Finding of anti-competitive means

Despite indications of discrimination, any market behaviour can only be qualified as unlawful within the meaning of antitrust law if conducted with anti-competitive means. A mere squeezing-out of competitors is not sufficient, since it is integral to competition law to some extent *and* eventually results from a better product and a more efficient business design.[100] It is important to focus on the anti-competitive nature of the presumably monopolistic behaviour and its potential or actual negative impact on the market in terms of an exclusion or restriction of competition[101] ('likely effect based approach') and thus the structure[102] and the competitiveness of the market, and especially specific market circumstances. Since the internet is highly dynamic and certain products and services are complex, such as a search machine algorithm which is constantly, rapidly and broadly changing,[103] the degree of innovation and the functionality are crucial criteria for the behavioural assessment.

c. Limited chances of a 'safe harbour'

Proven anti-competitive market behaviour can still be justified, at least in theory, considering the very high demands by the courts, such as in case of the so-called 'efficiency defence'.[104] Its success is very limited and its practicability low due to difficulties of measuring long-term dynamic efficiencies empirically. High requirements are necessary to avoid self-serving assertions. In case of the more practical

---

98 European Commission, press release, 5 May 2014, IP/14/116, available at http://europa.eu/rapid/press-release_IP-14-116_en.htm (March 2016).

99 See the resolution of the European Parliament to unbundle large online media companies, see more in C.II.1.

100 Cf. *Körber*, Thorsten, Google im Fokus des Kartellrechts, WRP 2012, 761–772 (p. 767 ff).

101 ECJ, decision, 19th of April 2012, case no. C-549/10 P (note 43) – *Tomra Systems.*

102 ECJ, decision, 13th of Feb. 1989, case no. 85/76, [1989] ECR 461 (note 120, 123) – *Hoffmann-LaRoche.*

103 Google has made 890 updates in its organic search algorithm in 2013, see http://searchengineland.com/google-made-890-improvements-search-past-year-201065 (March 2016).

104 Recognised in the field of article 102 TFEU, see ECJ, decision from the 17th of Feb. 2011, case no. C-52/09 (note 76) – *TeliaSonera.*

objective necessity defence,[105] it must be proven that the conduct in question was necessary for the company's productivity or even its survival. Legitimate objections include a lack of creditworthiness, repeated breach of contract[106] or a supply shortfall as a result of a changed economic situation, as long as the claimed economic behaviour alone determined the conduct, not the desire to strengthen its position in the market or to abuse it.[107] Reasons of justification must be proven by the undertaking in question which can be difficult, especially in case of a disclosure of sensitive information, business and corporate secrets (e.g. the unique search algorithm is the most important business secret of *Google*), and, in addition, may give competitors insights into the pricing policy of the monopolist.[108] Requirements and limits for rational business interests, including trading secrets or security measures, are not legally defined and often opaque. However, it seems rational to guarantee private consumers an objective online search free from spam links[109] or to delete websites with illegal content from the index and search result[110] to be in line with the law. That justifies a differentiation between search results. Generally, public security, especially consumer protection, product safety and quality as well as public health have been judicially acknowledged as reasons of justification[111] (so-called 'safety defence'). However, the actual implementation of health security and safety standards cannot lie in the hands of private companies,

---

105 ECJ, decision, 29th of June 1978, case no. 77/77 [1978] 1513 (note 24/28 f.) – *Benzine en Petroleum Handelsmaatschappij BV*; Commission, discussion paper 2005, note 78 and 80.

106 *Donoghue,* Robert O/*Padilla*, A. Jorge, Law and Economics of Art. 82 EC, Oxford 2006, p. 450.

107 ECJ, decision, 14th of Feb. 1978, case no. 27/76 [1978] ECR 207 (note 184/194) – *United Brands*; European Court of first Instance, decision, 1st of Jan. 1993, case no. T-65/89, [1993] ECR II-389, 418 (note 69) – *BPB Industries & British Gypsum.*

108 *Brand*, in: Frankfurter Kommentar-Kartellrecht, Band II, Art. 102 (75. Lfg. Oktober 2011) Rn. 345.

109 Cf. Chinese Supreme Court, Decision, 9 July 2010, Case No. 489 [2010] Gao Min Zhong Zi (高民终字), *Tangshan Renren Information Services Co., Ltd. versus Beijing Baidu Network Technology Co.* (唐山市人人信息服务有限公司与北京百度网讯科技有限公司垄断纠纷), Ltd., available at: www.bjgy.chinacourt.org/paper/detail/2011/08/id/542054.shtml.

110 *Körber*, Thorsten, Google im Fokus des Kartellrechts, WRP 2012, 761–772 (p. 771 f).

111 ECJ, decision, 6th of Oct. 1994, case no. T-83/91 [1994] ECR II-755 (at 138 and 207) – *Tetra Pak II*, affirmed by ECJ, decision, 14th of Nov. 11. 1996, case no. 333/94P [1996] ECR I-595 – *Tetra Pak II.*

since the authorities are responsible for public interests[112] and market participants usually have and determine different safety standards, which is why the defence's success is limited.

II. Antitrust needs in a digital economy

Due to political and media pressure, a discussion about the necessity of stricter antitrust measures has arisen in order to meet special antitrust needs in the constantly growing digital economy. However, on a closer look not all suggestions seem based on reason or even necessity.

1. Ownership unbundling?

The European Parliament suggested in its resolution in late November 2014 to split up huge online media companies, presumably referring to the *Google* group, i.e. to unbundle the original search service from other specialised, commercial services of the website in order to strengthen consumer rights in the digital internal market. Although it is not binding on the European Commission that has been investigating the 'media giant' since 2010, this suggestion may have some impact on its decision, or at least a symbolic importance and even an impact on national antitrust regulation.[113]

a. Factual and economic doubts

aa. In contrast to U.S. antitrust law, European competition law, especially the law against abuse of market power, does not include the remedy of ownership unbundling. It gives competition authorities the power to restore an inconstable market according to their own beliefs which might possibly ignore or conflict with the interests of the undertaking entirely.[114] However, most online media markets, for instance regarding social networks or the use of search engines, are not inaccessibly but rather contestable and open, as shown above. Apart from that, ownership unbundling is generally a very harsh structural measure and an 'ultima ratio' instrument, even within the antitrust enforcement policy of section 2 US

---

112 ECJ, decision, 14th of Nov. 11. 1996, case no. 333/94P [1996] ECR I-595 – *Tetra Pak II.*

113 See the German Government currently verifies whether a modification of the antitrust measures is necessary.

114 Cf. Monopolkommission, Sondergutachten 58 (gemäß § 44 Abs. 1 Satz 4 GWB, Bonn, 27. April 2010), Gestaltungsoptionen und Leistungsgrenzen einer kartellrechtlichen Unternehmensentflechtung, 2010, p. 14 f, online available at: http://monopolkommission.de/images/PDF/SG/s58_volltext.pdf (March 2016).

Sherman Act[115]. Its introduction in a national antitrust law system of a member state of the EU would most likely be in conflict with European regulation[116] which is superior and more appropriate to cope with cross-border activities of large online technology companies.

bb. Further doubts remain in terms of economic efficiency because unbundling is a fairly slow, costly, time-consuming and ineffective measure with respect to the innovation and quality competition process.[117] Negative impacts on the market are not unlikely, such as a decrease of incentives of the (quasi-)monopolist and the entire industry to invest and innovate,[118] since they cannot keep the fruits of their success. A company that grew powerful only by effective, desired rivalry would be punished for its accomplishments and not for illegitimate, anti-competitive conduct. Hence, a non-conduct-related ownership unbundling neglects the essence of the dynamics of economic competition and its preferable outcome.

b. Existing preventative instruments

Despite similarities, ownership unbundling is not comparable to the existing merger control. Although it does not focus on anti-competitive behaviour either, merger regulation prevents the development of market (media) power in the first place, considers the interests of the merging companies and is based on a company's decision.[119] There are no risks for investments that might result from later decisions of the authority, since they are analyzed in advance of the merger's legality after the notification process. The latter may include structural commitments[120] like a divestiture commitment. Authorities can deny approval for an acquisition of smaller 'unwanted' competitors by a powerful media company that endangers competition and consumer welfare within the framework of the

---

115 See an overview of the history of unbundling in the US Antitrust Law in *Nettesheim*, Martin/*Thomas*, Stefan, Entflechtung im Deutschen Kartellrecht: Wettbewerbspolitik, Verfassungsrecht, Wettbewerbsrecht, 2011, Mohr Siebeck, p. 24 ff.

116 An ownership unbundling imposed by a national authority is impossible, if the a merger was affirmed by the European Commission according to the prior European merger control (Council regulation (EC) Nr. 139/2004, 20th of Jan. 2004).

117 *Posner*, Richard A., Antitrust Law, 2. Edition, Chicago 2001 p. 268.

118 See *Verizon Communications, Inc. v. Law Offices of Curtis Trinko*, 540 U.S. 398, 407 ff. (2004).

119 *Klees*, Andreas/*Hauser*, Sebastian Max, Entflechtung von Unternehmen als Instrument des allgemeinen Wettbewerbsrechts? RATUBS Nr. 4/2010, S. 38 f.

120 *Nettesheim*, Martin/*Thomas*, Stefan, Entflechtung im Deutschen Kartellrecht: Wettbewerbspolitik, Verfassungsrecht, Wettbewerbsrecht, 2011, Mohr Siebeck, p. 75.

existing merger control. However, as within the framework of the 'relative abuse control', the determination of the likely elimination of future competition within the enforcement of the merger control requires a closer look at the special circumstances on online media markets, such as the constant growing data stream and the huge amount of transaction volume.

2. *Regulated internet structure?*

a. Especially in light of structural and normative limits of the current European regulation against an abuse of market power for the benefit of non-competitive aspects like media and information diversity, a partly regulated internet structure seems reasonable, and even practical, since any statutory regulation would be effective immediately. Indeed, the legislature more so than courts and competition authorities, is arguably the legitimate forum to regulate markets to both oversee the creation and use of market power of market participants for economic reasons *and* reduce a creeping deprivation in democratic governance.

b. However, there are numerous limits within the framework of the internet industry. First, the global scope of the 'World Wide Web' and the large amount of cross-border information restrains state influences[121] in principle, and therefore limits the territorial range of any state regulation. Second, a (wide) regulated internet structure is doubtful in light of information diversity anyway. For instance, China's central government currently restricts the digital access to data of foreign and English websites and by this influences the formation of opinion of its citizens. Third, any supplementary, or even case-by-case state regulation can only be justified if it has been proven that the market-inherent 'self-correcting' power is not working on digital media markets.[122] As shown above, most of the online market segments are currently open and competitive, and controlled by quality and innovation competition, which is why it is not rational nor in line with the purpose of antitrust law to impose rules on how to treat competitors. In particular, a general obligation to disclose the search algorithm of search engine that is the core of the business model of a search engine would rather endanger the existence

---

121 *Paal*, Boris P., Suchmaschinen, Marktmacht und Meinungsbildung, Rechtsstudie, Mai 2012, p. 53, available at http://i-comp.org/wp-content/uploads/2013/07/PAAL-Suchmaschinen-Marktmacht-und-Meinungsbildung-2012-final.pdf (March 2016).

122 Cf. *Körber*, Thorsten, Google im Fokus des Kartellrechts, Wettbewerbs in Recht und Praxis (WRP) 2012, 761 (763) with further reference.

of the provider and innovation in the entire industry.[123] Fourth, the internet sector evolves rapidly which is why any unification of rules involves the risk that a certain regulation will lag behind technical developments. Improvements and innovation in the field of technology cannot be determined in advance. Hence, a broad implementation of technical progress by a set of rules will most likely be behind technical standards. Especially with respect to a digital search engine, it would be hard to create an algorithm that ensures that a diversity of opinions is expressed in a generated search results list, since online search machines, like *Google*, answer daily to millions of different search requests automatically and the digital data constantly increase. The search machine constantly improves and changes up to six hundred times per year that includes mostly minor updates but occasionally major changes as well.[124] This differs from broadcasting and traditional telecommunication services, which is why the ex-ante control in that field is not suitable for search engines[125] as one may think at first glance.

3. *Case-by-case and guiding intervention*

Neither a 'free pass' for market participants nor blind interventionism by competition authorities will boost economic competition from which consumers benefit such as online media diversity, as modern competition theory[126] and antitrust enforcement policy[127] have pointed out over the last 50 years. Market interventions in a market process are not an end in itself.[128] In antitrust terms, such interventions aim to secure the possibility of entry into the market and assure equal market conditions, and hence to keep the market open for new competitive products and/or services that meet the needs and interests of consumers. Competition

123 *Paal*, Boris P., Suchmaschinen, Marktmacht und Meinungsbildung, Rechtsstudie, Mai 2012, p. 57, available at http://i-comp.org/wp-content/uploads/2013/07/PAAL-Suchmaschinen-Marktmacht-und-Meinungsbildung-2012-final.pdf (March 2016).

124 See *MOZ*, 'Google Algorithm Change History', available at: http://moz.com/google-algorithm-change (March 2016).

125 *Körber*, Thorsten, Google im Fokus des Kartellrecht, Wettbewerb in Recht und Praxis (WRP), 2012, 761–772 (p. 771).

126 See more *Fleischer*, Romy, Die Dynamik des Wettbewerbsschutzes, 2013, p. 18 f.

127 Cf. the antitrust enforcement policy in the USA during the 1960s, see *Hovenkamp*, Herbert J., The Antitrust Enterprise: principle and execution, Cambridge, Mass. 2005, p. 237; *Jones*, Alison/*Sufrin*, Brenda, EC Competition Law: Text, Cases, and Materials, 4. Edition, Oxford 2010, p. 22.

128 *Körber*, Thorsten, Google im Fokus des Kartellrecht, Wettbewerb in Recht und Praxis, 2012, 761–772 (p. 763) with further references.

authorities are not assigned to protect the economic wellbeing of rivals for their own sake but for that of the competition process in the entire industry, i.e. to guard the rivalry process and therefore to maintain a level playing field that allows market participants to compete and decide free from excessive state interventions (as well as private restrictions). Interventions must be case-by-case and guiding in order to sustain the market mechanism[129] and avoid an erosion of the market competition process, since an efficient antitrust enforcement policy could hardly be achieved by a harsh sanctions policy but rather by legal clarity that eventually leads to more legal security.

4. *Innovation is the strongest competition force*

a. In the field of software and telecommunication, many technological innovations have arisen in the market over the last decades but have not always been sustained. An effective or workable (innovative) competition is characterised by constant natural selection to the detriment of those goods that do not meet the needs and interests of consumers (any more). Only innovative suppliers survive in the market. An example of this social and economic Darwinism in economic markets is the rise and downfall of the floppy-disks which were displaced by CD's in the 1990s; the latter are now being forced out of the market by USB memory sticks because of their greater capacity to store more data and more convenient size. Whether market participants and online platform providers succeed in the market is determined by their accomplishments and achievements in the innovation and quality competition process which is with respect to a search engine an outstanding search algorithm.

b. The success of a 'media player' in the online industry depends mainly on how fast it adapts to changing consumer behaviour and interests, in particular privacy rights, data protection or copyrights. For instance, among online search engines *Startpage*[130] responded and introduced a platform that does not save search requests and thus does not assign requested data to individual users. In contrast, *Google* responded to ongoing complaints about advertising on the search results list with the introduction of an online service called *Contributor* – since November 2015 available, however, currently only in the U.S. – by which advertising can be blended out by paying a certain fee. The outcome of innovationary

129 Cf. German Government explanatory memorandum on the GWB 1958, German Bundestag Printed Paper 1158, 2nd election period, 1st attachment, p. 21 f.

130 See Startpage Website, available at: https://startpage.com/deu/protect-privacy.html (March 2016).

spirit may be uncertain and its success unsure, as seen, for example, with *Google's* failed project named 'Google Glass' in 2012,[131] since it entered a personal sphere of consumers which was not accepted in society; or its less successful attempt to enter the social network market with 'Google+' in 2013, perhaps being the result of the many technicians and engineers working with the Google Company who are less interested in social networking). However, this is exactly what economic competition is about and is also wanted from an antitrust perspective, namely an unpredictable search and discovery process that serves consumers.

D. Closing reflections

The internet with its constant changes and new digital inventions is a tool to express new forms of life but it is important that people and their opinion are not determined by the players involved, meaning online platforms. Concerns regarding equal opportunities on digital markets, social-political aspects like media and information diversity and the freedom to form an opinion suggest the need for baseline requirements for market conduct of powerful media companies. At the same time, it would be advisable for online platforms, such as search engines, to provide at least a bit more clarity about their policy and current market strategies to lower antitrust concerns, for their own sake. It would help to reduce the confusion between suspicions and facts that can be found quite often in printed and online media. Any unwanted politicisation of antitrust problems in society in the field of online platform rivalry that was striking in 2014 would be obsolete now as well. Anyhow, legal doubts can be dealt best and most effectively with the current European antitrust regulation against an abuse of market (media) power. It offers sufficient instruments, in spite of some remaining questions. Social-political challenges of the new online economy can be considered by the courts and authorities, since the existing provision against an abuse of market power is open for interpretation and the implementation of such values to some extent. Thus, an additional harsh structural instrument such as an ownership unbundling seems unnecessary and inapt, since it is hardly in line with the essence of competition. In the fast developing digital economy it is more rational to modify certain traditional evaluation standards within the antitrust assessment of a presumed abuse of market power, instead of replacing high standards and guiding principles completely. The structure of online markets is in constant flux anyway and changing rapidly due to

---

131 Also other large online companies failed in their attempt to enter different markets, like *Facebook* with its IPO in 2012 or *Zalando,* a multinational e-commerce company, with its IPO in 2014.

vast technological developments that change the circumstances to sustain effective media competition. With respect to online search engines, some modifications within the definition of the relevant product market is required due to presumably multi-sided characteristics and network effects, but also within the determination of a dominant market position where a shift from static to dynamic aspects in light of the special features of online media markets is necessary. The dynamic nature of the fast moving internet industry, especially online media markets being characterised by competitive innovation, is the basis for pioneering applications and services and therefore has to be preserved. Therefore, an excessive antitrust regulation that neglects these framework conditions has to be prevented in order to maintain beneficial innovative forces.

Michael Kling

Media diversity and competition law:
Merger control in the print media sector

Abstract: The article analyses the merger control law of the European Union, Germany and Australia with respect to print media mergers. Furthermore, it provides an overview on the respective case law. Also, it discusses the two-pillar-approach practiced in all three jurisdictions in order to secure media diversity.

"Fostering competition is the first step to promoting plurality in the media."

United Kingdom, Department of Trade and Industry and Department of Culture, Media and Sport, "A New Future for Communications", White Paper, 2000, para. 4.2.6

I. Overview

This essay discusses merger control regulation concerning media companies in the European Union, in Germany and Australia. The media sector has its own characteristics that need to be considered in a merger investigation. The article will primarily concentrate on print media products, i.e. newspapers and magazines. The reason for this limitation is to be found in the major changes of German competition concerning mergers of newspaper publishers that were recently made by the 8th Amendment to the *Gesetz gegen Wettbewerbsbeschränkungen* (Act Against Restraints of Competition; "AARC") of 2013. The analysis will be based on the recent jurisprudence and the decisions of the cartel authorities about concentrations of print media enterprises.

1. Theoretical background

Merger control regulation exists for the purpose of controlling the concentration of economic power of undertakings. The creation or the strengthening of a dominant position in the relevant market is not generally prohibited by competition law if it is only the result of "internal growth", i.e. the improvement of a company's position in the market (whether based on technological advance, the growth of financial resources, measures of successful expansion or other reasons).[1] But if the strengthening of a company's market position takes place through the concentration of previously independent companies, i.e. through so-called external growth, "the effects on competition may raise concerns"[2]. These concerns will be taken care of by the applicable merger control law regimes and the cartel authorities, whose task it is to decide about the notifications of concentrations. Merger legislation aims to prevent concentrations between previously independent companies that results in lasting damage to competition.[3] The concept of merger control can be qualified as a preventive "ex ante" control, contrasted with the control of the abuse of market power of undertakings, e.g., which functions as an "ex post" control, because the growth of enterprises in the market is lawful. Competition law provisions apply to all industries, i.e. to all kinds of economic entities, following an "universal" approach (so-called "principle of universality"). That said, it has to be made clear, though, that the media sector has indeed its own unique characteristics. As economic sectors vary a lot, every sector could theoretically claim that the relevant law shall not apply due to these special characteristics. That is not a convincing argument: the law does indeed apply to all sectors, and special characteristics are to be taken into account while applying it.[4]

---

1 Kling/Thomas, Kartellrecht, 2nd edition, 2016, § 6 para. 5; see also Kling/Fleischer, Zur Leitidee des Wettbewerbsschutzes in den Kartellrechtsordnungen der Europäischen Union und Australiens – eine rechtvergleichende Analyse, (2010) 27 Nihon University Comparative Law, p. 139 et seq., p. 142 et seq.

2 Rosenthal/Thomas, European Merger Control, 2010, A. 3.

3 Rosenthal/Thomas, European Merger Control, 2010, A. 5.

4 See ACCC, Paper "Merger Law", 2006/2001, p. 4: "The media sector, like all other sectors of the economy, has its own unique characteristics that will need to be considered in a merger investigation. The ACCC's informal clearance process enables these characteristics to be identified and given proper weight when determining whether a merger is likely to substantially lessen competition or not."

2. Structure of the analysis

The following analysis will take a look at the legal framework concerning concentrations in the print media sector, both a supranational level (i.e. within the European Union) and in national law (i.e. in Germany and in Australia). This will be followed by a review of the relevant case law. Finally, a legal comparison will be made covering the three jurisdictions that are subject of this analysis.

II. The legal framework of merger control in the European Union, in Germany and Australia

1. European Union

a) Regulation No. 139/2004 and Articles 101, 102 TFEU

The main legislative texts for merger decisions within the European Union are the EC Merger Regulation No. 139/2004[5] on the one hand and the so-called Implementing Regulation No. 802/2004[6] on the other.[7] The EC Merger Regulation (which first entered into force in 1990)[8] contains the main rules for the assessment of concentrations, whereas the Implementing Regulation concerns procedural issues (notification, deadlines, right to be heard, etc.). Due to the so-called "effects doctrine", the European merger control regime also applies to mergers in which both parties are located outside the European Union, if the merger has a *foreseeable, immediate* and *substantial effect* in the European Union.[9] This is likely if the turnover thresholds in Article 1 of the Regulation No. 139/2004 are exceeded, though it may not necessarily always be the case.[10] Even though Article 21 (1) of Regulation No. 139/2004[11] aims at avoiding the review of concentrations under

---

5 Council Regulation (EC) No. 139/2004 on the control of concentrations between undertakings, OJ No. L 24, of 29/01/2004, p. 1.

6 Commission Regulation No. 802/2004 implementing Council Regulation (EC) No. 139/2004 on the control of concentrations between undertakings, OJ No. L 133, p. 30.

7 For further merger-related legal texts, see Rosenthal/Thomas, European Merger Control, 2010, A. 15.

8 Council Regulation (EEC) No. 4064/89 on the control of concentrations between undertakings, of 03/12/1989, OJ No. L 395, p. 1.

9 GC, Decision of March 25, 1999, case T-102/96, [1999] E.C.R. II-753 para. 90 – *Gencor v. Commission.*

10 Rosenthal/Thomas, European Merger Control, 2010, A. 31.

11 The cited provision states: "This Regulation alone shall apply to concentrations as defined in Article 3, and Council Regulations (EC) No 1/2003, (EEC) No 1017/68, (EEC)

both the Regulation and Articles 101 and 102 TFEU,[12] secondary legislation cannot exclude primary legislation within European law. Consequently, Articles 101 and 102 TFEU continue to be applicable to concentrations,[13] as held by the European Court of Justice in *Continental Can*[14] and the *British-American Tobacco*[15] case.[16] This, of course, is rather a theoretical aspect than a practical problem,[17] so I will not discuss it further.[18]

Article 21 (4) of the Regulation No. 139/2004 states that

> [...] Member States may take appropriate measures to protect legitimate interests other than those taken into consideration by this Regulation and compatible with the general principles and other provisions of Community law. Public security, *plurality of the media* and prudential rules shall be regarded as legitimate interests within the meaning of the first subparagraph.

Article 21 (4) of the Regulation No. 139/2004 aims to protect legitimate interests of the EU Member States. It applies when there are non-economic interests that should be into account in favour of the concentration.[19] The rationale behind this provision is the conviction that competition cannot in every case guarantee the non-economic media-specific model of plurality of opinion.[20] The cited article grants the EU Member States the right to prohibit a concentration for the purpose

---

No 4056/86 and (EEC) No 3975/87 shall not apply, except in relation to joint ventures that do not have a Community dimension and which have as their object or effect the coordination of the competitive behaviour of undertakings that remain independent".

12 Rosenthal/Thomas, European Merger Control, 2010, A. 55.

13 Rosenthal/Thomas, European Merger Control, 2010, A. 55.

14 ECJ, Decision of April 18, 1975, case 6/72, [1973] E.C.R 215 – *Continental Can v. Commission* (also named: *Europemballage*).

15 ECJ, Decision of, November 17, 1987, joint cases 142/84 and 156/84, [1986] E.C.R. 1899 paras. 37 et seq. – *BAT and Reynolds v. Commission.*

16 For details about the so-called "Continental Can doctrine", see Bechtold/Bosch/Brinker, EU-Kartellrecht Kommentar, 3rd edition, 2014, Introduction to FKVO paras. 7 et seqq.

17 For the remaining practical situations see Rosenthal/Thomas, European Merger Control, 2010, A. 56 et seq., who also concluded that it would be "highly unlikely that the Commission would apply Articles 101 and 102 TFEU rather than the EUMR [i.e. Regulation No. 139/2004]".

18 See Kling/Thomas, Kartellrecht, 2nd edition, § 8 paras. 336 et seqq.

19 Paal, Medienvielfalt und Wettbewerbsrecht, 2010, p. 295.

20 Paal, Medienvielfalt und Wettbewerbsrecht, 2010, p. 295.

of protecting the plurality of media[21] in cases when the Commission approves it;[22] the opposite case (the Commission prohibits the concentration, but the national authority approves it) is not covered by this provision, though.[23]

b) *EU Merger Guidelines*

In the field of mergers, notices and guidelines of the European Commission play an important role for the interpretation of the EC Merger Regulation. Therefore, the Commission developed Guidelines on the assessment of horizontal mergers[24] as well as Guidelines on the assessment of non-horizontal mergers.[25] The latter Guidelines serve as a means for the assessment of mergers between companies

---

21 EG-Kommission, Erklärungen für das Ratsprotokoll vom 19. Dezember 1989 (Engl. statements for the Council minutes), WuW 1990, 240 (243): „Die Möglichkeit der Mitgliedstaaten, sich auf die „Medienvielfalt" zu berufen, entspricht dem berechtigten Anliegen der Aufrechterhaltung diversifizierter Informationsquellen im Interesse des Meinungs- und Ausdruckspluralismus."

22 As an example, see the EC Commission's Newspaper Publishing case, http://europa.eu/rapid/press-release_IP-94-208_en.htm. This case is discussed in Paal, Medienvielfalt und Wettbewerbsrecht, 2010, p. 296 et seq. The Commission's press release reads as follows:

> After its first scrutiny of a concentration in the newspaper sector, the Commission has approved the public bid for joint acquisition of the UK company Newspaper Publishing plc (NP), publishers of 'The Independent' and 'The Independent on Sunday', by a consortium consisting of the Spanish media company Promotora de Informaciones S.A. (PRISA), the Italian media group Editoriale l'Espresso S.p.A. (Espresso) and the UK newspaper publishing company Mirror Group Newspapers plc (MGN). […] The Spanish and Italian parents operate on geographic markets which are separate from the UK newspaper publishing market. The tabloid newspapers published by Mirror Group Newspapers plc on the one hand, and 'The Independent' on the other hand, are not significantly substitutable from the viewpoint of the consumer, either readers or companies which purchase advertising space. In view of this absence of overlap, the Commission has decided not to oppose the operation. The operation has been notified concurrently under the UK *Fair Trading Act* to the UK authorities, whose jurisdiction relates to issues such as accurate presentation of news and free expression of opinion. This is in compliance with the Merger Regulation, which provides that Member States may take measures to protect legitimate interests other than those taken into consideration by the Regulation, such interests to include plurality of the media.

23 Paal, Medienvielfalt und Wettbewerbsrecht, 2010, p. 295.

24 OJ No. C 31, of 05/02/2004, p. 5.

25 OJ No. C 265, of 18/10/2008, p. 6.

that are in a so-called vertical or conglomerate relationship. As far as the merger procedure is concerned, the Commission's "Best Practice Guidelines" clarify the relationship between the case team and parties/third parties during the procedure (pre-notification contacts, meetings, provision of documents). To provide better guidance to the parties when it comes to offering commitments, the Commission has also published model texts for divestiture commitments and for trustee mandates and an explanatory guideline.[26]

c) *Relevance of European merger regulation for the media sector*

There are no specific Guidelines that deal with mergers of media companies, but the European Commission nonetheless publicly claims to keep an eye on the "rapidly evolving" media sector:

> "One of the Commission's main concerns is that mergers in the media sector do not significantly impede competition and that access to key elements (whether content, technology or interconnection) is not affected."[27]

Regarding the print media sector, supranational concentrations are relatively rare.[28] A systematic analysis of the relevant case law makes clear that such mergers typically won't have *foreseeable*, *immediate* and *substantial effects* as demanded by the ECJ. They may very well affect competition on the domestic market, though. As a consequence of the fragmented European media market, the member states of the EU play the decisive role when it comes to the question of protecting media diversity (by the means of public media law or merger control law).[29] Article 21 (4) of Regulation No. 139/2004 clarifies that the European Commission supports

---

26 http://ec.europa.eu/competition/mergers/legislation/legislation.html.

27 http://ec.europa.eu/competition/sectors/media/overview_en.html#mergers.

28 Cf. BKartA, Decision of April 18, 2011, case B 6–28/11 – Hearst Corp./Elle-Verlag: Hearst Corporation, New York, purchased a 50% share of ELLE-Verlags GmbH, Munich ("ELLE Deutschland").

29 Cf. DoC, Policy Background Paper No. 3, June 2014, "Media control and ownership", p. 52:

> The EU, through the European Commission, has tended to focus on competition factors and competition law to regulate media businesses, leaving specific content and media diversity protection to member states. It has argued that competition laws can respond to abuses of market power or dominance and set the principles to reflect market conditions it deems appropriate, but that national regulators have jurisdiction over issues of media pluralism, diversity and freedom of information.

the management of media-related issues by the member states' authorities.[30] Even though European merger law provisions and the Commissions guidelines may not apply, their "role model effect" should be born in mind. To a remarkable extent, national authorities and even national courts are being influenced by the Commission's view as laid down in the respective texts.

2. Germany

a) *Specific protection and regulation of the media sector by German law*

aa) *Constitutional law – the Basic Law of Germany*

When applying German merger control law, one has to obey the constitutional guarantees which are provided by the Basic Law of Germany (which forms the constitution of the Federal Republic of Germany). The basic rights function as a means of interpretation of the ordinary law, thus setting limits for its scope, too.

The so-called "freedom of the press", i.e. Article 5 (1) (second and third sentence) of the Basic Law, applies to media enterprises of all sectors, not only to the print media. The named paragraphs state:

> "(1) […] Freedom of the press and freedom of reporting by means of broadcasts and films shall be guaranteed. There shall be no censorship."

According to Article 5 (2), these rights "shall find their limits in the provisions of general laws, in provisions for the protection of young persons, and in the right to personal honour".

Obviously, Article 5 grants media enterprises basic individual rights. But this may not be the most interesting aspect of this provision. According to the Federal Constitutional Court of Germany, Article 5 also contains a guarantee of the press as a legal "institution", i.e. a functional guarantee of the press as such.[31] Surprisingly, this aspect of the freedom of press is not covered by the primary

---

30 See also DoC, Policy Background Paper No. 3, June 2014, "Media control and ownership", p. 52 et seq.: "However Article 21 (4) of the *139/2004 Merger Regulation* stipulates that member states can apply additional controls in order to protect pluralism in the media, showing the EU's support for the management of these issues by national regulators."

31 Cf. Nieschalk, Folgerungen aus deregulierten Medienlandschaften für die Reformdiskussion um das Pressefusionsrecht, 2012, p. 25 et seqq., 39 et seqq.; see also Zohm, Der verfassungsrechtliche Rahmen der Pressefusionskontrolle, 2010. The government is obliged to practise a policy of neutrality with respect to media, which restricts the scope of activity of the German authorities; for a detailed analysis, see Zagouras, WRP 2007, 1429 (1434).

European law (i.e. by the Charter of Fundamental Rights), because fundamental rights granted on the European level are generally interpreted as individual rights of natural or legal persons (i.e. publishers, media enterprises, etc.). This does not mean, of course, that there are no functional guarantees at all in European law. There is one guarantee for competition, e.g., which was developed by the European courts by interpretation of Articles 101 et seqq. of the Treaty on the Functioning of the European Union (TFEU), which belongs to the primary European law.

bb) Further regulation in Germany aiming at media diversity

Within Germany, the country's States (*Bundesländer*) are given exclusive powers to regulate the broadcasting (i.e. television and radio) sector, because the *Bundesländer* have maintained their own cultural sovereignty. TV and radio are therefore subject to a high degree of regionalism. Notwithstanding this regionalism and the exclusive powers of the *Bundesländer* to provide safeguards against concentration of ownership in order to prevent dominant influence on public opinion, there are legal provisions that apply in all of the country's States. Insofar as plurality of opinion is concerned, Section 25 et seqq. of the German "Inter-State Broadcasting Agreement" (*Rundfunkstaatsvertrag*) aims at preventing dominant power of opinion in the private television sector in Germany. The protection of plurality of opinion in nationally-transmitted nationwide private television – as regulated by Section 26 of the Broadcasting Agreement – is not only secured by the courts,[32] but it is also the main task of the Commission on Concentration in the Media ("Kommission zur Ermittlung der Konzentration im Medienbereich", abbreviated "KEK"). The KEK is an independent regulatory body that assesses mergers that exceed certain thresholds; an average annual audience share of 30 per cent or more is deemed to be a "controlling influence" for the purpose of media diversity. So far, the KEK has published five "Reports on the Development of Media Concentration and Measures to Secure Plurality of Opinion in the Private Broadcasting Sector".[33]

---

32 See as an example BVerwG, Decision of November 24, 2010, case 6 C 16/09, BVerwGE 138, 186 = NVwZ-RR 2011, 279 – Springer/ProSiebenSat1. The Springer/ProSiebenSat1 case, which dealt with a cross-media concentration, was also decided according German merger law, see BGH, Decision of June 8, 2010, case KVR 4/09, WuW/E DE-R 3067 – Springer/Pro Sieben II; see also Steger, WuW 2010, 282 et seqq.; Paal, ZWeR 2012, 380 et seqq.; Esser, NZKart 2013, 135 et seqq.

33 http://www.kek-online.de/information/publications/media-concentration-reports.html?L=1:

The application of the Broadcasting Treaty provisions and the activities of the KEK will not be analysed in particular here, as the television sector is not an object of analysis for this article. From now on, we may turn to print media markets, and newspaper markets, especially. There are basically two different kinds of newspapers in Germany, newspapers which are distributed nationwide (such as Frankfurter Allgemeine Zeitung, Süddeutsche Zeitung, Die Welt) and regional newspapers. It is fairly true to say, as the Australian Department of Communications does of Germany: "The newspaper sector is almost wholly regional and there is a relatively small press market".[34] However, this situation has rather historic causes than legal ones. Contrary to what the DoC indicates, in my opinion the regionalism of the German newspaper market cannot be based on the exclusive powers of the *Bundesländer* for "culture" or other legal peculiarities. Although Germany was unified in 1871 for the first time, and consequently has ever since been regarded as being a "nation", its regionalism has survived in most fields of social life. Germany is a "country of regions", and the newspaper market is no exception to this. There is a definitive interest of the "ordinary German reader" to receive regional and local news on a regular basis. This is why many subscribe to "their" local newspaper. Obviously, the situation is not much different in rural Australia,[35] where "it is far from clear, however, that the online media is any better than a local newspaper or radio station at serving geographically-clustered individuals whose only common interest is local news."[36]

If one were to search for a legal basis (not only social or historic ones) for the existence of so many regional papers in Germany, one should cite Article 5 (1) of the Basic Law again, as it contains the right of "freedom of the press". This

First Report: "Securing diversity of opinion against media concentration"; Second Report: "Ensuring Plurality of Opinion in Times of Major Change"; Third Report: "Cross-Media Relations: A Challenge for Media Concentration Control"; Fourth Report: "On the Way towards Securing Plurality across Different Media"; Fifth Report: "Turning from a Television-Centred View to a Broader Focus on Media Requirements for a Present-Day Regulation to Secure Plurality of Opinion in the Media". The KEK website provides summaries of the mentioned reports in English.

34 DoC, Policy Background Paper No. 3, June 2014, "Media control and ownership", p. 51.

35 ACCC, Paper "Merger Control", 2006/2011, para. 93: "[…] local advertising generally remains geographically restricted. Small businesses in rural and regional areas may find little utility in being able to advertise on national websites and face a relatively restricted range of ways to send their message to local customers." Para. 24 reads: "[…] These local markets are likely to continue for the foreseeable future and will impinge on media mergers in rural and regional Australia."

36 ACCC, Paper "Merger Control", 2006/2011, para. 50.

provision, of course, is valid nationwide, and it gives every publisher the right to print and distribute a newspaper, whether nationwide or restricted to a certain geographic region.

b) Merger control according to Sections 35 et seqq. AARC

Within the German Competition Law, the relevant legal framework concerning mergers was incorporated into the AARC since the second amendment of 1973. The set of rules dubbed "Zusammenschlusskontrolle"[37] (merger control) is to be found in Chapter 7, Sections 35 to 43 AARC.[38] Mergers of print media enterprises are covered by the cited provisions. Special rules governing only press mergers were established in 1976, as a result of the third amendment to the AARC. Ever since, Section 38 (3) AARC contains the so-called turnover multiplier for concentrations of print media undertakings.[39]

According to a renowned practitioner, merger review by the Federal Cartel Office in the press sector has always been "strict" in order to support journalistic diversity ("publizistische Vielfalt" in German) – even though the written law was the same for all undertakings.[40] According to the same practitioner, major changes

---

37 The terms "Zusammenschlusskontrolle" and "Fusionskontrolle" are often used synonymously in the German language. While the first term is used for merger control within German competition law, the latter is more common within European competition law, as the German translation for "Council Regulation No. 139/2004" is "Fusionskontrollverordnung".

38 See also Zagouras, Konvergenz und Kartellrecht, 2002, p. 95 et seqq., 132 et seqq.

39 Kling/Thomas, Kartellrecht, 2nd edition, 2016, § 22 paras. 76 et seqq. For further details about the history of Section 38 AARC, see Zagouras, Konvergenz und Kartellrecht, 2002, p. 134 et seq.

40 Klumpp, WuW 2013, 344 (345):

> Zudem prüft das Bundeskartellamt Pressezusammenschlüsse im Rahmen der materiellen Beurteilung - obwohl der gesetzliche Kontrollmaßstab an sich der gleiche ist wie für andere Branchen - regelmäßig besonders streng. Dies hat dazu geführt, dass in der Vergangenheit viele Vorhaben vom Bundeskartellamt untersagt oder schon im Vorfeld einer Untersagung von den beteiligten Unternehmen aufgegeben wurden. Gerechtfertigt wird der strenge Maßstab unter anderem mit der publizistischen Vielfalt, die durch die Pressefusionskontrolle jedenfalls indirekt mit geschützt werden soll. Dies war auch der Grund dafür, dass in Reaktion auf die zunehmende Konzentration im Pressewesen in den 70er-Jahren eine gesetzliche Sonderbehandlung von Pressezusammenschlüssen überhaupt eingeführt wurde.

in the economic framework that happened in recent decades left the authorities' strict review practice unaltered.[41]

As Section 35 (3) AARC states, the German merger control is applicable only if the European merger provisions of Council Regulation No. 139/2004 do not cover the case in question, as Recital 8 states:

> The provisions to be adopted in this Regulation should apply to significant structural changes, the impact of which on the market goes beyond the national borders of any one Member State. Such concentrations should, as a general rule, be reviewed exclusively at Community level, in application of a 'one-stop shop' system[42] and in compliance with the principle of subsidiarity. Concentrations not covered by this Regulation come, in principle, within the jurisdiction of the Member States.

This means that the European Commission has exclusive jurisdiction if a concentration falls within the scope of the Council Regulation No. 139/2004.

A concentration used to be unlawful under the earlier version of Section 36 (1) AARC if it was expected to create or strengthen a dominant position. In this case, it could be prohibited by the Bundeskartellamt, unless the undertakings concerned were able to prove that the merger would also lead to improvements of the conditions of competition and that these improvements would outweigh the disadvantages of dominance. Since the eighth amendment to the AARC of 2013, the so-called SIEC test has to be applied. The abbreviation SIEC stands for "*s*ignificant *i*mpediment to *e*ffective *c*ompetition".[43] The former "dominance test" has since been a part of the SIEC test, which means that for our purposes, the basic criteria for merger control as we have known them since 1973 (prevention of the creation of dominance on the relevant market) are still relevant.

The eighth amendment to the AARC of 2013 brought a couple of other interesting changes for mergers of media enterprises:

41 Klumpp, WuW 2013, 344 (345): „Die wirtschaftlichen Rahmenbedingungen für Zeitungsverlage haben sich in den vergangenen Jahrzehnten jedoch massiv verändert. Insbesondere das Internet hat zu gravierenden strukturellen Veränderungen sowohl auf den Leser- wie auch auf den Anzeigenmärkten geführt. […] An der strengen Prüfungspraxis des Bundeskartellamts hat sich trotz dieser massiven Veränderung der Rahmenbedingungen im Ergebnis kaum etwas geändert."

42 Cf. Article 21 (3): "No Member State shall apply its national legislation on competition to any concentration that has a Community dimension."

43 See Bechtold, GWB Kommentar, 7th edition, 2013, § 36 para. 1; Bechtold/Bosch/Brinker, EU-Kartellrecht Kommentar, 3rd edition, 2014, Art. 2 FKVO para. 1; see also Bechtold, NZKart 2013, 263 (265) for details about the SIEC test.

Firstly, according to Section 38 (3) AARC, mergers between media companies benefit from a reduction of the turnover multiplier from 20 to eight for revenues derived from the publication, production and distribution of newspapers and magazines. The threshold for the notification of a mergers of print media undertakings is as follows: the worldwide turnover of the concerned undertakings is at least €62.5 million (previously: €25 million; generally: €500 million); one of the undertakings concerned must have an annual domestic turnover of at least €3.125 million (previously: €1.25 million; generally: €25 million), whereas another undertaking concerned must have a domestic turnover of at least €0.625 million (previously: €0.25 million; generally: €5 million). The reasoning behind the raising of the relevant threshold in the press sector is quite simple: many of the German print media undertakings have suffered from severe financial losses over a couple of years. The number of subscribers to print media has dropped significantly, and so has the number of occasional readers, it seems – obviously, potential readers are more likely go online nowadays to gain information[44] instead of purchasing print media as it was common to do in the past. Consequently, in some cases, local newspapers had to be "rescued" by larger media companies who still maintain financial power. In order to maintain media diversity in the press market, as demanded by Article 5 of the Basic Law of Germany, the legislator felt the need to take action.

---

44 The rise of online news is discussed in DoC, Policy Background Paper No. 3, June 2014, "Media control and ownership", p. 24 et seq.:

> The usage of news websites as a proportion of the Australian adult population is also significant. In 2013 (calendar year), an estimated 41 per cent of Australians over 14 years of age visited a news website each week, on average, during the year. In 2011, research from the ACMA found that 22 per cent of respondents had accessed news through a social media website, including Facebook (83 per cent) and Twitter (17 per cent). Not only are news websites regularly accessed by Australians, they are also important in terms of the value ascribed to them by users. In 2012, 34 per cent of respondents identified the internet as their main source of news [...]. Similar patterns were evident in 2013. [...] The preferences and demographics of online news consumption are also noteworthy. In 2013, 68 per cent of Australians aged 16 and over accessed online news content weekly or more often, with the highest regular use (75 per cent) in the 35 to 44 age bracket. This is notable as other forms of online information seeking (such as conducting a search or general web browsing, for example) tend to be more popular among younger age groups (16 to 34 years). There are also clear differences in terms of gender, with males more likely to be accessing news online on a weekly basis (74 per cent) than women (63 per cent).

This leads us to the second and third major changes of law made by the eighth amendment. From 2013 onwards, the so-called "Anschlussklausel" ("connection clause") of Sec. 35 (2), second sentence No. 1 AARC has been applicable to press mergers as well. This provision states that merger control law (i.e. Sec. 35 (1) AARC) shall not apply where an undertaking which is not dependent within the meaning of Sec. 36 (2) AARC and had a worldwide turnover of less than €10 million in the last business year, merges with another undertaking. Consequently, takeovers of small and medium independent publishers do not have to be notified, as long as the annual turnover of the company does not exceed €1.25 million. The third relevant change especially deals with rescue mergers, which are privileged by Sec. 36 (2) (second sentence No. 3) AARC in cases where a small or medium publishing company has suffered substantial annual loss ("erheblicher Jahresfehlbetrag") over a period of three consecutive years, so that its future existence is doubtful.

c) *Price maintenance for newspapers and magazines according to Section 30 AARC*

When applying the AARC to the press sector, one should bear in mind that Sec. 30 AARC contains special resale price maintenance for newspapers and magazines as well. According to Sec. 30 (1) (first sentence) AARC, the prohibition of cartels (Sec. 1 AARC) "shall not apply to resale price maintenance by which an undertaking producing newspapers or magazines requires the purchasers of these products by legal or economic means to demand certain resale prices or to impose the same commitment upon their own customers, down to the resale to the final consumer". This basically leads to a total lack of price competition as far as consumers are concerned. Sec. 30 AARC is interpreted in a strict manner.[45]

3. Australia

a) *Specific regulation of the media sector in Australia*

As in Germany, there is a specific regulation of the media sector in Australia. Media diversity is primarily protected by the restrictions on cross-media mergers in the *Broadcasting Services Act* 1992 ("BSA").[46] Besides that, the ACCC whose purpose is to protect competition in markets in Australia will apply the relevant

45 LG Hamburg, Decision of June 8, 2011, case 315 O 182/11, GRUR-RR 2012, 38 = MMR 2012, 172 – studibooks.de, paras. 29 et seqq.

46 ACCC, Paper "Media Mergers", 2006/2011, p. 5 and para. 11.

provisions of the *Competition and Consumer Act* 2010 ("CCA") to mergers of media companies.[47]

The media-related legislative framework is overseen and administered by the Australian Communications and Media Authority (ACMA). In January 2014, the Department of Communications (as part of the Australian Government) published a Policy Background Paper on "Media control and ownership", which summarises the relevant regulation. The regulation aims at the protection of media diversity, which means ensuring that there are different "voices" to be heard in the media sector.[48] "Media diversity" is defined in the cited paper as follows:

> Media diversity refers to the ability of citizens to access and consume a wide range of viewpoints without any one media owner or controller exercising too much influence. Among other factors, this is seen to support an informed citizenry and more effective democracy. [...] Media diversity regulation seeks to ensure access to a wide variety of influential media 'voices', with ownership or editorial control of these voices spread over a number of organisations. A 'voice' could be described as a media owner – whether that owner controls a television service or network, a radio service or network, a newspaper, a website, or a combination of these. This is based on the premise that the media is able to influence the issues audiences pay attention to by 'framing' (setting the context in which an issue is analysed) and 'agenda-setting' (identifying, promoting and ordering news content in such a way that affects the relative importance of a given issue).[49]

The Australian regulation of the media sector covers all kinds of media, i.e. commercial radio and television broadcasting, regulated media platforms, and associated print newspapers, for each of which different "control rules" exist. Since this

47 ACCC, Paper "Media Mergers", 2006/2011, p. 5.

48 For two definitions of the terms "diversity" and "plurality", see also G. Hewitt, "Media Mergers: Background Note", [2004] OECD Journal: Competition Law and Policy, Vol. 5, No. 4, p. 79 (112): "Diversity [...] refers to the variety of content on offer, while pluralism refers to the number of different providers of media services, i.e. the number of different voices competing for attention." The author's definitions are based on a 2001 "Media Ownership Consultation paper" by United Kingdom's Department on Trade and Industry and Department of Culture, Media and Sport), which read: "Diversity refers to the variety of available programmes, publications and services, whereas plurality is about the choice people can make between different providers of those services." These definitions may serve as a helpful tool to clarify the meaning of the words used by the author, but this conceptual perception is of course not mandatory. One could just as well declare "diversity" and "plurality" synonyms; for further discussions on how to define the terms "diversity" and "plurality", see also Paal, Medienvielfalt und Wettbewerbsrecht, 2010, p. 71 et seqq.

49 DoC, Policy Background Paper No. 3, June 2014, "Media control and ownership", p. 4.

chapter is restricted to print media only and Georgios Gounalakis's and Simon Rößs chapter takes the broader view, we may reduce the analysis to print newspapers only. From the view of an "outsider" like the present author, the most interesting aspect of the Australian regulatory concept in that respect is the fact that it covers only so-called "associated newspapers". The Policy Background Paper defines this term as follows:

> An 'associated newspaper' is one that that is linked in terms of circulation with the relevant licence area. Specifically, a newspaper is 'associated' with a commercial television broadcasting licence if more than 50 per cent of its circulation is within the relevant licence area, while a newspaper is associated with a commercial radio broadcasting licence if more than 50 per cent of its circulation is within the relevant licence area and the newspaper's circulation covers at least 2 per cent of the licence area's population."[50] Consequently, "[m]ost small, community papers do not meet this threshold. Perhaps more importantly, this also excludes the national newspapers, *The Australian* and the *Australian Financial Review*. As a consequence, the ownership of these papers is not regulated through the media control rules.[51]

The limitation of the regulation to "associated newspapers" is striking. One may speculate if it were mainly driven by the fear of the government that cross-media conglomerates owned by "media moguls" could gain control over "public opinion". Limitations on the number of "voices" that are to be heard on the different Australian media sectors can happen in different ways, though. In the author's view, the general exclusion of national newspapers from the regulation seems to be particularly dangerous for the protection of media diversity and an effective democracy. Here, the "Frankfurter Rundschau" case[52] may serve as an example: if the owner of a national newspaper with a liberal-conservative political tendency (like the "FAZ") bought the majority of the shares of a national newspaper with a clear tendency to the political left (like the "FR") – is there not a danger that the new owner might influence the political direction of its target, thus limiting the number of "voices"? When looking at local newspaper markets, the definitions of which by the Department of Communications are "rigid and relatively local"[53], the phenomenon that occurred in Germany – i.e. the reduction of "voices" by (threats

50 DoC, Policy Background Paper No. 3, June 2014, "Media control and ownership", p. 5 et seq.

51 DoC, Policy Background Paper No. 3, June 2014, "Media control and ownership", p. 6.

52 This case will be discussed later, see below III. 1. a).

53 DoC, Policy Background Paper No. 3, June 2014, "Media control and ownership", p. 6: "The concept of a 'market' for media services, at least in terms of this regulation, is therefore rigid and relatively local."

of) insolvency of local newspapers –[54] could very well occur everywhere else in the world as well and thus in Australia, too. The author suggests that the number of subscribers to regional and local newspapers will likely become smaller as younger generations of potential readers are not willing to subscribe to printed newspapers nowadays. The industry trend for Australian newspapers is negative, according to PWC.[55] We may let the question remain unanswered, though, if the situation might possibly change if local and regional newspapers manage to overcome the obstacles of entering the "online" world.

The Department of Communications explained the limits of the current media control rules by "weighting" only three traditional media forms – commercial television, commercial radio and certain newspapers associated with those broadcasting services. It also explained that this "weighting" reflected the "views of the Parliament in 1992".[56] Notwithstanding the discretion every authority should have, and a relatively old view of the Australian Parliament, the concept is not fully satisfactory if media control regulation should really aim at protecting media diversity as a whole. Rather, it seems that regulatory concepts are often to be seen as a direct reaction to current threats, but not as a more general and objective legislative action.

The limitations of the regulatory concept concerning media control and ownership in Australia, which were pointed out above, raise the question whether the relevant provisions of the Australian competition law are able to cover the "gap cases" (i.e. mergers of national newspapers, mergers of local and regional newspapers). It is undoubted that the Australian media control regulation does not exclude the application of the national merger control law on a "case-by-case basis"[57].[58]

---

54 The relevant cases will be discusses later, see below III. 1. b).

55 See DoC, Policy Background Paper No. 3, June 2014, "Media control and ownership", p. 28: "The average weekday readerships for Australia's major newspapers have declined between 5 and 32 per cent over the five years to 2013. This trend has been well documented in Australia and is a pattern that has also been evident in newspaper readership in other countries." These facts are also true for the advertising market, see DoC, Policy Background Paper, ibid., p. 22: "[…] the share of total advertising revenue for the 'traditional' media is expected to fall between 2013 and 2017: newspapers from 22 to 13 per cent […]".

56 DoC, Policy Background Paper No. 3, June 2014, "Media control and ownership", p. 7.

57 ACCC, Paper "Merger Control", 2006/2001, para. 113; DoC, Policy Background Paper No. 3, June 2014, "Media control and ownership", p. 7.

58 DoC, Policy Background Paper No. 3, June 2014, "Media control and ownership", p. 10: "The ACCC's assessment of media mergers occurs separately from, and is not obliged to take account of, the media-specific control and ownership rules established in the

b) Section 50 CCA

aa) Introduction

Merger control in Australia is, as in Germany, part of the written domestic competition law. Section 50 of the *Competition and Consumer Act 2010* ("CCA"), applies to transactions that involve the acquisition of shares or assets by any person or corporation, which have the effect or are likely to have the effect of substantially lessening the competition in any market. For the assessment of every case, a prior definition of the relevant market is mandatory.[59]

The CCA is overseen by the Australian Competition and Consumer Commission (ACCC). Like the European Commission, the ACCC "actively monitors the media sector for potential threats to competition".[60]

bb) General criteria for market definition

When assessing a merger under Section 50 CCA, the ACCC seeks to define the appropriate product, geographic and functional markets. The appropriate *product* market includes all suppliers of products to whom consumers would be likely to switch so as to avoid a price rise by the merged company.[61] The relevant *geographic* market includes all suppliers who currently supply the area supplied by the merged company or who would be likely to commence supplying this area if the merged company raised its prices.[62] The definition of the relevant *functional* market involves the identification of the vertical stage of production and/or distribution relevant to the proposed merger. These criteria reflect the general principles of market definition, which are "fairly similar across countries".[63]

BSA. This means that the ACCC may oppose proposed mergers that might otherwise be permitted under the media control rules, or vice versa. Unlike the BSA control rules, the ACCC's assessment of merger activity is not governed by predetermined and specific rules."

59 For a very detailed analysis of market definition, see ACCC, Paper "Media Mergers", 2006/2011, paras. 67 et seqq., ibid., Attachment 1, paras. 30 et seqq.

60 DoC, Policy Background Paper No. 3, June 2014, "Media control and ownership", p. 11.

61 ACCC, Paper "Media Mergers", 2006/2011, Attachment 1, para. 30.

62 ACCC, Paper "Media Mergers", 2006/2011, Attachment 1, para. 32. This is particular relevant as geographic distinctions in competition have to be considered between urban and rural Australia, see ACCC, ibid., para. 60.

63 OECD, Paper "Media Mergers: 3. Summary of the discussion", [2004] OECD Journal of Competition Law and Policy, Vol. 5, No. 4, p. 147 (148).

cc) *Print media markets*

According to this market definition, we therefore must differentiate between different print media products – such as newspapers and magazines, e.g., the reader market and the advertising market of newspapers, and the geographic territory of distribution; consequently, national newspapers and local newspapers belong to two different geographic markets.[64]

In 2006, the ACCC stated, with respect to newspaper advertising markets:

> These markets will be determined by considering the relevant product, geographic and functional dimensions of the markets. [...] When considering the relevant product dimensions of the advertising markets relevant to the merger of two newspapers, the ACCC needs to consider what substitution possibilities, if any, exist both between different types of advertising products provided by newspapers and across different modes of delivery.[65]

The so-called hypothetical monopolist test[66] may be used to assist in determining the breadth of the relevant markets.[67]

With respect to defining newspaper product markets, according to a more "traditional view", online news content would form a product market different from printed newspapers. In the past, the ACCC based its assumptions on this "classic" standard:

> Media outlets have traditionally been characterised by their modes of delivery. Thus, FTA television, pay-TV, radio and print media have generally been considered to be in separate markets.
>
> Technological developments have added two additional delivery modes to those listed above. The online media now represents a specific mode for the delivery of media content

---

64 ACCC, Paper "Media Mergers", 2006/2011, Attachment 1, para. 34.

65 ACCC, Paper "Media Mergers", 2006/2011, para. 116 et. seq.

66 ACCC, Paper "Media Mergers", 2006/2011, para. 121:

> A simple economic test (the hypothetical monopolist test) is used to assist in determining the breadth of the relevant markets. In the current example, this test would ask whether or not the substitution by advertisers from newspaper classified advertising to online classified advertising is sufficient to render unprofitable a small but significant price increase in classified advertising by the merged newspaper. If substitution is sufficient to render the newspaper price increase unprofitable then it is reasonable to conclude that online classified advertising places a significant competitive constraint on newspaper classified advertising so that, for the purpose of evaluating the competitive effects of the newspaper merger, online and newspaper classified advertising should be considered as part of a single integrated classified advertising market.

67 ACCC, Paper "Media Mergers", 2006/2011, para. 117.

> through the internet. Other wireless services, and in particular 3G mobile telephony, also provide an alternative media delivery mode.[68]

However, this concept of market definition could very well change in the medium term, as print and online media content seem to have converged increasingly in a relatively short period of time.[69] The ACCC rightly pointed out – some 10 years ago already – that

> [a]s traditional media boundaries blur, focus may shift from the way information is delivered to the actual products media companies offer […] In the past, the ACCC has regarded the media as four distinct products—free-to-air television, pay television, radio and print. Those products have been thought of as having little overlap in content or advertising. Convergence of technology means we can no longer take that view. Some advertising and content is now being packaged across a number of delivery platforms such as newspapers, 3G mobile phones and internet news sites.[70]

Later, in the same paper, the ACCC summarised the media divergence developments as follows:

> Clearly a number of the developments summarised above indicate that different modes of media might be 'converging'. The digitisation of print, audio and audio-visual content and the ability to access these alternative forms of content through a single delivery device, such as a laptop computer or a 3G telephone, is likely to lead to competition between media outlets that traditionally provided separate and distinct products."[71] […] The traditional view of media products has been changing over recent years and is likely to change further in the future, for at least three reasons. This will impinge on the markets that are relevant for merger analysis under the Act. First, any changes to cross media laws make feasible some mergers that previously would have been impossible. Thus mergers that involve aggregations across modes of delivery become more relevant and raise competition issues that cross delivery modes.[72]

In the view of the ACCC, "[d]evelopments in the internet mean that newspapers and online media directly compete for some types of advertising".[73] When considering the merger between two newspapers, or between a newspaper owner and a major online classified advertiser, and depending on the specific facts of the merger under analysis,

68 Cf. ACCC, Paper „Media Mergers", 2006/2001, para. 73 et seq.

69 See also Paal, Medienvielfalt und Wettbewerbsrecht, 2010, p. 55 et seqq.; 59 et seqq., 62 et seqq.; Zagouras, Konvergenz und Kartellrecht, 2002, p. 1 et seqq.

70 ACCC, Paper "Media Mergers", 2006/2011, p. 4 et seq.

71 ACCC, Paper "Media Mergers", 2006/2011, para. 48.

72 ACCC, Paper "Media Mergers", 2006/2011, para. 80.

73 ACCC, Paper "Media Mergers", 2006/2011, para. 81.

> a relevant market may be the market for the provision and distribution of classified advertising to advertisers through print and online media in Australia [...] depending on the specific merger under consideration, a market that considers only one type of classified advertising could be relevant, such as the provision and distribution of employment classified advertising to advertisers through print and/or online media in Australia.[74]

All this, of course, does not mean that a market definition according to the "classical" distinction between the two modes of TV broadcasting, radio broadcasting and print media is to be regarded as generally outdated already. Rather, according to the ACCC, "[t]he key element when determining whether different media are in the same market for merger analysis is substitution".[75] Substitution is indeed the "simple" answer to the difficult question of product market definition.

The question whether two products, which belong to two different modes of media, are interchangeable substitutes or not, is dependent on the specific elements of the merger under consideration; it has to be answered on a case-by-case basis. It is quite possible, though, that two products which belong to the same media mode may form two markets. This especially applies to different forms of newspaper advertising that are not so-called "close substitutes" for each other. Consequently, "a rise in the relative price of classified advertising, by itself, would not lead to significant substitution to other forms of newspaper advertising".[76] The abstract concepts behind the case-by-case analysis of media mergers are (1) the so-called demand-side oriented market concept, i.e. the customer's view ("Bedarfsmarktkonzept" in German),[77] and (2) the so-called "SSNIP test" (which stands for "*s*mall but *s*ignificant *n*on-transitory *i*ncrease in *p*rice").[78] Both of these concepts are relevant for the review of merger cases according to European and German competition law as well. Different media may also function as *complements* rather than *substitutes* for each other, depending on the messages that advertisers want to send to their target audience, e.g., and the consumer's behaviour during the week or during the working day.[79]

74 ACCC, Paper "Media Mergers", 2006/2011, para. 84.
75 ACCC, Paper "Media Mergers", 2006/2011, p. 5. The ACCC further elaborates on the concept of "substitution", paras. 79 and 115. In the latter paragraph, "substitution" is once again dubbed as "the key issue"; cf. Paal, Medienvielfalt und Wettbewerbsrecht, 2010, p. 189 et seqq.
76 ACCC, Paper "Media Mergers", 2006/2011, para. 119.
77 Cf. Paal, Medienvielfalt und Wettbewerbsrecht, 2010, p. 185 et seq., 189 et seqq.
78 Cf. Paal, Medienvielfalt und Wettbewerbsrecht, 2010, p. 186.
79 ACCC, Paper "Media Mergers", 2006/2011, para. 127.

Over the years, the ACCC has assessed quite a number of proposed media transactions on a case-by-case basis.[80] However, for the purpose of this article, most of these are not suitable, as they mostly deal with television and radio services, or cross-media mergers. Insofar as print media enterprises were involved, they will be discussed in a short case analysis.[81]

dd) Predictive character of merger review

One should always bear in mind that in all jurisdictions, the application of merger law is based on prognosis.[82] Prognosis is difficult ground – it may fail due to wrong data or by using wrong analytic concepts, it may falsely rely on wishful thinking on the authority's side or contain other errors. Consequently, the ACCC rightly stressed that media mergers must always be analysed on the basis of "hard evidence", but not on "wishful thinking".[83]

ee) The SLC test as the material decision criterion

The material decision criterion of *substantial lessening of competition* – the so-called SLC test – is widespread in the jurisdictions of English-speaking countries, e.g. in the United Kingdom.[84] The SIEC test of the European and German merger law, as analyzed earlier in this essay, closely resembles the SLC test. This does not come as a surprise, because the SLC test served as a model in the creation of the

80 For the details, see ACCC, Media Mergers, 2006/2011, p. 1–48; DoC, Policy Background Paper No. 3, June 2014, "Media control and ownership", p. 10 et seq.

81 See below, IV. 2., IV. 3.

82 For the "with or without test" in Australian merger law see ACCC, Paper "Media Mergers", 2006/2011, para. 110: "When considering a merger, the ACCC must use the with-or-without test. Put simply, the ACCC must consider the likely future of competition if the merger occurs versus the likely state of competition if the merger does not proceed. This analysis requires the ACCC to consider both current competition in the relevant market and how this competition will develop over time". See also DoC, Policy Background Paper No. 3, June 2014, "Media control and ownership", p. 11: "Moreover, the competition test is 'forward-looking', examining the likely competition effects of a merger in the foreseeable future, rather than examining the situation as it stands. The competition assessment undertaken by the ACCC is a future 'with or without test', assessing the future state of competition <u>with</u> the merger, and <u>without</u> so as to isolate the merger's impact on competition from other changes."

83 ACCC, Paper "Media Mergers", 2006/2011, para. 25, 57

84 For a comparative analysis of merger review in Gemany, USA, UK, France and the EU concerning print media enterprises see Wiring, Pressefusionskontrolle im Rechtsvergleich, 2008.

latter.[85] It is questionable if there are any substantial differences to be found both in the abstract concepts of these tests and in their application in practice. For the purpose of this article, we may simply ignore them. Both of these tests mainly aim at the prevention of market domination of undertakings by external growth, i.e. by mergers of economic entities that operated independently before. As a part of the SIEC test, market dominance is still a major criterion for the assessment of a case. The ACCC obviously shares this view, because in its 2006 paper on merger control, it made clear:

> "Broadly, merger analysis aims to determine whether existing or potential constraints in the relevant markets would be likely to prevent the merged firm from exercising market power. Market power may be exercised unilaterally by the merged company or by market participants in a co-ordinated manner. [...]"[86]

The basic "extra feature" of the German SIEC test in comparison to the former market dominance test lies in the eligibility of so-called uncoordinated effects.[87] However, a learned German practitioner, Professor Rainer Bechtold (who is a senior partner of a renowned German law firm specialising in competition law), voiced the opinion that most of the relevant cases that are being discussed in that respect could be solved without major problems by singularly using the market dominance test.[88] I clearly support Professor Bechtold's view. The SIEC test is

---

85 Bechtold/Bosch/Brinker, EU-Kartellrecht Kommentar, 3rd edition, 2014, Art. 2 FKVO para. 2.

86 ACCC, Paper "Media Mergers", 2006/2011, para. 170. The AARC's analysis does not stop at this point, of course. The subsequent paragraphs of the named paper make clear that the analysis can become very complex when applied to a single case. The analytic instruments of the AARC closely resemble those of the European Commission and of the German Bundeskartellamt. For further reading see the in-depth analysis by Stefan Thomas in: Kling/Thomas, Kartellrecht, 2nd edition, 2016, § 8 and § 20.

87 Bechtold/Bosch/Brinker, EU-Kartellrecht Kommentar, 3rd edition, 2014, Art. 2 FKVO para. 3.

88 Bechtold, NZKart 2013, 263 (266):

> Es ist nach wie vor offen, ob der SIEC-Test auch Fälle erheblicher Behinderungen wirksamen Wettbewerbs erfasst, die nicht schon die Voraussetzungen des Regelbeispiels erfüllen, nämlich Begründung oder Verstärkung einer marktbeherrschenden Stellung. [...] U. E. können die Fälle, die insoweit erörtert werden, durchweg auch mit dem Marktbeherrschungstest erfasst werden. Das gilt insbesondere auch für Zusammenschlüsse, an denen der Marktführer nicht beteiligt ist, sondern zwischen den nach Marktanteilen nächstfolgenden, insbesondere unter dem Gesichtspunkt des Zusammenschlusses der closest competitors.

nothing but a rather strange compromise between the widely accepted market dominance test of old and the "modern" SLC test; its incorporation into the German AARC reflects the political will at the time of the 7th amendment to the AARC of 2005 to incorporate economic ideas into the German competition law without giving up the traditional concept in the first place. In the recent ten years, it has neither improved nor damaged the legal analysis of merger cases, simply because practitioners will start it with looking at market dominance, however under the "flag" of a possible substantial lessening of competition.

Considering the SLC test, the Australian Department of Communications pointed out in 2014, that

> [k]ey focal points in the process of assessing the competition impacts of a given merger are the extent and nature of rivalry between firms and market power in the pre-merger and post-merger environments. The greater the degree of competition in a market [...] the less market power each participant will possess. The level of market power will therefore be dependent on whether alternative supply options or substitutes (actual or potential) are available post-merger to effectively constrain the merged firm. If the merged firm can increase prices for a sustainable period, or otherwise reduce some other aspect of the service offering (lowering the product quality, range or levels of customer service, for example), the merger may decrease economic efficiency and reduce the gains from trade and total welfare.[89]

III. German case law concerning merger control in the print media sector

In the next chapter of this essay, I will analyse the relevant German case law. There is a plethora of cases that deal with media-related mergers alone, and it would be impossible to analyse even the print media-related case law as such, either. Therefore, the facts force us to narrow down the analysis to what we consider to be exemplary cases.

As far as German merger control law is concerned, the print media sector has been of major importance due to the struggles for survival that publishers of newspapers and magazines have had to fight in recent years. However, on a supranational level, concentrations that cross the borders of EU Member States are rare, as pointed out earlier. This is the reason why the analysis is restricted to domestic case law.

89 DoC, Policy Background Paper No. 3, June 2014, "Media control and ownership", p. 9.

1. So-called "rescue mergers" of daily newspapers

Within the German merger control practice of the Federal Cartel Office, the relevant provisions of the AARC are mainly applied to so-called "rescue mergers" ("Sanierungsfusionen" in German) concerning daily newspapers. This is an issue which mainly occurs in connection with regional and local news papers. In the German press sector, one would usually find only one local newspaper in the relevant local market. This applies to the whole geographic area of Germany. The only exception to this was the local Mainz area, where two local newspapers have competed with each other for circa 25 years, the "Mainzer Allgemeine Zeitung" and the "Rhein Zeitung" – until the latter went bankrupt in 2013. The problematic market structure has to be taken into account when applying Sec. 36 AARC, as Article 5 of the Basic Law of Germany does not only grant individual basic rights, but also guarantees the free press as an institution.

a) The "Frankfurter Rundschau" case[90]

A remarkable "rescue merger" case within the print media sector is the "Frankfurter Rundschau" case. It deals with a concentration between the Frankfurter Allgemeine Zeitung and the Frankfurter Rundschau, both of which are daily subscription newspapers that are distributed nationwide. The first of these two newspapers has a liberal-conservative tendency, whereas the latter clearly supports the political left. In 2013, FR filed for insolvency. Its termination was expected by the end of January, 2013. The owner of the FAZ newspaper intended a "rescue merger". The German Federal Cartel Office approved the concentration.

Insofar as FR operated on a national reader market and on a corresponding national advertising market, there were no specific competition problems to be seen by the authority in these respects. Therefore, the Federal Cartel Office concentrated on the regional markets within the Rhine-Main region, where competition could possibly be harmed by the concentration:

On the local reader market in the Frankfurt city area, FR was (and still is to this day) the only competitor of FAZ. As far as the advertising markets were concerned, there were several other regional markets, in which the BILD-Zeitung was present as an additional competitor, because BILD operated with regional booking units. Furthermore, there were several regional advertising supplements in the Frankfurt area as well. The question arose whether these regional advertising markets formed a common market. This would be the case if the regional booking

90 BKartA, Decision of February 27, 2013, case B 6 – 9/13.

units were essentially identical (in German: "im Wesentlichen deckungsgleich"). In the view of the authority, it was not necessary to analyse the latter criterion in detail, because the criteria for a rescue merger were fulfilled.

There are three criteria for a "rescue merger" ("Sanierungsfusion") in German merger law:

(1) the target requires restructuring
(2) there is no alternative to the concentration which is less harmful to competition (especially no alternative buyer in sight)
(3) in case of a (hypothetical) market exit of the target, its the market shares would fall to the buyer.

In the "Frankfurter Rundschau" case, the need for restructuring of FR (i.e. criterion no. 1) was not in question, as FR had already filed for insolvency. There was an alternative buyer (a Turkish media operator named Burak Akbay) who had not been active in the relevant market before, which is a fact that could have raised doubts in the Federal Cartel Office in respect to the second criterion. The so-called "alternative view" could lead to the conclusion that FR could remain on the market as a competitor without the concentration with FAZ. But the authority's assessment of the case was different, as several factual circumstances made it highly improbable that the merger with the Turkish media operator would have been successful. The market exit of FR was to be expected by 1 March 2013. Until that date, the alternative transaction with the Turkish media operator could not have been completed successfully. After a market exit of FR, the Federal Cartel Office held that a re-entry would have seemed highly improbable, due to "the special characteristics of the newspaper market".[91] Therefore, the second criterion was met as well, at least in the view of the Federal Cartel Office.

Finally, in the view of the authority, the third criterion was met as well. Considering the reader market, in the main distribution area of FR, no other competitor existed than FAZ. On the advertising market, BILD could at least theoretically have profited from an expected market exit of FR on the local advertising market, because of the important role of the regional booking units of FR. But factually, this would not have lead to a shift of market power from FR towards BILD (or towards other competitors) in future, because BILD had never been a "close competitor" to FR. The closest competitors on the advertising market were the FAZ and a regional newspaper named Frankfurter Neue Presse (FNP) with their booking units. Consequently, the Federal Cartel Office concluded that BILD or

91 BKartA, Decision of February 27, 2013, case B 6 – 9/13, p. 3.

other advertising supplements would have been unable to absorb a significant part of FR's advertising budget after FR's market exit. In sum, all three criteria for a rescue merger were fulfilled.

b) "Rescue merger" cases concerning regional newspapers

The "Frankfurter Rundschau" case can without a doubt be regarded as a key decision regarding newspaper mergers. But there are a couple of other "rescue merger" cases concerning regional newspapers that deserve a honourable mention, namely the "Münchener Abendzeitung" case[92], the "Westfälische Rundschau (WR)/Westdeutsche Allgemeine Zeitung (WAZ)"[93] case, and the "Münstersche Zeitung" case,[94] all of which were decided by the Federal Cartel Office in the Summer of 2014. They are particularly interesting because they were decided after the 8th Amendment to the AARC came into force. Consequently, the new press exemption clause in Article 36 (1), second sentence No. 3 AARC[95] was applicable. Due to the given space limitations, we may concentrate on the issues of main importance, which are as follows:

(1) The "Münchener Abendzeitung" case

Firstly, the "Münchener Abendzeitung" case could be solved easily by the authority, because the distribution areas of the buyer's newspaper titles (i.e. Straubinger Tagblatt/Landshuter Zeitung) and the target's did not overlap. Therefore, the German Cartel Office approved the merger.

---

92 BKartA, Decision of June 24, 2014, case B 6 – 82/14.

93 BKartA, Decision of July 22, 2014, case B6 – 89/13.

94 BKartA, Decision of September 1, 2014, case B 6 97/14.

95 The provision reads as follows:

> (1) [1]A concentration which would significantly impede effective competition, in particular a concentration which is expected to create or strenghten a dominant position, shall be prohibited by Federal Cartel Authority [Bundeskartellamt]. [2]This shall not apply, if [...] no. 3 the dominant position of a newspaper or magazine publisher aquiring a small- or medium-sized newspaper or magazine publisher is strenghtened, where it is proven that the publisher that is aquired had a significant net annual deficit within the meaning of § 275 (2) no. 20 of the German Commercial Code [Handelsgesetzbuch] in the last three years and its existence would be jeopardised without the concentration. Furthermore, it must be proven that before the concentration, no other aquirer was found that could have ensured a solution that would have been less harmful to competition.

(2) The "Westfälische Rundschau" case

Secondly, the authority had to disapprove the merger in "Westfälische Rundschau" case, because it would have resulted in the buyer's (i.e. Medienhaus Lensing's) monopoly on the relevant market. It should be pointed out that the new press exemption clause in Section 36 AARC 2013 did not change one basic rule of German merger law: the creation of a monopoly by the means of concentration remains unlawful in general. The buyer of the target should not be its only competitor on the relevant economic market. The main objective of the press exemption clause is to support small and medium as well as local publishers in managing structural change. Basically, it aims at solving the problems of regional daily newspapers.[96] The limited scope of economic activity and the lack of financial resources on their side may create many problems in regard to the digital structural change of this economic sector when compared to larger daily newspaper chains.[97]

Only if the very strict rules of the "rescue merger" apply, which were explained above, the creation of a monopoly can be lawful; basically, these are the cases where a (threat of) insolvency of the target is beyond doubt.[98] In the "Westfälische Rundschau" case, the authority discussed a "rescue merger" in the special form of a "failing division defence", but it came to a negative conclusion, because several local issues of newspapers published by the undertaking Funke Medien NRW could not be regarded as "divisions" in that sense.[99] Finally, Lensing withdrew its application on 22 July 2014.

---

96 Bechtold, GWB Kommentar, 7th edition, 2013, § 36 para. 53.

97 BKartA, Decision of July 22, 2014, case B6 – 89/13, p. 5 et seq.

98 BKartA, Decision of July 22, 2014, case B6 – 89/13, p. 2:

> Der Regelfall der Sanierungsfusion ist dabei die beantragte oder zumindest unmittelbar bevorstehende Insolvenz eines ganzen Unternehmens ("failing company"). An diesem durch objektive und gesetzlich geregelte Tatbestände gekennzeichneten Regelfall sind die Sanierungsbedürftigkeit und die Marktaustrittsprognose bei einem bloßen Unternehmensteil zu messen. In der Variante der "failing division" ist aus Sicht des Bundeskartellamts ein mit dem Regelfall vergleichbarer objektiver Nachweis nur möglich, wenn der fragliche Betriebsteil in organisatorischer und wirtschaftlicher Hinsicht eigenständig geführt wird. An den Nachweis der zwingenden Notwendigkeit des Austritts eines Betriebsteils sind hohe Anforderungen zu stellen, weil Unternehmen bei der Unterscheidung über den Marktaustritt eines Unternehmensteils über erhebliche Spielräume verfügen.

99 BKartA, Decision of July 22, 2014, case B6 – 89/13, p. 2 et seq.

(3) The "Münstersche Zeitung" case

Thirdly, the "Münstersche Zeitung" (MZ) case proves that the "failing division defence" concept is not just a theoretical one. In that very case, the concentration concerning another regional daily newspaper would have led to a quasi-monopoly of the buyer (i.e. Aschendorff GmbH & Co.) in the regional reader market of the Münsterland region. The Federal Cartel Office could only approve the merger if the criteria of a "rescue merger" or the criteria of the press exemption clause were met. Since the parties could prove that the conditions of a "failing division defence" were indeed met, the authority did not have to assess the case under the press exemption clause.[100] Whereas the "rescue merger" demands a (threat of) insolvency to the whole undertaking ("failing company defence"), it is sufficient for the application of the "failing division defence" if an economically and in organisational terms independent "division" within that company is affected.[101] In this case, MZ's market exit as an independent entity was deemed to be impending.[102]

2. Other press-related merger cases – the "Haller Tagblatt" case as an example

The Federal Cartel office is not always concerned with concentrations that are mainly driven by insolvency threats of media companies. Rather, there are also "normal" mergers of "healthy" undertakings. In the "Haller Tagblatt" case,[103] e.g., the reason for the merger was to be found in the old age of the owner of the company that published the daily newspaper "Haller Tagblatt" (i.e. Schwäbisch Hall GmbH (ZSH)). The owner simply wanted to secure the future economic existence of the newspaper and its "editorial orientation" by the sale.

In the "Haller Tagblatt" case, controversy arose about an expected monopolistic structure of the relevant reader market (due to a lack of actual or potential competition). The problem of the case was the expected strengthening of a dominant

---

100 BKartA, Decision of September 1, 2014, case B 6 – 97/14, p. 2, 5. The Federal Cartel Office therefore did not have to decide if the press exemption clause is applicable if the creation of a dominant position is to be expected.

101 This test is of course much more complex than the summary presented here may suggest. For the details concerning the "failing division defence", see BKartA, Decision of September 1, 2014, case B 6 – 97/14, p. 2 et seqq.

102 BKartA, Decision of September 1, 2014, case B 6 – 97/14, p. 3.

103 BKartA, Decision of April 21, 2009, case B 6 – 150/08; OLG Düsseldorf, Decision of December 22, 2010, case VI-Kart 4/09 (V), WuW/E DE-R 3173; BGH, Decision of June 16, 2012, case KVR 15/11, WuW/E DE-R 3695 = NZKart 2013, 36; see also Klumpp, WuW 2013, 344 et seqq.

position on the reader market concerning subscription newspapers in the southwestern region of Germany as well as on the local advertising market.[104] Both participants (i.e. the publisher of the daily newspaper "Haller Tagblatt", ZSH, and the Neue Pressegesellschaft Ulm [NPG], publisher of "Hohenloher Tagblatt") were monopolists on the reader market of their respective sales areas,[105] which were adjacent to each other.[106] Also, prior to the concentration, a connection between these two undertakings had existed through Südwest-Presseverbund (i.e. a cooperation agreement about a centrally designed newspaper cover as well as joint advertising activities).[107]

The Federal Cartel Office disapproved the merger. Because of the fact that the seller already had a dominant position in the relevant market, the authority expected a strengthening of the dominant position in both the reader market and the advertising market. Also, the authority argued that the increase of resources for the second participant, which would be a consequence of the merger, could discourage actual or potential competitors from accessing the advertising market.

Like the authority, and according to the "demand-side oriented market concept" ("Bedarfsmarktkonzept" in German), the judges of Sixth Civil Senate of the Higher Regional Court Düsseldorf (OLG Düsseldorf) identified two markets (i.e. a reader market and an advertising market).[108] But contrary to the authority, the judges approved the merger.[109] It held that the existing monopolies and cooperation agreements resulted in a total lack of "residual competition" ("Restwettbewerb" in German) which could be harmed by the merger in the future;[110] its rationale seems to be: "If there is neither actual nor potential competition on the

104 OLG Düsseldorf, Decision of December 22, 2010, case VI-Kart 4/09 (V), WuW/E DE-R 3173, para. 71 et seq.

105 BGH, Decision of June 16, 2012, case KVR 15/11, WuW/E DE-R 3695, para. 4 = NZKart 2013, 36.

106 OLG Düsseldorf, Decision of December 22, 2010, case VI-Kart 4/09 (V), WuW/E DE-R 3173, para. 74 et seq.

107 BGH, Decision of June 16, 2012, case KVR 15/11, WuW/E DE-R 3695, para. 5 = NZKart 2013, 36.

108 OLG Düsseldorf, Decision of December 22, 2010, case VI-Kart 4/09 (V), WuW/E DE-R 3173, paras. 48 et seqq.

109 OLG Düsseldorf, Decision of December 22, 2010, case VI-Kart 4/09 (V), WuW/E DE-R 3173, paras. 45, 96 et seqq.

110 OLG Düsseldorf, Decision of December 22, 2010, case VI-Kart 4/09 (V), WuW/E DE-R 3173, para. 99: „Die fusionsbedingte Beeinträchtigung eines aktuellen Restwettbewerbs kommt im Entscheidungsfall schon deshalb nicht in Betracht, weil ein solcher auf den relevanten Märkten nicht vorhanden ist."

relevant market, residual competition cannot be harmed by a concentration" – this is a remarkable statement! As no market access of third parties was in sight and no third-party competition was to be expected during forecasting horizon, the reasoning of the judges of the Higher Regional Court Düsseldorf on the lack of potential competition[111] is factually correct. The authority, however, had argued on the basis of an elimination of potential competition as a consequence of the strengthening of market power between the participants.

Finally, the German Federal Supreme Court (BGH) decided the case. It upheld the decision of the Higher Regional Court Düsseldorf for the most part, rejecting the complaint of the Federal Cartel Office. The grounds of the judgment mainly deal with requirements for predictive decisions concerning a strengthening of a dominant position of the buyer, the main criterion which was not met in the case, according to the two courts who opposed the view of the Federal Cartel Office. Generally, in the view of the Federal Supreme Court, the strengthening of a dominant position must be "likely", need not be "very likely" (as provided by the Higher Regional Court Düsseldorf, which allegedly "erred" in that respect). According to the Federal Supreme Court, the mid-term prediction period is about three to five years long.[112] In the view of the judges of the Court, an elimination of future potential competition by the concentration was only "possible" ("möglich") in the case, but not "probable" ("wahrscheinlich" in German).[113]

---

111 For a detailed analysis, see OLG Düsseldorf, Decision of December 22, 2010, case VI-Kart 4/09 (V), WuW/E DE-R 3173, paras. 101 et seqq.

112 BGH, Decision of June 16, 2012, case KVR 15/11, WuW/E DE-R 3695, para. 38 = NZKart 2013, 36.

113 In detail, BGH, Decision of June 16, 2012, case KVR 15/11, WuW/E DE-R 3695, para. 32 et seq. = NZKart 2013, 36 argues as follows:

> 32 c) Eine Verhinderung der künftigen Entstehung potentiellen Wettbewerbs infolge des Zusammenschlusses ist im Streitfall allenfalls möglich, indes nicht aufgrund konkreter Anhaltspunkte mit einiger Wahrscheinlichkeit zu erwarten. Das Beschwerdegericht hat deshalb im Ergebnis zu Recht die Verstärkung einer marktbeherrschenden Stellung auch unter diesem Aspekt verneint.
>
> 33 aa) Der Zusammenschluss könnte im Streitfall wegen der Verhinderung künftigen potentiellen Wettbewerbs nur untersagt werden, wenn nach den bei Schluss der mündlichen Verhandlung vor dem Beschwerdegericht bestehenden Wettbewerbsbedingungen aufgrund konkreter Anhaltspunkte ohne den angemeldeten Zusammenschluss mit einiger Wahrscheinlichkeit drei Voraussetzungen erfüllt werden. Zunächst müsste ein vom Südwest Presseverbund unabhängiger Dritter kurz- oder mittelfristig den ZSH erwerben. Er müsste zweitens die bestehende Mantel- und Anzeigenkooperation mit NPG beenden. Nach den danach

3. Concentrations concerning publishers of so-called "special interest" magazines

With respect to magazines, the Federal Cartel Office differentiates between so-called "general interest" magazines and so-called "special interest" magazines. The latter deal with issues of the reader's private lives only, such as different kinds of sports or other hobbies.[114] The situation on the market for "special interest" magazines seems to be different from other print media markets insofar as high market shares or a significant addition of market shares ("bedeutende Marktanteilsaddition") will not necessarily be regarded as being harmful to competition by the authorities. There are different reasons for this, as the following examples will make clear.

a) The "Pegasus" case[115]

"Pegasus" is a popular German horse riding sports magazine which is distributed nationwide. The Top Special Verlag (which is a joint venture owned by Jahr Verlag GmbH and Axel Springer Verlag) wanted to buy the title. The same publisher

bestehenden Wettbewerbsbedingungen müsste drittens ein wirtschaftlich sinnvoller Markteintritt von ZSH in das Vertriebsgebiet von NPG oder umgekehrt möglich sein. Nur dann, wenn NPG aufgrund konkreter Tatsachen gegenwärtig zu befürchten hätte, dass ohne den Zusammenschluss mit einiger Wahrscheinlichkeit künftig alle drei Bedingungen erfüllt werden, könnte eine die Untersagung des Zusammenschlusses rechtfertigende Verstärkungswirkung durch Verhinderung potentiellen Wettbewerbs angenommen werden.

114 Women's magazines, e.g., are "special interest" magazines in that sense. They are subdivided into five different categories by the Federal Cartel Office, i.e. "yellow press magazines" ("Yellow-Press-Zeitschriften"), "simple women's magazines" ("Einfach-Frauenzeitschriften"), "quality women's magazines" ("Qualitäts-Frauenzeitschriften"), "premium women's magazines" ("Premium-Frauenzeitschriften"), and "life style magazines" ("Life-Style-Magazine"), see BKartA, Decision of December 3, 2013, case B 6 – 97/13, p. 2 – Funke Mediengruppe; BKartA, Decision of April 2011, case B 6 – 28/11, p. 2 – Hearst Corp./Elle-Verlag. "COSMOPOLITAN" belongs to the category of "quality women's magazines", while it also contains "life style content". "ELLE" is part of the adjacent market of "premium women's magazines", as pointed out by the Federal Cartel Office in the "Hearst" case, ibid., p. 2: „Die COSMOPOLITAN ist zu den Qualitäts-Frauenzeitschriften zu zählen und weist auch Lifestyle-Inhalte auf. Die Zeitschrift ‚ELLE' ist dem benachbarten Markt der Premium-Frauenzeitschriften zuzuordnen. Heftpreis, redaktioneller Inhalt – wie z.B. die künstlerisch anspruchsvollen und hochwertig produzierten Modestrecken – sowie die einkommensstarke Leserinnenzielgruppe der ELLE weichen von der COSMOPOLITAN hinreichend ab."

115 BKartA, Decision of November 22, 2011, case B 6 – 77/11.

already owned two other "special interest" magazine titles that were related to horses, i.e. "St. Georg" and "Mein Pferd" ("My Horse"). After the purchase of "Pegasus", Top Special Verlag would have a total market share of almost 50% on the reader market for horse magazines. Nonetheless, two independent competitors (the magazines "Cavallo" and "Reiter Revue" ["Rider's Revue"]) were active in the same market as well. In the view of the authority, the reader market for horse magazines is very much subdivided, and the barriers for market entry by other publishers are relatively low. To produce the content of horse magazines, comparably low economic effort is necessary. Consequently, it would be relatively easy for the competitors of Top Special Verlag to enter the market for horse magazines with new titles of their own. This fact reduces the economic scope for action of Top Special Verlag. Due to these circumstances, the Federal Cartel Office decided in 2011 that the creation of a dominant position of Top Special Verlag was not to be expected (and we should add that based on the German merger law which as been applicable since 2013, a significant impediment to effective competition would seem improbable as well). From the view of the consumer, the high market share of Pegasus magazine does not prevent him from choosing an alternative among the existing "special interest" magazines.

The "Pegasus" case is particularly interesting, because a high market share of 50% or more normally would indicate the creation of a dominant position (according to the so-called AKZO-rule of the ECJ).[116] Of course, this is not a strict rule that applies everywhere because the lower the barriers for market entry are, the more fragile is the position of a presumably "dominant" undertaking.

Judging from earlier case law, the "special interest" magazine reader markets in Germany are a bit special insofar as market entry seems to be easier than in other fields of print media; at least, the respective reader markets are competitive ones.[117]

---

116 ECJ, Decision of July 3, 1991, case C-62/86, Slg. 1991, I-3359, para. 60 – AKZO: "With regard to market shares the Court has held that very large shares are in themselves, and save in exceptional circumstances, evidence of the existence of a dominant position [...]. That is the situation where there is a market share of 50% such as that found to exist in this case." This case was decided under Article 86 of the Treaty, which is today Article 102 TFEU.

117 See BKartA, Decision of October 15, 2015, case B 6 – 93/10 concerning mountain bike riding magazines, e.g., where the authority argues that notwithstanding a high market share of the magazine "Mountainbike Rider", potent competitors will be active on the relevant market after the concentration.

b) *The "needleworks magazines" case*[118]

In another remarkable "special interest" magazine case, which was decided by the Federal Cartel Office in 2011 also, two needleworks magazine titles named "Anna" and "Verena" were purchased by 2 ME Holding from Vicant Crafts Publishing GmbH. These magazines publish crochet, knitting and embroidery patterns, which they receive for free from the producers of fabric, cloth and cotton – which means that only a few original editorial contributions are included. As the revenues from advertising made up only 10% of the total revenue, the analysis of the Federal Cartel Office therefore concentrated on the reader market. The entry barriers to this market were regarded as low, due to the lack of original editorial contributions. Since "Anna" and "Verena" only present third party content, these magazines function as a sort of "platform"; their readers have plenty of alternatives to choose from, also. Consequently, the concentration was approved by the authority.

IV. Australian case law concerning merger control in the print media sector

1. Introduction

Australian case law concerning mergers of two print media companies is rare. The focus seems to be more on cross-media mergers. As pointed out above, media diversity in Australia is mainly secured by the BSA of 1992, which covers cross-media mergers. Insofar as the ACCC has investigated mergers of media companies under Section 50 CCA, TV and radio play a much more important practical role that print media.

2. Fairfax / Rural Press Limited

On December 6, 2006, Fairfax Media announced that it would acquire Rural Press Limited. Rural Press then owned 170 newspaper and magazine titles, among which the "Canberra Times" was the most prominent. From the viewpoint of securing media diversity and competition, the acquisition of such a large number of newspapers by an already large media company like Fairfax could be evaluated as problematic. However, the major issue of the case seems to have been the acquisition of a number of regional commercial radio station licences.[119] The merger

118 BKartA, Decision of April 29, 2011, Case B 6 – 29/11.

119 DOC, Policy Background Paper No. 3, June 2014, "Media control and ownership", p. 15 et seq.

was completed as early as May 8, 2007. In 2011, Fairfax sold its eight regional commercial radio licences to Grant Broadcasters for a reported $ 15 million.[120] The ACCC approved the merger. The ACCC's Chairman, Graeme Samuel, said in April 2007 that the proposed acquisition was unlikely to reduce competition.[121]

3. West Australian Newspaper Holdings / Mid West Times

In 2005, the ACCC had to decide a print media merger case. WAN proposed to acquire the "Mid West Times", a free, weekly home-delivered newspaper published in the Geraldton region of Australia. WAN owned the other free weekly regional newspaper in the market, i.e. the "Mid-West Mail". The ACCC did not oppose the acquisition because entry barriers were low.[122] The ACCC considered the relevant markets to be the markets for: (1) publishing and supply of newspapers; and (2) supply of newspaper advertising services in the area comprising Geraldton and the mid-west region of West Australia. The ACCC analysed the acquisition as follows:

> While West Australia Newspapers Limited owns the other free weekly regional newspaper in the market (the Mid West Mail), the ACCC considered that barriers to entry are relatively low given technological advancements in desk-top publishing. In addition, the practice of letterbox delivery makes it easier for a new free newspaper competitor to attract readers. Consequently the ACCC decided that the proposed acquisition is unlikely to substantially lessen competition in the relevant markets.[123]

The ability of new players to enter the market is as decisive for the case-by-case analysis under Section 50 CCA as it is under German competition law.[124] The ACCC's assumption that barriers for market entry were low could certainly not have been made if the merger had taken place somewhere in Germany. This is because the market for regional newspapers is hardly accessible in Germany;

---

120 DOC, Policy Background Paper No. 3, June 2014, "Media control and ownership", p. 16.

121 See the article „ACCC accepts Fairfax, Rural Press merger" of April 18, 2007, to be found here: http://www.theage.com.au/news/Business/ACCC-accepts-Fairfax-Rural-Press-merger/2007/04/18/ 1176696904341.html.

122 ACCC, Paper "Media Mergers", 2006/2011, para. 14.

123 ACCC, Summary of December 6, 2005 "West Australian Newspapers Holdings Limited - proposal to acquire the Mid West Times (a free, weekly home-delivered newspaper)", file number C2005/1461.

124 ACCC, Paper "Media Mergers", 2006/2011, p. 5: "However, the ACCC must also, among other things, assess the ability of new players to enter the market. If barriers to entry are low, then a merger leaving few media outlets in a market might not raise competition concerns."

broadly speaking, each region has its own (single) regional newspaper. Obviously, the factual situation differs significantly in Australia. The different market structure in Australia is to be welcomed, as low market entries to the regional newspaper market serve the aims of media diversity and effective competition better than the German market structure does.

V. Conclusion

In Germany and in Australia, there are two pillars to secure media diversity:

- The first pillar is represented by a public authority, whose media-specific regulation aims at having a multitude of "voices" in the (commercial) television, (commercial) radio and the newspaper sectors.
- The second pillar is represented by merger control regulation. Merger control law primarily aims at securing "workable competition" on the respective relevant market by the means of preventing the creation or the strengthening of economic dominance by external growth.

Merger control law is therefore not focused on media companies; rather, it applies in general, i.e. to all economic sectors. Even though there is no direct link between competition law and media law, diversity of ownership as promoted by merger law indirectly guarantees a variety of media "voices" as well.[125] This is especially true for the news genre and print media. Plurality of opinion could easily be endangered if there were no restrictions to concentrations of print media enterprises at all.

Thus, on a higher plane, both regulatory concepts secure media diversity and plurality of opinion in democratic societies. Consequently, media law and competition law represent two sides of the same coin when it comes to the protection of media diversity in modern democratic societies.[126] The United Kingdom Communications White Paper of 2000 rightly stated that fostering competition was "the first step to promotion plurality in the media" (a suitable expression which formed the motto to this essay).[127] In the convincing view of the British authorities,

125 Cf. DoC, Policy Background Paper No. 3, June 2014, "Media control and ownership", p. 12.

126 Cf. G. Hewitt, "Media Mergers: Background Note", [2004] OECD Journal: Competition Law and Policy, Vol. 5, No. 4, p. 79 (80): "The question of who owns our newspapers, television and radio is vital to democracy".

127 See also Paal, Medienvielfalt und Wettbewerbsrecht, 2010, Dritter Teil „Vielfalt durch Wettbewerb", p. 119: „Auf generell-abstrakter Ebene ist zunächst von der Prämisse auszugehen, dass das Auswahl- und Entdeckungsverfahren Wettbewerb einen prinzipiell förderlichen Mechanismus für die Sicherung publizistischer Vielfalt bildet. Die

a competitive market is "likely to be one with many voices and diverse content, though there is no guarantee that this will be the case".[128]

As far as competition law is concerned, the level of media diversity depends, as the ACCC put it, "on the outcome of individual merger investigations" undertaken by the authorities.[129] One should always bear in mind that competition is a dynamic process,[130] and the outcome is typically unpredictable[131]. In general, a plurality of media enterprises will promote journalistic competition and a plurality of "voices".[132] Of course, this essay does not promote the inapt idea of abandoning media laws in order to reduce the legal control of media company activities to competition law or even merger review alone; the concept of "primacy of economic

---

Entstehung von Meinungs- und Medienvielfalt profitiert nach dieser Konzeption von der Existenz eines funktionierenden ökonomischen und publizistischen Wettbewerbs." The author limits this view a few pages later, though; for detailed information see the author's statement, ibid., p. 135–137.

128 United Kingdom, Department of Trade and Industry and Department of Culture, Media and Sport, "A New Future for Communications - Communications White Paper", 2000, para. 4.2.6.

129 ACCC, Paper "Merger Control", 2006/2011, p. 6.

130 See J. M. Clark, Competition as a Dynamic Process, 1961.

131 See F. A. v. Hayek, Wettbewerb als Entdeckungsverfahren, 1968 (Freiburger Studien, 1994, p. 249 et seqq.); Die Anmaßung von Wissen, 26 ORDO (1973), p. 12 et seqq.

132 See also a self-contradictory reasoning by Paal, Medienvielfalt und Wettbewerbsrecht, 2010, p. 146 et seqq.:

> [...] Somit bildet die ökonomische Vielzahl von Medienunternehmen weder eine zwingend erforderliche noch überhaupt eine hinreichende Bedingung für die angestrebte publizistische Vielfalt. [...] Allerdings kann eine erhöhte Unternehmenskonzentration auf dem Medienmarkt zu erheblichen Gefahren und sogar zu irreversiblen Strukturveränderungen führen, welche dauerhaft die Sicherstellung von Meinungs- und Medienvielfalt zu beeinträchtigen vermögen. [...] Folgerichtig besteht ein zumindest hinreichend plausibler Kausalzusammenhang zwischen Vielzahl und Vielfalt. Keine absolute Geltung beanspruchen können zwar die Thesen ‚Vielzahl garantiert Vielfalt' oder sogar noch weitergehend ‚Vielzahl ist Vielfalt'. Nach den bisherigen Ergebnissen dieser Arbeit gilt aber jedenfalls: ‚Vielzahl begünstigt Vielfalt' und weiterhin zumindest dem Grunde nach ‚Vielfalt durch Vielzahl'. Eine entsprechend ausgeprägte Vielzahl an Medienunternehmen ist dem Anliegen der Sicherstellung von Meinungs- und Medienvielfalt in hohem Maße zuträglich.

With respect to the question of securing media diversity and pluralism of opinion, Paal's book offers a variety of different, opposing views (ibid., p. 143 et seqq.), and it sometimes remains unclear which opinion the author supports.

law" ("Primat des Wirtschaftsrechts" in German) deserves no support,[133] because there is a vast number of special characteristics to the media which have to be taken into account by lawmakers and regulators. The media "serve as watchdogs to inform the public of shortcomings and wrongdoings both by private and public actors", and they "constitute the channels through which alternative political choices are communicated to the public, and subjected to critical assessment".[134] Public media law is therefore needed to ensure the functioning of the media and media diversity. Competition law is only *one* means among several of securing the plurality of opinion,[135] and it has a relatively limited scope.[136] Consequently, competition law alone would be insufficient to preserve the decisive role that media have for modern democratic societies.[137] The interesting subsequent question

---

133 For citations and a subsequent discussion of the problem, see Paal, Medienvielfalt und Wettbewerbsrecht, 2010, p. 300 et seqq., 308 et seqq.

134 G. Hewitt, "Media Mergers: Background Note", [2004] OECD Journal: Competition Law and Policy, Vol. 5, No. 4, p. 79 (116).

135 The question how exactly merger review contributes to media pluralism (even though it is not explicitly concerned with that objective) is elaborated on in detail by G. Hewitt, "Media Mergers: Background Note", [2004] OECD Journal: Competition Law and Policy, Vol. 5, No. 4, p. 79 (119 et seqq.). According to the 2004 OECD paper on media mergers, the competition authorities seem to have an "aversion to dealing with pluralism" (ibid., p. 169) or at least a kind of "uneasiness" (p. 170). The reasons for this criticism are based on three grounds, (1) the absence of objective measures for pluralism, (2) reputational concerns in regard to the authorities' reputation for objectivity and (3) the desire to reduce risks associated with possibly being wrong. Against the background of the case law analysed in this essay, we may conclude that the authorities preserved media diversity without leaving the "safe harbour" of the respective competition law regimes or making "political" decisions. There seems to be no reason for being uneasy with the results of the cases, as the decisions were based on hard evidence, not speculation or vague ideas of what pluralism of media could be.

136 See also Paal, Medienvielfalt und Wettbewerbsrecht, 2010, p. 310: „Wo die ökonomische Konzentrationskontrolle nur ein ‚stumpfes Schwert' bereithält, kann und soll die publizistische Konzentrationskontrolle in Fällen des Bestehens einschlägiger Gefährdungslagen für die Meinungs- und Pressevielfalt ihre besondere Wirkungskraft entfalten."

137 G. Hewitt, "Media Mergers: Background Note", [2004] OECD Journal: Competition Law and Policy, Vol. 5, No. 4, p. 79 (82) sub 6: "Merger review can make a positive contribution to preserving media pluralism, but cannot alone adequately protect it". See also Paal, Medienvielfalt und Wettbewerbsrecht, 2010, p. 299, who identified several gaps of protection („[…] verschiedene (zumindest partielle) Unzulängli-

whether it is possible to harmonise media law and competition law with the aim of reducing inefficiencies could be discussed here.[138]

Summing up, this chapter has shown that the theoretical concepts and the material criteria of merger law analysis vary slightly between Germany and Australia, but their regulatory basis is identical: merger law aims at preventing the creation and the strengthening of market power by external growth, i.e. by concentrations of formerly independent companies. It does not come as a surprise that the outcome of individual merger investigations in Germany is sometimes different from the outcome in Australia, even though the cases seem at first sight to be quite similar. The reason can be found rather in the facts than in the law; e.g. when the level of market entry is different, as it is in the local and regional newspaper sector, the use of the same methodology demands different results. These are differences in the legal outcomes of legal review that we must accept without asking for a major change of methodology.

Bibliography

Australian Competition and Consumer Commission (ACCC), Media Mergers, August 2006 (updated 2011), download: https://www.accc.gov.au/system/files/Media%20Mergers%20-%202011.pdf (latest check: October 10, 2015).

Australian Government, Department of Communications (DOC), Policy Background Paper No. 3, June 2014, "Media control and ownership", download: http://www.presscouncil.org.au/uploads/52321/ufiles/Control_Background_Paper_Australian_Government_Department_of_Communications.pdf (latest check: October 10, 2015).

Bechtold, Rainer, Die 8. GWB-Novelle, Neue Zeitschrift für Kartellrecht (NZKart) 2013, 263–269.

Bechtold, Rainer, GWB. Kartellgesetz. Gesetz gegen Wettbewerbsbeschränkungen (§§ 1–96, 130, 131), Kommentar, 7th edition, Munich 2013.

---

chkeiten und Schutzlücken des bestehenden wettbewerbsrechtlichen Ansatzes zur Vielfaltssicherung im Medienbereich").

138 For further reading, see Paal, Medienvielfalt und Wettbewerbsrecht, 2010, p. 306 et seqq., 310, 313 et seq., 336 et seq., 339 et seq. The author, a renowned scholar of both German media law and competition law, clearly opposes the concept of (full) harmonisation of media law and competition law regimes (ibid., p. 310). Nonetheless, the author supports harmonisation within European law, while the European Union currently lacks legislative powers to secure plurality of opinion (ibid., p. 337, 339). See also Gounalakis, Konvergenz der Medien – Sollte das Recht der Medien harmonisiert werden?, Gutachten C zum 64. Deutschen Juristentag, 2002.

Bechtold, Rainer/Bosch, Wolfgang/Brinker, Ingo, EU-Kartellrecht, Kommentar, 3rd edition, Munich 2014.

Clark, John Maurice, Competition as a Dynamic Process, Westport, Connecticut 1961 (Reprint 1980).

Esser, Michael, Medienkonvergenz und Zusammenschlusskontrolle - Zur fusionskontrollrechtlichen Bewertung medienübergreifender Transaktionen, NZKart 2013, 135–142.

Gounalakis, Georgios, Konvergenz der Medien – Sollte das Recht der Medien harmonisiert werden?, Gutachten C zum 64. Deutschen Juristentag, München 2002.

Hayek, Friedrich August von, Wettbewerb als Entdeckungsverfahren, in: Freiburger Studien, 2nd edition 1994, 249–265.

Hewitt, Gary, Media Mergers: Background Note, OECD Journal: Competition Law and Policy, 2004, Vol. 5, No. 4, p. 79–146, download: http://www.oecd-ilibrary.org/governance/media-mergers-background-note_clp-v5-art16-en (latest check: October 10, 2015).

Kling, Michael/Fleischer, Romy Nicole, Zur Leitidee des Wettbewerbsschutzes in den Kartellrechtsordnungen der Europäischen Union und Australiens – eine rechtvergleichende Analyse, (2010) 27 Nihon University Comparative Law, p. 137–166.

Kling, Michael/Thomas, Stefan, Kartellrecht, 2nd edition, Munich 2016.

Klumpp, Ulrich, Neues in der Pressefusionskontrolle: Zur geplanten Änderung der Pressefusionskontrolle durch die 8. GWB-Novelle - Zugleich Besprechung der BGH-Entscheidung „Haller Tagblatt“, Wirtschaft und Wettbewerb (WuW) 2013, 344–356.

Nieschalk, Malte, Folgerungen aus deregulierten Medienlandschaften für die Reformdiskussion um das Pressefusionsrecht, Hamburg 2012.

OECD, “Media Mergers: 3. Summary of the Discussion”, OECD Journal: Competition Law and Policy, 2004, Vol. 5, No. 4, p. 147–170.

Paal, Boris P., Medienvielfalt und Wettbewerbsrecht, Tübingen 2010.

Paal, Boris P., Crossmediale Zusammenschlüsse, Marktabgrenzung und Medienmacht - Springer/ ProSieben II, Zeitschrift für Wettbewerbsrecht (ZWeR) 2012, 380–402.

Rosenthal, Michael/Thomas, Stefan, European Merger Control, Munich 2010.

Steger, Jens, Konglomerate Medienzusammenschlüsse in der deutschen Fusionskontrolle - unter besonderer Berücksichtigung der Entscheidung AxelSpringer/ ProSiebenSat.1 -, Wirtschaft und Wettbewerb (WuW) 2010, 282–291.

United Kingdom, Department of Trade and Industry and *Department of Culture, Media and Sport*, A New Future for Communications – White Paper, 2000.

Wiring, Roland, Pressefusionskontrolle im Rechtsvergleich: Eine Untersuchung zur Rechtslage in Deutschland, den Vereinigten Staaten von Amerika, dem Vereinigten Königreich, Frankreich und auf der Ebene der Europäischen Union, Baden-Baden 2008.

Zagouras, Georgios.

- Konvergenz und Kartellrecht: Die Regulierung des Wettbewerbs im Bereich der Medien und Kommunikationsplattformen nach GWB, TKG und RStV sowie Optionen für eine Umstrukturierung, München 2002.
- Die Ministererlaubnis nach § 42 GWB und überragende Interessen der Allgemeinheit bei Zusammenschlüssen von Medienunternehmen, WRP 2007, 1429–1436.

Zohm, Ann-Kathrin, Der verfassungsrechtliche Rahmen der Pressefusionskontrolle, Berlin 2010.

John Duns

Media diversity and the role of competition law

Abstract: This chapter considers the extent to which competition law is an effective guardian of media diversity and, to the extent that it is not, whether it should be reformed to better play such a role. It is argued that competition law plays an important although limited role in this respect but that reform of competition law is nevertheless not the answer.

1. Introduction

The aims of this chapter are to assess the extent to which competition law can and should play a role in the protection and promotion of media diversity. Indeed, there have been calls for competition to be the *sole* means by which media diversity is regulated. This is the approach taken in New Zealand, for instance, and some media commentators expect to see a stronger trend in this direction. Hardy, for example, suggests that one of the key trends in communications policy is a shift from 'sectoral [that is, specific media policies such as media ownership rules] to general competition regulation, and from broader public policy considerations towards limited regulatory intervention on economic and consumer welfare grounds'.[1] And Iosifides[2] has identified an 'increased reliance on competition regulation as one of the defining features of contemporary 'global media and

1 Hardy J, *Western Media Systems*, London, Routledge, 2008, at 141, quoted in Smith P, 'Too much or not enough? Competition Law and television broadcasting regulation in the United Kingdom' (2013) 9(3) *Westminster Papers* 145 at 145.

2 Iosifides P, *Global Media and Communication* Policy, Palgrave Macmillan 2011 at 81, referred to in Smith, supra at 145.

communication policy.' This stance has also been supported by economists and, significantly, the EU Commission.[3]

A concern of this chapter is to assess whether the promotion of media diversity would be in safe hands if left solely to competition law. It will be suggested that the answer to this question is 'No'. It will be argued that while competition law does indeed have a role to play in the promotion of media diversity, this role is an indirect one only, with the consequence that competition law can be ineffectual to promote media diversity. Specifically, competition law becomes an unreliable protector of media diversity where the objectives of competition law and the promotion of media diversity conflict. This conclusion in turn leads to the further question of whether competition law should be adjusted in some way so that its impact is direct. That is, should competition law have, as a direct objective, the promotion of media diversity? On this point it is argued that, while there is some merit in this proposal, on balance it is not one that should be pursued.

My primary perspective in examining these issues is from the Australian competition law viewpoint. However other perspectives, particularly from the EU, are also taken into account. It will be seen that there are some features of Australian law that provide a helpful contrast with EU law but for the most part Australian and EU competition laws adopt a similar approach to the questions discussed.

The next part of this chapter considers the extent of the compatibility between competition law and the promotion of media diversity - how competition law does in fact work to promote media diversity. The following part looks at the limitations of competition law in this role. The next part considers whether, in view of these limitations, it is appropriate to extend competition law so that it can play a more direct role in the promotion of media diversity and, if so, how this might be done. Conclusions are drawn in the final part.

2. How competition law can promote media diversity

The value of media diversity in a democracy is generally accepted but to convert this into a legislative goal, or to assess whether media diversity is in fact being promoted, requires some clarity around its meaning. In a recent Policy Background Paper on 'Media Control and Ownership' by the Australian Department of Communications, media diversity was described as 'the ability of citizens to access and consume a wide range of viewpoints without any one media owner or controller

---

3 See generally Smith op cit at 145–146, referring to the EU Commission Press Release of 12 July 2000 in which the Commission proposed an overhaul of the rules governing electronic communication.

exercising too much influence.'[4] At a minimum, then, media diversity requires a variety in the *sources* of media (particularly news and opinion). However it is more than this. It is not simply a matter of having a greater number of media sources. Media diversity requires not only diversity of control but also diversity of output.[5] This suggests that there may not be a simple correlation between competition among media firms and media diversity.[6] 'Diversity' is a relative concept and so media diversity depends on there being diversity within society generally. Further, media diversity can be either 'reflective' or 'open'. Reflective diversity means that the media devotes coverage to issues etc in similar proportions to the interests of those who hold them (if 80% of society is interested in sport, 80% of media coverage would be devoted to sport). 'Open' diversity, on the other hand, occurs where media coverage gives weight to all preferences etc, regardless of the proportion of society that holds those interests.[7]

Media services are often stated to be fundamentally different in nature from other goods and services. This is said to be 'due to the role that media plays in and for democracy.'[8] As stated by Van Cuilenburg, 'Media diversity in society is being promoted because of its wholesome effects on democracy. The very essence of democracy seems to be divergent opinions and political parties, from which people can elect their political representatives in parliament and congress… diversity is not only an end in itself, but also a means to securing important democratic values, like the great class ones of freedom, equality and fraternity.'[9] The implication of the special nature of media is generally thought to be that the media requires its own, separate, legal treatment.

Nevertheless there is also a view that, at least to some extent, competition among media providers may be seen to be like competition for any other

---

4 Department of Communications Policy Background Paper *Media Control and Ownership, Policy Background Paper No 3*, June 2014, at 4.

5 Doyle G, *Media Ownership: The Economics and Politics of Convergence and Concentration in the UK and European Media*, Sage, London, 2002, cited in Smith op cit 152.

6 Van Cuilenburg J, 'On competition, access and diversity in media, old and new', (1999) 1 *news, media & society* 183 at 189.

7 Van der Wurff R and van Cuilenburg J, 'Impact of Moderate and Ruinous Competition on Diversity: The Dutch Television Market' (2001) 14 *Journal of Media Economics* 213 at 214.

8 Bania K, 'European merger control in the broadcasting sector: Does media pluralism fit?' 9 *The Competition Law Review* 49 at 50. Likewise, the Australian Department of Communications has stated that media diversity 'is seen to support an informed citizenry and more effective democracy': *Media Control and Ownership*, op cit, 4.

9 Van Cuilenburg, op cit, 197–98.

product.[10] Competition is valued for a variety of benefits that it brings, but it is generally accepted that the most valued benefit is the efficiency that results from the forces of competition in meeting consumer demand. Firms are forced, through the process of competition, to meet consumer demands. A failure to do this will be disciplined by the market – consumers will turn to other firms that are prepared to meet their requirements. An absence of competition, on the other hand, allows firms the discretion to prioritise matters other than maximum consumer welfare.[11] The objective of competition law is thus to promote the efficient achievement of consumer demands or, to put it in the more negative terms of its legislative context, to prohibit conduct that substantially lessens competition.[12]

This objective of competition law can work to promote media diversity. That is, media firms, by being prevented from behaving anti-competitively, will be forced to compete to meet consumer demand. This competition will thereby lead to a 'variety of voices'. In this way there is a consistency between the promotion of competition and the promotion of media diversity. As stated by Arino, 'in most situations, what is good for competition would also be good for pluralism, as generally, a plurality of competitors (voices) will allow for a variety of products (discourses).'[13] After considering cases where both competition and pluralism were in issue, Arino concludes that 'in the majority of cases, competition enforcement not only furthered economic efficiency but also indirectly ensured the protection of pluralism.'[14] As Arino goes on to acknowledge, and as discussed further below, this is a generalisation only, but it is a starting point.

It is true that an analysis of conduct by media firms, such as a merger between two media firms, may raise its own particular issues in a competition law context. One prominent issue has been how the relevant 'market' should be defined in a case involving media firms. How the market is defined in a particular case is often

10 Van Cuilenburg, op cit, 194.

11 Of course there will still be the incentive for a firm with market power to meet consumer demand, in order to maximise profits, but the absence of competition will tend to dilute the strength of this incentive.

12 It was suggested by a former Chair of the Australian Competition Regulator, not completely tongue in cheek, that the whole of competition law could be reduced to a single prohibition: 'any conduct that substantially lessens competition is prohibited.' There are important exceptions to this generalisation but it nevertheless contains an element of truth.

13 Arino M, 'Competition Law and Pluralism in European Digital Broadcasting: Addressing the Gaps', (2004) 54 *Communiations & Strategies* 97 at 101.

14 Arino, op cit 117.

significant.[15] A wide market definition, for example, may make conduct that might otherwise appear anti-competitive to be, on closer examination, of less concern. In contrast a narrow market definition may magnify the impact of the conduct under review. Markets are not static and so may change over time as, for example, technology changes and new competitors emerge. There are potentially interesting issues in defining the market in which media firms operate, not least because of changing technology. One issue has been over the products to be included in the market - do free to air and pay television compete and hence belong in the same market? Print and electronic media? And so forth.

A recent illustration was provided by the Foxtel/Ten Network acquisition in Australia. In this case Foxtel, the leading subscription television provider in Australia, sought to acquire 10% of the shares in the Ten Network, a free to air television provider. The Ten Network, in turn, sought to acquire 24.9% of Foxtel's advertising agency. The Australian competition regulator, the Australian Competition and Consumer Commission (the ACCC) provisionally considered the relevant market to include both free to air and subscription service television and possibly extended to subscription video on demand services.[16] This contrasts with an earlier decision in which the ACCC had treated free to air and subscription television services as being in separate markets.[17] The European Commission has generally treated pay and subscription service television as in separate markets, although has acknowledged that they seem to be moving towards the one market.[18] It is well known, of course, that technology now allows different forms of media (print, television, radio) to cross more readily into other forms, such as print media operating an online presence, and this 'convergence' may eventually

15 The 'market' consists of the competitors for the product at issue. Identifying the market is the first step in determining the state of competition (within that market) and ultimately the impact of the relevant conduct on that competition.

16 See ACCC *Statement of Issues, 14 September 2015 Foxtel Management Pty Ltd and Ten Network Holdings Ltd proposed acquisitions*, available on the ACCC website: http://registers.accc.gov.au/content/index.phtml/itemId/1190276/fromItemId/751043. The acquisition was ultimately cleared by both the ACCC and the media regulator. At the time of writing, the ACCC had not released its reasons for its decision.

17 See ACCC *Statement of Issues Foxtel proposed acquisition of Austar United Communications Limited*, available on the ACCC website at http://registers.accc.gov.au/content/index.phtml/itemId/1044881/fromItemId/751043, at paras 35–37.

18 See Bania, op cit, at 54.

lead to the emergence of a 'media market', in which traditionally separate forms of media will compete.[19]

Market definition in media cases may also be complicated by the fact that media typically involves what economists refer to as a 'two-sided' market. That is, media firms play a role of bringing together two different groups (advertisers and consumers) who benefit from their connection but who would otherwise have difficulties in connecting. This not only means that there will be at least 2 markets typically involved in a media case but may also have implications for determining whether the conduct in issue is anticompetitive.[20]

But despite the interest of these issues to competition lawyers, the key point here is that, apart from the politically sensitive nature of the media, the economic principles brought to bear in the consideration of other products can also apply to media firms and products. It is this that allows for a consistency between the aims of competition law and the objective of media diversity. This has been noted, for example, by the ACCC. The ACCC has a specific policy on 'media mergers' and in this document it states that 'the ACCC will consider the impact of media mergers on market concentration, and therefore on the number and market share of media outlets in a market. The ACCC will also consider whether a merged media business could exercise market power by reducing the quality of the content it provides consumers, which could include reducing the diversity of the content it provides.'[21] European commentators have made a similar point.[22]

In this sense, at the heart of competition policy is the objective of providing choice to consumers and the promotion of choice in the media is consistent with the aims of media diversity. This complementarity between competition law and media objectives has been one reason that some jurisdictions are placing a growing reliance on competition law rather than specific media legislation to deal with media diversity.

---

19 Compare Smith, op cit, at 153. See ACCC *Media Mergers* 2006 (revised in 2010), available at http://www.accc.gov.au/publications/media-mergers at paras 48–53.

20 See, further, for example Evans D and Schmalensee R, 'Markets with Two-Sided Platforms' (2008) 1 *Issues in Competition Law and Policy* 667 (ABA Section of Antitrust Law); Rysman M, 'The Economics of Two-Sided Markets' (2009) 23 *Journal of Economic Perspectives* 125; Filistrucchi L, Geradin D, van Damme E and Affeldt P, 'Market Definition in Two-Sided Markets: Theory and Practice' (2014) 10 *Journal of Competition Law & Economics* 293.

21 ACCC *Media Mergers*, op cit, at para 12.

22 Arino, op cit, at 101.

Turning to the competition laws themselves, in practice it is merger law that has been the most prominent. Indeed, as noted, the Australian regulator has a specific policy dealing solely with media mergers. Merger law is concerned to prevent acquisitions that may create excessive market power in the merged firm. EU competition law prohibits mergers that 'would significantly impede effective competition in the common market or a substantial part of it.'[23] Australian competition law, based on the United States' antitrust merger provisions, prohibits acquisitions that 'have the effect or likely effect of substantially lessening competition in a market.'[24] Significantly, Australia competition law also provides for the option of allowing ('authorising') mergers (and other anti-competitive conduct) where the merger can be shown to generate a 'public benefit' that outweighs its anti-competitive and other effects. The possibility of using the authorisation provisions to authorise mergers (or other conduct) on the ground that the promotion of media diversity is a 'public benefit' is taken up below.

Potential mergers of media firms, leading to greater concentration in the media, may thus be blocked under the merger provisions. A merger, under the Australian provisions, will be prohibited[25] if it is, or is likely, to result in a substantial lessening of competition in a market. The relevant analysis involves identification of the markets in which the merging firms operate, assessing the state of competition in that market and then determining whether the future, if the acquisition proceeds, is likely to be more anticompetitive than the future without the acquisition.[26]

There have been a number of merger decisions involving media firms in both Australia and the EU (and EU nations) and these provide an illustration of how competition law may be used to promote media diversity. An interesting example was the attempted acquisition in the UK by BSkyB of ITV. BSkyB, a leader in UK pay television, was prevented by the UK competition regulator from acquiring 17.9% of ITV on the ground that this would substantially lessen competition.

---

23 European Council Regulation 139/2004/EC of 20 January.

24 *Competition and Consumer Act 2010* (Cth) s 50.

25 If found to be in breach there is a range of possible sanctioning options but in practice an injunction is most likely to apply. An order requiring the acquirer to divest itself of the offending acquisition or a declaration that the acquisition is in breach of the Act have also been used in practice.

26 This is known as the 'future with and without test'. See further ACCC, *Media Mergers* op cit 'Part B: A framework for analysing media markets'.

This was despite the fact that the acquisition would not have been in breach of the cross-media ownership laws.[27]

Australian media merger decisions have been less striking. Despite initial announcements of opposition to media mergers[28] as being anticompetitive, in practice few end up being opposed,[29] though sometimes compromises are reached in order to allow the merger to proceed.[30]

In theory at least, other provisions of competition law are also potentially applicable to promote media competition and hence media diversity. These include prohibitions against abuse of market power[31] and against media firms entering into anti-competitive agreements or practices with their customers or suppliers.[32] These provisions are available, at least in principle, to deal with conduct that interferes with competition among media firms and may, in turn, have an impact on media diversity, such as media firms entering into anticompetitive agreements to prevent potential new entrants to the market or a powerful media firm using its

27 See https://assets.digital.cabinet-office.gov.uk/media/55194c63ed915d1424000382/sky_berr_decision.pdf See Smith op cit at 152.

28 Such as, for example, The Seven Network's acquisition of Consolidated Media Holdings and Macquarie's acquisition of certain of Fairfax's radio assets. See ACCC *Statement of Issues 13 September 2012, Seven Group Holdings Limited – proposed acquisition of Consolidated Media Holdings Limited* available at http://registers.accc.gov.au/content/item.phtml?itemId=1078827&nodeId=ab37d0276ff950c430be436f59106a10&fn=Seven%20%20Group%20Holdings%20Limited%20proposed%20acquisition%20of%20Consolidated%20Media%20Holdings%20Limited%20-%2013%20September%202012.pdf.

29 Thus, for example, the outcomes in the 2 decisions just referred, both of which were ultimately unopposed: ACCC *Public Competition Assessment 15 February 2013 Seven Group Holdings Limited – proposed acquisition of remaining shares in Consolidated Media Holdings Limited* and ACCC, *Macquarie Radio Network Limited (MRN) – proposed acquisition of the radio assets of Fairfax Media Limited (FML) and FML's proposed acquisition of 54.5% of MRN*, both of which are available on the ACCC website respectively at http://registers.accc.gov.au/content/index.phtml/itemId/1084318/fromItemId/751043 and http://registers.accc.gov.au/content/index.phtml/itemId/1185004/fromItemId/751043.

30 For an example of this, see Fairfax acquisition of Rural Press newspapers, which was allowed after Fairfax gave an undertaking to divest itself of certain newspapers – see ACCC website; the undertaking is also available on the website. See http://registers.accc.gov.au/content/index.phtml/itemId/784990/fromItemId/751043.

31 Article 82 of the Treaty on the Function of the European Union (TFEU) and s 46 of the Australian *Competition and Consumer Act 2010* (Cth).

32 Article 81 of the TFEU and Div 1 and ss 45 and 47 of the *Competition and Consumer Act*.

market power to maintain or extend an existing absence of competition. In practice non-merger provisions have had little role to play. There are various reasons for this. A difficulty with the abuse of market power provisions, for example, is the burden of establishing an 'abuse' under the relevant competition provisions. An illustration has been provided by Smith who traced the problems the British competition regulator faced in attempting to establish that BSkyB had misused its market power.[33] Further, common to all actions under competition law, the generally ex post nature of competition proceedings and the time needed for proper investigation of a breach have made these provisions particularly difficult to be used effectively.[34]

3. The limitations of competition law as a champion of media diversity

The previous section suggested that there is a consistency in the objectives of competition law and the promotion of media diversity. This congruency gives rise to the argument that competition law may therefore be an appropriate policy tool for the promotion of media diversity. However, I think it needs to be conceded that there is an unsatisfying generality about the discussion in the previous section. This is because, while it is true that there is generally a consistency between the objectives of competition law and the goal of media diversity, this leaves at least two further questions unanswered. The first is whether media diversity can be explicitly taken into account in an analysis of whether conduct is anti-competitive. The second, and related question, is how media diversity as an objective will be treated in the event that it clashes with the objective of promoting competition.

These questions raise a basic problem for those who seek to use competition law as the sole promoter of media diversity. This is that the link between the promotion of competition and the promotion of media diversity turns out to be a weak one.[35] We can accept that competition law is concerned to prevent the acquisition of media market power (through merger) and the misuse of market power by media firms and by promoting competition among media firms competition law will thereby assist media diversity. But, as noted at the beginning of this chapter,

---

33 Smith op cit 154-5.

34 See generally Bania op cit and Smith op cit. The latter looks generally at how competition law has been applied to UK television.

35 This is a point recognised by a number of commentators. See, for example, Smith, op cit, at 146 (in the 'safeguarding of media plurality … competition regulation is of only limited value.'

diversity of media ownership is not necessarily the same thing as media diversity. As pointed out in a report to a Canadian body that examined the approach of various jurisdictions (including Australia and Germany) to the promotion of media diversity, 'Many analysts and observers equate media pluralism with a diversity of ownership and that concentration of ownership will skew public discussion by not exploring all viewpoints and interests. … While ownership is an important criterion in measuring diversity, other factors are important, including rural/urban accessibility, number of services available, licensing requirements, etc.'[36] This point has also been explicitly recognised by the Australian competition regulator. In its *Media Mergers* the ACCC states that 'A key purpose of the Act [the Australian Competition and Consumer Act 2010] is to protect competition in markets in Australia, including media markets. Media diversity is primarily protected by the restrictions on cross-media mergers in the Broadcasting Services Act.'[37] The latter Act is concerned with rules limiting cross-media ownership, which are considered elsewhere in this book. Thus the competition regulator does not see media diversity as a direct responsibility of competition law and policy but rather as a matter of specialist media legislation. A recent Australian Policy Background Paper into media control and ownership in Australia makes a similar point when it states that 'It also needs to be highlighted that the focus on diversity in the *control* of broadcasting licences and associated newspapers does not equate to a diversity of *services* or *products*.'[38] And so the point is that competition law can be effective in ensuring that there is competition among media firms but this will not, in itself, result in media diversity. In fact, as seen below, the reverse may even by the case.

The proposed acquisition by News Corporation of BSkyB provides a good illustration of this competition/diversity divide.[39] This was an acquisition which gave rise to concerns about media diversity but ultimately such concerns were

---

36 Media Strategy Policy Limited *A Report to the Canadian Radio and Television Commission. Media Ownership; Rules Regulations and Practices in Selected Countries and Their Potential Relevance to Canada*, July, 2007, at 1.

37 ACCC Media Mergers op cit at para 12.

38 *Media control and ownership: Policy Background Paper No 3*, op cit at 7.

39 See Smith, op cit, at 153 and generally European Commission *Case No COMP/M.5932 – News Corp*/BSKyB, at http://ec.europa.eu/competition/mergers/cases/decisions/m5932_20101221_20310_1600159_EN.pdf Report *on Public Interest Test on the Proposed Acquisition of British Sky Broadcasting Group plc by News Corporation* available at http://stakeholders.ofcom.org.uk/binaries/consultations/public-interest-test-nov2010/statement/public-interest-test-report.pdf and http://stakeholders.ofcom.org.uk/binaries/consultations/public-interest-test-nov2010/statement/uils-further-advice.pdf.

not considered relevant to the competition assessment. In this case, the European Commission undertook a detailed analysis of the potential anti-competitive impact of the acquisition and concluded that it was not sufficiently anti-competitive to be in breach of the competition laws. It acknowledged that media plurality was not its concern and that this aspect had not been taken into account. In its decision the Commission made it clear that '[t]he present decision is based solely on competition-related grounds under the Merger Regulation and is without prejudice to the media plurality review of the relevant UK authorities. Given that the purpose, legal frameworks, and focus of a competition review by the Commission on one hand, and a media plurality review by the relevant UK authorities on the other hand are different, the findings in the present decision are without prejudice to the UK media plurality review of the proposed transaction.'[40]

The media plurality review referred to by the Commission was in fact undertaken by the UK media regulator, Ofcom. Ofcom's initial assessment was that the impact of the acquisition on plurality (particularly in relation to news and current affairs) was of sufficient concern to render the acquisition against the public interest. This led to negotiations between the parties which resulted in agreed measures to guarantee the independence of BSkyB's news channel.

This illustrates a broader issue about the relationship of competition and media diversity. This is that, at their heart, they have different notions of 'public interest' and these notions may clash. As explained by Arino, 'Both the safeguard of competition and of pluralism are said to be in the public interest, but they are understood differently. For the purposes of competition, the public interest primarily equals the 'satisfaction of consumer preferences'. By contrast, under the pluralism paradigm, the public interest is sees as the collective benefit resulting from an informed public debate on civic issues. Thus, reference is made to something that goes beyond what 'interests the public' to include another two fundamental functions of the media: that of informing and that of acting as a 'watchdog' of government.'[41]

And so in the event of a clash between competition and media diversity, in a competition case it will be competition that will be given priority. In fact it is even starker than this. Issues of plurality and diversity are generally not even seen as relevant to the competition analysis, as can be seen above. They are, at best, a fortunate indirect effect, a happy coincidence. Arino, in a summary of the EU Commissioner's approach to media mergers, observes that 'non-economic constraints

40 Ibid, at para 309.

41 Arino, op cit, 101–102.

[such as plurality] have not been openly incorporated into the competition law framework' and that any benefits of competition decisions to plurality and diversity were 'only an indirect effect'[42] and concludes that the courts in competition cases cannot 'depart altogether from questions of efficiency or evidence of expected prices and flow of goods in a relevant market' and that 'therefore, given that the extent to which competition law can take into account non-economic considerations is so limited, there will be situations in which competition law will not suffice to protect pluralism.'[43] A more recent study by Bania supports this, showing the Commission's reluctance to intervene in media mergers.[44]

It has already been noted that media diversity is not the same thing as media competition, that is, there is not a simple positive correlation between competition and diversity.[45] But there may be a further, important, complication to this relationship. This is that the more highly competitive a media market is, the *less* this may promote media diversity. This is because the greater degree of competition the more likely it is that the products will tend towards homogeneity. Vigorous competition leads to effective pressure on price, forcing it down to its most efficient level. But this same competition may also force firms to offer what consumers as a whole demand, which in turn can restrict diversity. A competitive, but nevertheless less than highly competitive market ('monopolistic competition'), may be necessary to allow media firms sufficient room from price pressure to cater to minority views. Van Cuilenburg suggests that this explains the lack of content variety in the highly competitive commercial television stations in the UK in contrast with the greater diversity in the less competitive daily newspapers.[46] A similar study on the Dutch television market was to a similar effect.[47] The implications for the promotion of media diversity are that a highly competitive market may need, through specific media regulation, to be *discouraged* rather than promoted.[48]

For these various reasons, it is difficult to resist the conclusion that the promotion of competition is not a reliable proxy for the promotion of media diversity.

42 Arino, op cit, 112.
43 At 113.
44 Bania, op cit, esp 59–71.
45 Van Cuilenburg, op cit, 189.
46 Van Cuilenburg, op cit, 198–202.
47 Van der Wurff R and van Cuilenburg J, op cit.
48 Id at 228.

4. Should competition law be extended so that it promotes media diversity?

The story so far is that there is a weak link between promoting competition and promoting media diversity and that even this link is likely to be broken when there is a clash between these two objectives. This conclusion is not surprising. As Arino states, 'In short, pluralism is not a goal of competition, but simply a consequence of it'.[49] This part now considers whether competition law *should* take into account the impact of conduct on media diversity (that is, whether the link between the two should be strengthened) and, if so, how this might be achieved.

In relation to the first issue, some have argued that competition law should in fact take into account the impact on media diversity of the conduct being examined. There are different ways this might be achieved. The boldest arguments involve creating special rules in competition law to deal with media diversity directly. Arino, for example, suggests that, when analysing the conduct of media firms, competition law should embrace a 'marketplace of ideas' or a 'market for pluralism'.[50] This would be used to identify firms with power in such a market ('opinion power') and the task for the court would then be to determine whether the conduct of the media firm was likely to lessen media diversity. This analysis would be undertaken in a similar fashion to the way in which we now determine whether conduct lessens competition. A similar approach, recommended in a report by economists to the EU Commission,[51] was that when defining the market for a media merger, the 'quality' of products rather than the usual test of a product's price, should be the guiding factor. That is, it seeks to alter the test that is usually used for determining the outer boundaries of a market for a product when dealing with media products. The usual test is to ask what reaction, if any, there would be to a small increase in *price* of that product. If a small increase would result in customers turning to another firm, then that other firm is considered to be a competitor and hence its product is to be included in the market. This Report suggests that, in the case of a media product, to determine the relevant market

49 Arino, op cit at 117.

50 Arino, op cit at 117.

51 Europe Economics, 'Market Definition in the Media Sector: Economic Issues. Report for the European Commission, DG Competition (2002), available at http://ec.europa.eu/competition/sectors/media/documents/european_economics.pdf referred to in Bania op cit at 55.

the question would become – if there were a small decrease in the *quality* of the product, to whom, if anyone, would customers turn?[52]

There are other less ambitious approaches. These would not alter the usual approach of competition law to the definition of markets but would nevertheless acknowledge that media diversity is a *relevant* consideration when conduct of a media firm is being assessed under competition law. That is, in determining whether conduct engaged in by a media firm is anti-competitive, the court (or Tribunal in some cases) would be entitled to take into account the impact of the conduct on media diversity as well as on competition. And so conduct might be prohibited under competition law, not solely on the ground that it is anti-competitive, but also, on a separate ground, that it will have a negative impact on media diversity.

Despite the fact that this approach involves a less radical change to competition law principles than the 'marketplace of ideas' or 'opinion power' concepts considered above, the use of competition law in this way is highly contentious. Many years ago, before his involvement with the US antitrust regulator, Robert Pitofsky argued for such a broader role for competition law generally. He argued that 'it is bad history, bad policy and bad law to exclude certain political values in interpreting the antitrust laws. By 'political values' I mean, first, a fear that excessive concentration of economic power will breed antidemocratic political pressures, and second, a desire to enhance individual and business freedom by reducing the range within which private discretion by a few in the economic sphere controls the welfare of all.'[53]

This line of argument has been taken up more recently by European commentators to suggest that media diversity should be a legitimate factor in assessing anti-competitive conduct.[54]

The problem with using competition law in this way is that it requires balancing the different objectives of competition and media plurality without weakening them both in the process. The use of competition law to promote media plurality is, in this sense, a compromise. The argument for its use in this way is strongest where there is no specific legislation dealing with media diversity. In effect, the argument is that competition law is better than nothing or, putting it more positively, that when the conduct of media firms comes before the court in a competition case, the

52 The change in advertising minutes per hour was a suggested proxy for quality. See Bania, op cit, 75–76.

53 Pitofsky R, 'The Political Content of Antitrust' (1979) 127 *University of Pennsylvania Law Review* 1051 at 1051.

54 See generally Arino, op cit and Bania, op cit.

court should not waste this opportunity and take into account only competition issues but should also deal with the media diversity concerns that the conduct raises. This argument therefore has particular force in the EU, where, for constitutional reasons, there is an absence of specific legislation at the EU level dealing with media diversity. The only legislation is state based and this is likely to be insufficient to deal with transnational issues.[55] So despite the difficulties, some still advocate that competition law should play a direct role in promoting media diversity. This argument has been put by Arino as follows: 'Without advocating a multi-purpose use of competition law as the optimal vehicle to advance all the public interest in terms of media objectives, I still take the view that it is possible, desirable and legitimate for competition law to openly take media pluralism into consideration. This could be achieved by putting a stronger emphasis on issues other than price, for instance on analysis of its impact on quality and choice.'[56]

One of the most intriguing aspects of this whole issue is the scope that already exists, particularly in Australian competition law, for media diversity to be taken into account in a competition decision. It has been seen that it is unlikely to be given any recognition in the assessment of whether conduct is anti-competitive. However Australian, and to a lesser extent EU, competition law allows for 'public benefits' to be taken into account in a competition case and potentially to override the limited 'lessening of competition' analysis. Australian competition law makes provision for the ACCC to 'authorise' (future) conduct. Conduct that is authorised is immune from liability under the competition provisions of the Act.[57] The ground for authorisation is, in general terms, that the relevant conduct generates a 'public benefit' and that this public benefit outweighs any anti-competitive or other detriment that the conduct may cause.[58] 'Public benefit' has been broadly construed to include 'anything of value to the community generally, any contribution to the aims pursued by the society.'[59] It is apparent from this how the impact of conduct on media diversity could be raised. The argument would be that a negative impact on media diversity would be a relevant 'other detriment' to be

55 Arino op cit at 122–124.

56 Arino op cit at 121–122.

57 See generally Part VII of the Act. Authorisation is not available for misuse of market power but is available for other conduct. Note that in the case of mergers, it is the Australian Competition Tribunal, not the ACCC, with power to authorise.

58 See s 90 and generally *Re Qantas Airways* [2004] ACompT 9.

59 *Re Queensland Cooperative Milling Association Ltd; Re Defiance Holdings Ltd* (1976) 25 FLR 169, at 210.

taken into account or that a positive impact on media diversity would be a 'public benefit' to be weighed against any anti-competitiveness.

EU competition law has a more restricted version of this 'public benefit' exemption. Article 101(3) of the TFEU provides for the prohibition against anti-competitive agreements (in Art 101(1)) to be declared inapplicable if the particular agreement creates certain economic benefits. More promisingly, the EU merger regulation requires the Commission to take into account 'the interests of the intermediate and ultimate consumers, and the development of technical and economic progress provided that it is to consumers' advantage and does not form an obstacle to competition.'[60]

Despite these provisions being available, it is clear that, in practice, assessment of conduct, even by media firms, is dominated by considerations of the efficiency of the conduct, not its impact on media diversity. As Bania notes, broader public policy considerations have 'at the most, played a marginal role'.[61] The same is true for Australia.[62]

It is thus not the inability of competition law, certainly in Australia at least, that holds it back from playing a direct role in the promotion of media diversity. It is the unwillingness of regulators, or the Competition Tribunal, to embrace a role for competition law that extends beyond anti-competitive and efficiency considerations.

Is this unwillingness appropriate? In my view it is. The greatest justification for competition law to take into account 'non-competition' issues, such as the promotion of media diversity, is where these issues can best, or only, be dealt with by a competition court or tribunal. To deal with media diversity arguments in a competition case legitimately raises concerns that (i) these issues will receive inadequate ('inexpert') treatment by the competition body (what expertise does a

---

60 Council Regulation (EC) No 139/2004 of 20 January 2004 on the Control of Concentrations between Undertakings, Article 1(b). Bania argues, op cit at 72, that other provisions may also be relevant, including Article 167(4) of the TFEU and Arts 11(2) and 51(1) of the Charter of Fundamental Rights.

61 Bania, op cit, 71. Some examples are given of where media diversity seems to have been taken into account in a merger decision but these are conceded to be 'rather exceptional' (at 108).

62 Duns J, 'Competition Law and Public Benefits' (1994) 16 *Adelaide Law Review* 245; Fels A and Grimwade T, '(2003) 'Authorisation: is it still relevant to Australian Competition Law?' (2003) 11 *Competition and Consumer Law Journal* 187; Officer R and Williams P, 'The Public Benefit Test in an Authorisation Decision' in Richardson M and Williams P (eds) *The Law and the Market* (Federation Press 1995).

competition body have to deal with media diversity issues?) and (ii) promotion of these other issues will undermine the primary task of competition law, namely to promote competition for the range of benefits this creates. So while there may be some justification for EU competition bodies to take into account media diversity issues, on the basis that there is no EU wide law on the subject, this is a second-best solution. It is also one that is hard to justify in the Australian context, where there is specific media legislation.[63]

5. Conclusion

There is little doubt about the fundamental importance of media diversity in a democratic society. One of the aims of this chapter was to examine whether we need specific legislation dealing with media diversity or whether media diversity is in safe hands if left to competition law. There are certainly advantages in relying on competition law for this role. Competition law is a specialised area, with specialised regulators, familiar with the tools required to promote competition. Competition law is very capable of accommodating media products into its analysis. Competition among media firms will promote media diversity. In the absence of specific media legislation, competition law will provide support for media diversity. It is therefore not surprising that this approach has its proponents.

As this chapter has sought to explain, however, there are also a number of problems in relying on competition law to promote media diversity. A fundamental question is whether the aims of competition and the aims of media diversity are ad idem. As explained in this chapter, I think this is where competition law ultimately fails as a sole regulator of media products. The promotion of competition will generally coincide with the promotion of media diversity. But the two objectives may certainly clash and, in this event, competition law will choose the promotion of competition over the promotion of media diversity. The chapter considered whether competition law should be amended to accommodate media diversity as an objective but concluded that this would be a second best solution. The optimal regulation of media diversity requires competition law to be supported by specific media legislation.

---

63 Namely, the Australian *Broadcasting Services Act 1992* (Cth). This is not to say, of course, that this media specific legislation is up to the task. In a recent speech, the ACCC chairman raised some significant queries about the effectiveness of the *Broadcasting Services Act*. See the speech of Mr Rod Simms, 5 November 2015, 'Promoting innovation through competition' available on the ACCC website: https://www.accc.gov.au/speech/promoting-innovation-through-competition.

Greg Taylor*

Diversity within government broadcasters

Abstract: This chapter compares the legal arrangements for ensuring freedom from governmental control for state broadcasters in Germany and Australia. While Germany has an impressive set of principles reinforced by a recent decision of the Federal Constitutional Court and Australia has no such systemic constitutional protections, the situation in Germany in reality is different from, but scarcely superior to the Australian position.

1. Introduction

In common-law countries media diversity law centres around the avoidance of monopolies or excessive degrees of market dominance by one provider or group of providers across an entire market. That is without doubt an important topic, and it is the one to which other chapters of this book are largely devoted. If thought is given in Australia to ensuring the independence of public broadcasters from the government – as it frequently is – we do not consider this a question of media diversity, still less of constitutional law on which the legislature's range of options might be constrained by overarching, judicially enforceable constitutional principles.

---

* Honorary Professor, Marburg University, Germany; Associate Professor, Graduate School of Business and Law, R.M.I.T. University, Melbourne, Australia. Warmest thanks are due to those who read and commented upon a draft, including and above all one very eminent person involved with the governance of the Z.D.F.

It is otherwise in Germany, as this chapter will show. The starting point is that the constitutional guarantee of media freedom in Article 5 I 2 of the Basic Law[1] has a much broader function than appears at first sight. It is not merely a right of media organisations to defend themselves against attempted interference by the state.[2] Rather, in accordance with the now reasonably well-known concept that rights guarantees may impose positive as well as negative duties upon the state, Article 5 I 2 also requires the state to take positive action to ensure that media freedom is a reality, not just a possibility.[3] In relation to public broadcasters,[4] this principle requires them to be set up in a manner that ensures that a variety of voices participates in their governance, which in turn requires their independence (although not, as we shall see, their complete separation) from the state to be promoted.[5] As with so many other features of modern German constitutional law, this principle is a reaction to abuses under the Nazis: Dr Goebbels' media remain notorious, and the point requires no labouring.[6]

The decision of the German Federal Constitutional Court of 25 March 2014[7] that forms the basis of the discussion in this chapter illustrates these principles

---

1 'Freedom of the press and freedom of reporting by means of broadcasts and films shall be guaranteed' – from www.iuscomp.org/gla/statutes/GG.htm#5. All other translations from German in this chapter are by its author. The reference to reporting by means of films now seems rather odd, but newsreels were common at the time at which the Basic Law was written.

2 In this chapter, I use "State" to refer to the sixteen German federal States and "state" to refer to the general concept of a state.

3 BVerfGE 12, 205, 260f; 57, 295, 322; 119, 181, 241; Bryde, "Fundamental Rights as Guidelines and Inspiration : German Constitutionalism in International Perspective" (2007) 25 Wisconsin Int LJ 189, 199–201; Grzeszick, "The 'Serving' Freedom to Broadcast – Subjective *versus* Objective Dimensions of a Fundamental Right" in Pünder/Waldhoff (eds.), *Debates in German Public Law* (Hart, Oxford 2014), p. 84; Schulze-Fielitz in Dreier (ed.), *Grundgesetz : Kommentar* (3rd ed., Mohr Siebeck, Tübingen 2013), pp. 643, 709, 714f, 724f; Stern *et al.*, *Das Staatsrecht der Bundesrepublik Deutschland* Vol. IV/1 (C.H. Beck, Munich 2006), pp. 1703f; Wittemann, "Constitutionalising Communications : The German Constitutional Court's Jurisprudence of Communications Freedom" (2010) 33 Hastings Int & Comp LJ 95, 102.

4 Not private ones : BVerfGE 121, 30, 50f.

5 BVerfGE 12, 205, 262f; 121, 30, 50, 53; BVerfGE 136, 9, 30; OVGE 34, 439, 441 (OVG Lüneburg).

6 Hahn, *Die Aufsicht des öffentlich-rechtlichen Rundfunks : Bestandsaufnahme und Zukunftsperspektiven* (Peter Lang, Frankfurt/M. 2010), p. 163.

7 As with all German decisions, this one is published without a name and is referred to officially simply by its citation : BVerfGE 136, 9. However, the series of Broadcasting

very well. In brief, the Court decided that both governing bodies of the *Zweites Deutsches Fernsehen* (Z.D.F.),[8] run by the sixteen State governments of Germany, were not set up in a manner that guaranteed the independence of the channel from the state and assured a variety of voices and were therefore constitutionally invalid. This was because too many appointments to the two boards in charge of the Z.D.F. were in the gift of politicians or were actually occupied by them. In addition to this decision, which few commentators indeed found surprising given the highly politicised make-up of the boards and the long series of decisions which threw their composition into doubt,[9] the Court proclaimed, by a majority of five to three Judges, a new[10] principle of transparency in the operation of the boards to which legislative effect was also required to be given.

At first sight this sounds thought-provoking, and far ahead of what could be expected in the common-law world. While the idea of diversity within one organisation may remind the historically inclined of Stalin's forcible advocacy of socialism within one country, neither is a self-contradictory idea, and diversity within one organisation will doubtless do more good in the end. We should first of all observe, however, that with us the problem attacked by the judgment of 25 March 2014 could hardly exist in the same form in the first place, as no-one would think of staffing the board of the A.B.C. or for that matter of the B.B.C. – the odd stray Lord aside – with practising politicians. The real problem comes, however, with making these fine principles a reality – as we shall see, and as dissenting Justice Andreas Paulus pointed out in his judgment in the German Federal Constitutional Court's decision. It is hard to break the dominance of the political parties in public life in general and in appointments to public office in particular – even more so in Germany than in Australia, for there virtually every public appointment of note has a party background. Thus, for example, Justice Paulus himself is associated with and was elected to the German Federal Constitutional Court at the

---

Decisions have acquired unofficial numbers, and this case is therefore likely to become known informally as the "Fourteenth Broadcasting Case". In this chapter it is referred to simply by its date, or, in the footnotes, by its citation.

8 Second German Television, *i.e.* Channel Two.

9 Cornils, Casenote, ZJS 2014, 447, 448; Dörr, „Die Mitwirkung des Verwaltungsrats bei der Bestellung des Z.D.F.-Chefredakteurs und das Problem der Gremienzusammensetzung" K&R 2009, 555, 559; Hahn in Hahn/Vesting (eds.), *Beck'scher Kommentar zum Rundfunkrecht* (5th ed., C.H. Beck, Munich 2012), p. 659; Hesse/Schneider, Casenote, NVwZ 2014, 881, 881. There were even some hints of what was to come in 2008 in BVerfGE 121, 30, 55.

10 Degenhart, Casenote, K&R 2014, 340, 341.

behest of a political party – the Free Democrats, since expelled from the *Bundestag* at the elections of 2013. All Justices of the Court are associated with and owe their positions to one or other of the political parties in this way, and this is not considered scandalous, as it might be in many parts of the common-law world. Rather, party-based election and affiliation form the principle by which appointments are organised and a spectrum of views assured as well as a high quality of appointments maintained by means of mutual veto rights among the parties.[11] In an atmosphere permeated with party-political patronage it will, however, not be easy to create boards for the Z.D.F. or any other broadcaster which, unlike the Court, have little or no connexion with party political life.

We shall see that there is, therefore, perhaps less to the decision of 25 March 2014 than meets the eye. It may be that these fine-sounding German principles will cash out, as the philosophers say, in a way that betrays their promise – not for the first time in a legal system which is fond of top-down reasoning and high-sounding principles but which has to operate in a setting that is just as imperfect and prone to compromise, and as full of distorting real-world power concentrations, as that of common-law countries.

The crucial test will be whether it is possible – whether the politicians are willing – to banish not just the formal influence of state office-holders over appointments but the informal, behind-the-scenes influence of the parties, such as is also exercised in relation to appointments to the Federal Constitutional Court, for example. The first difficulty, even assuming that this task is taken seriously in hand, will be merely identifying some organising principle for making such decisions other than party parity.[12] Another difficulty arises from the inherent paradox that it is both politicians who make the rules and against whom the rules are supposed to protect us, the media-consuming public.[13]

Having thus cautioned the reader against comparing the law of common-law countries as it actually operates against an idealised view of German law based on its advertised principles alone, I turn to a brief review of the position in Australia.

---

11 I describe this system in brief and give further references in Taylor, "Conventions by Consensus : Constitutional Conventions in Germany" (2014) 12 Int Jo Const Law 303, 320–322.

12 As is pointed out in a blog post by Lenski, „Der lange Schatten von Art. 21 GG – Staatsferne, Staatsfreiheit und Machterhalt im ZDF-Staatsvertrag" at http://www.verfassungsblog.de/lange-schatten-von-art-21-gg-staatsferne-staatsfreiheit-und-machterhalt-im-zdf-staatsvertrag/.

13 Wittemann, (2010) 33 Hastings Int & Comp LJ 95, 137.

2. A comparative overview: the A.B.C.

One commentator claims:

> Freedom of broadcasters from the state is a very German constitutional principle. It can be understood only against the background of experiences with the Nazi regime and has no equivalent in most countries of the European legal area.[14]

However, even taking into account Germany's unique history it is inherently unlikely that there would be no equivalent felt need for independence on the part of the public broadcaster from the government in societies as similar, in broad terms, as Germany and those of the rest of western Europe (including Australia, which derives its institutions from western Europe). Equivalent constitutional principles do exist in some other European civil-law countries and on the non-constitutional level in others, as well as also in Japan.[15]

Although no constitutional principle mandates such measures, it is noticeable that legislation in Australia also makes provision for members of the governing body, the Board, of the Australian Broadcasting Corporation[16] to be appointed in a manner which is designed to ensure some distance from the government. The background to this change, made in 2010, is that the Howard government (1996–2007) formed the view that the A.B.C. was a hotbed of anti-conservative bias against it – similar accusations are regularly made against its sister organisation in the United Kingdom – and consequently decided to appoint certain prominent conservative identities to the Board of that body in an endeavour to correct

14 Huber, „Die Staatsfreiheit des Rundfunks – Erosion und Neujustierung" in Detterbeck *et al.* (eds.), *Recht als Medium der Staatlichkeit : Festschrift für Herbert Bethge zum 70. Geburtstag* (Duncker & Humblot, Berlin 2009), p. 497.

15 Grzeszick, "The 'Serving' Freedom", pp. 90–93. There seem to be no equivalents in the Royal Charter of the B.B.C. (Cm 6925 (2006)) or in Part III of the Canadian *Broadcasting Act*, S.C. 1991, c. 11, but see *Television New Zealand Act* 2003 (N.Z.) s 28; *Prasar Bharati (Broadcasting Corporation of India) Act* 1990 (India) s 4 (1); *Broadcasting Act* 1999 (S. Af.) s 13 (1), (2). The Indian provision is particularly interesting as it sets up a permanent nomination panel; however, I lack any information about its operation in practice and cannot therefore pursue the topic here.

16 And also the Special Broadcasting Service : see *Special Broadcasting Service Act* 1991 (Clth) s 17 (2A), (2AA), (2AB), (2B), Part 3A. I concentrate here on the A.B.C. as the larger and more important entity in relation to which allegations of bias are much more frequently made, and also simply to avoid doubling the number of all statutory citations.

that perceived bias.[17] The succeeding Labor government (2007–2013), for its part, perceived no such bias in its own favour and considered these appointments an example of political interference:

> It is well known that lack of due process has in the past resulted in appointments to the A.B.C. and S.B.S. boards that were primarily motivated by political concerns rather than the best interests of the national broadcasters and the Australian public. There is widespread concern in the community that such political appointments have diminished the level of expertise on both boards and have weakened the ability of those boards to perform their duties.[18]

As a consequence Part IIIA of the *Australian Broadcasting Corporation Act* 1983 (Clth) was passed to establish a Nomination Panel for Board appointments. It is not subject to governmental direction (s 24C) and provides nominations to the government for Board members; in the case of the appointment of the Chairperson, the Leader of the Opposition must also be consulted (s 24X (1)). The government retains the right to appoint persons other than those recommended by the Panel but in that case is required to explain its choice to Parliament by tabling a statement of reasons and an assessment of the person chosen against the selection criteria (s 24X (2), (3)).

The selection criteria published by the responsible government minister are intended to provide a further degree of accountability, objectivity and transparency in the selection process.

It was furthermore provided that members of Australian legislatures and senior political staff members,[19] and also those who held such positions for a period of twelve months after they cease to hold them, cannot be appointed to the Board at all; former politicians and staff members can be appointed after the expiry of the twelve-month ban only if recommended by the Nomination Panel (s 12 (5A), (5AA), (5AB), (5B)). Australian law is thus, despite its lack of constitutional requirements, ahead of German law as far as keeping politicians off boards of government broadcasters is concerned.

While it cannot be denied that these rules represent an advance on what had gone before, it requires only a little acquaintance with the realities of power to perceive that much will now depend upon the composition of the Nomination

17 Strictly speaking the appointments are made by the Crown, but in reality the Crown always acts on the advice of the government.

18 Hon. A. Albanese in Commonwealth Parliamentary Debates, House of Representatives, 22 November 2010, p. 3231. On the S.B.S., see above, fn 16.

19 As defined in the *Australian Broadcasting Corporation (Definition of Senior Political Staff Member) Instrument* 2014 (Clth).

Panel which will take the leading role in selecting board members. The most recent appointees to it at the time of writing, under the conservative government that took office in 2013, are two prominent and outspoken conservative lawyers and publicists, Dr Janet Albrechtsen and the Hon. N.A. Brown Q.C.[20] Indeed, Dr Albrechtsen was, from 2005 to 2010, one of the members of the A.B.C. Board to whom objection was taken by the non-conservative side of politics; Brown Q.C. was a minister in an earlier conservative government.

These appointments were made even though s 24F (1) of the *Australian Broadcasting Corporation Act* 1983 (Clth) confides appointments to the Nomination Panel, in a further attempt to reduce political influence, not to the government or indeed any politician, but to the Secretary (permanent civil-service head) of the Prime Minister's Department. While Dr Albrechtsen and Brown Q.C. are both distinguished members of society and hardly unfit members of a government body, it is fair to say that credulity has been stretched by the idea that, of all those who might have been considered for the job, the Secretary chanced across these two names with no input from politicians such as the Prime Minister.

But it should also be pointed out that there is no Pope-like figure who can infallibly pronounce on and forever settle for everyone the question whether left-wing bias at the A.B.C. is a real problem which must be dealt with in this (and other) ways, or whether it is all a figment of conservative politicians' imaginations, they should stop claiming that there is bias and the appointments of Dr Albrechtsen and Brown Q.C. were another outrageous example of political interference. There is no substitute for value judgments on this score, and they will inevitably involve political assessments on which there will be perfectly legitimate disagreement. Nor can it be gainsaid that the present Chairman of the Board of the A.B.C., the Hon. J.J. Spigelman A.C. Q.C., who was appointed under the previous Labor government in 2012, is clearly associated with the Labor side of politics even though his immediate past role was Chief Justice of New South Wales.[21] While, in both roles, his contribution appears generally agreed to have been unaffected by his political sympathies, that too is a contestable value judgment.

---

20 See http://www.dpmc.gov.au/pmc/media/2014/nomination-panel-abc-and-sbs-appointments.

21 Thus it is obviously the case that some Judges in Australia may also be more or less loosely associated with one side or other of politics, as some have been in England at least since the nineteenth century, but the system in Germany mentioned in passing earlier is of a different in type as well as degree given that party nomination is the chief organising principle for appointing Judges of the Federal Constitutional Court in the first place.

3. The *Z.D.F. Case* – background

The Z.D.F. was set up in 1961[22] following the famous decision of the German Federal Constitutional Court of 28 February 1961[23] that the federal government's peremptory creation of its own television station was outside its constitutional powers. Then as now the Z.D.F.'s legal basis was an agreement among all the federal States – the new States added at Reunification acceded smoothly to the *Z.D.F. Agreement*.

As well as its Director-General (*Intendant*), the Z.D.F. possesses, as is usual in German public broadcasting, two governing bodies. The larger is the Television Council, which is often compared to the broadcaster's parliament given its functions of advising the Director-General about and setting and enforcing guidelines for programming.[24] When the Federal Constitutional Court's decision was rendered, the Z.D.F.'s Television Council was the largest of all German public broadcasters',[25] at seventy-seven members:

- one from each State government (sixteen);
- three from the federal government;
- twelve from political parties in accordance with their representation in the *Bundestag*;

22 An account may be found in Grzeszick, "The 'Serving' Freedom", pp. 83f; Williams, *Broadcasting and Democracy in West Germany* (Bradford U.P., 1976), pp. 31–34.

23 BVerfGE 12, 205. A brief account of this and succeeding cases in this field in English is in Kommers/Miller, *Constitutional Jurisprudence of the Federal Republic of Germany* (3rd ed., Duke U.P., 2012), pp. 510–518. See also pp. 90–95, for it is this decision that also launched, in the case law, the famous concept of *Bundestreue* (federal comity), for which it is probably better known abroad.

24 *Z.D.F. Agreement*, § 20 (1); Frank in Schiwy/Schütz/Dörr (eds.), *Medienrecht : Lexikon für Praxis und Wissenschaft* (5th ed., Carl Heymann, Cologne 2000), p. 505; Hahn in Hahn/Vesting (eds.), *Beck'scher Kommentar*, p. 659; Stuiber, *Medien in Deutschland* Vol. 2 (U.V.K. Medien, Constance 1998), pp. 728–730.
Nevertheless it would be wrong to compare the Z.D.F.'s Television Council with the A.B.C. Advisory Council, for example, as the powers of the Television Council are clearly much stronger. It must also approve the statute of the Z.D.F. and the budget and annual accounts, and, as we shall see, elects the majority of the Administrative Council. Under § 26 (3) of the *Z.D.F. Agreement*, both bodies must act together to dismiss the Director-General.

25 Hahn in Hahn/Vesting (eds.), *Beck'scher Kommentar*, p. 657; Stuiber, *Medien in Deutschland*, p. 720.

- two from each of the two major Churches and one from the Central Council of Jews in Germany;
- twenty-five representatives from assorted named interest groups such as trades unions, employers' bodies, local councils, journalists' bodies, charities, the Association of Victims of Stalinism, *etc.* – nominated by the interest groups concerned but selected by the State Premiers;[26]
- finally, sixteen representatives – again selected by the State Premiers – for general interest areas such as the Universities, youth, the higher professions, consumer protection, animal welfare and art and culture – the distinction between this and the previous category is that these representatives do not come from specific, named interest groups, but rather general fields of human endeavour.[27]

This structure, often referred to as "internal pluralism", is a result of the Federal Constitutional Court's insistence, since its very first broadcasting decision of 1961 disallowing federal government broadcasting within Germany,[28] that 'all societally relevant interests'[29] should be represented in the governing bodies of public broadcasters to ensure diversity. Taken literally, this direction would be impossible to fulfil: rather, a selection must be made by the legislature, which the Courts will not refuse endorsement to unless it is grossly unbalanced.[30]

As can be seen from the list, the main criterion for its composition might be thought to be ensuring that those already blessed with power and a strong voice in society are not excluded![31] But nor could it be called grossly unbalanced. At one stage the Central Council of German Romany[32] sued seeking inclusion in the charmed circle, but was told that no body had a right to admission and the Central Council of Jews in Germany was there as a religious group and not as victims of

26 Hahn, *Aufsicht*, p. 168 points out that this is unusual in German public broadcasting – normally there is no filter and the interest groups simply nominate members of the board directly.

27 *Z.D.F. Agreement*, § 21 (1) – (4).

28 See above, fn 23. There are no difficulties with federal broadcasting outside Germany, *e.g.* the Deutsche Welle.

29 BVerfGE 31, 314, 327f appears to be the first case in which this exact phrase was used.

30 BVerfG-K, NVwZ 1999, 175; Hahn in Hahn/Vesting (eds.), *Beck'scher Kommentar*, p. 657.

31 Wittemann, "West German Television Law : An Argument for Media as Instrument of Self-Government" (1984) 7 Hastings Int & Comp LR 145, 166–168.

32 *I.e.* the gypsies' central representative body, but the equivalent word to "gypsy" in German is now taboo after its misuse under the Hitler regime – and as a result even a food item, the gypsy schnitzel, will probably have to be re-named sooner or later.

the Holocaust.[33] This however immediately raises the question why there was no Islamic representative,[34] or for that matter a Buddhist or Hindu one, although no case has been brought by any other interest group seeking admission.

While § 21 (8) of the *Z.D.F. Agreement* stated that all but the first two classes of members listed above may not include members of the State or federal governments,[35] clearly the provisions allowed for a huge degree of political influence over the composition of the Television Council. In addition to the seats formally reserved for governmental or party appointees (the first three classes above) there was (unlike in Australia) no prohibition on members of Parliament taking up other positions such as those allocated to interest groups, and they frequently do.[36] While it was the custom for the twenty-five interest-group nominees to be approved by State Premiers without objection,[37] it will be seen that all members other than the five Christian and Jewish members – a total of 93.5% of members – were appointed by, or from the ranks of, politicians,[38] although that does not mean that all of them must necessarily identify very strongly with a political party.

The Z.D.F.'s second governing body is the Administrative Council, a much smaller committee of fourteen members at the time of the Court's judgment. It consisted of five State and one federal government representative (the State representatives being in practice usually State Premiers)[39] as well as eight further members elected by the Television Council with a three-fifths majority of all its

33 BVerfG-K, NVwZ 1999, 175.

34 Hesse/Schneider, NVwZ 2014, 881, 882; expert witnesses at a closed session of the *Bundestag* Committee for Culture and the Media : press release available at www.bundestag.de/presse/hib/2014_04/01/263120.

35 Nevertheless a minority of the sixteen State representatives are not former politicians. An outstanding example is Rhineland-Palatinate's appointment of Prof. Brun-Otto Bryde, a former Judge of the Federal Constitutional Court (loosely affiliated with the Greens Party in accordance with the system explained earlier, fn 11, but hardly a political hack; in fact he is not even a party member). However, it is the integrity of structures that is the important point, not whether a bad structure could be made to work well.

36 Huber, „Staatsfreiheit", p. 502.

37 BVerfGE 136, 9, 53.

38 Hahn, *Aufsicht*, pp. 189f.

39 Degenhart, „Wozu die Aufregung? Anmerkungen zur *Causa* Brender aus verfassungsrechtlicher Sicht" K&R 2010, 8, 8. At the time of writing this section (early 2015) two members were recently retired State Premiers and the other three were serving Premiers.

members; these latter must not belong to any government or legislature.[40] The Administrative Council also appoints and supervises the Director-General and approves the budget and annual accounts.[41] Thus the Administrative Council, as its name suggests, is concerned largely with financial, personnel and technical matters; advice on and guidelines about programme content come from the Television Council.[42]

So much for the rules as they appear on paper; for, as so often, they conceal a different and more complicated reality – one that is even more saturated with party-political influence. The starting point for the real story are the so-called "friendship circles". Behind this innocent moniker lurk informal party groupings: both the Television Council and the Administrative Council are staffed by persons who belong to these groupings. There are two of them, one for the Social Democrats and one for the conservative Union parties, and they meet on the night before the formal meeting of the board in question just like a party caucus, although their decisions are not binding in any formal or informal sense upon the members; they discuss and vote informally upon the matters to be considered the next day.[43] At last report, about two-thirds to three-quarters of the Television Council were members of "friendship circles", and at least ten of the fourteen members of the Administrative Council belonged to them (until 2012, it was virtually all of them).[44]

This practice is obviously of very long standing, as it was established by the time that Professor Arthur Williams wrote his study of *Broadcasting and Democracy in West Germany*[45] in 1976. Indeed, he recorded that this practice was thought to have originated in German broadcasting with the Z.D.F. and added loftily, 'The

40 § 24 (1) (b) of the *Z.D.F. Agreement*.

41 § 23 of the *Z.D.F. Agreement*.

42 Frank in Schiwy/Schütz/Dörr (eds.), *Medienrecht*, p. 505; Hahn in Hahn/Vesting (eds.), *Beck'scher Kommentar*, pp. 663f.

43 BVerfGE 136, 9, 18; Stuiber, *Medien in Deutschland*, p. 871.

44 Hahn, *Aufsicht*, p. 183; Heinicke, „„Mainz bleibt Mainz'? : Das Z.D.F. und die *Causa* Brender" KJ 2010, 458, 460; Huber, „Staatsfreiheit", p. 502; Kepplinger/Hartmann, *Stachel oder Feigenblatt? : Rundfunk- und Fernsehräte in der Bundesrepublik Deutschland – eine empirische Untersuchung* (Institut für Medienentwicklung und Kommunikation, Frankfurt/M. 1989), p. 62. BVerfGE 136, 9, 18, 62 states that almost all members of the Television Council belong to a "friendship circle", but I prefer the more conservative figure.

45 Bradford U.P., 1976.

manner in which the political parties have on occasion conducted themselves is evidence of the immaturity that persists in political life in the Federal Republic'.[46]

Perhaps a kinder view would be that, in a body of seventy-seven members like the Television Council, some organising principle is required, and in the German polity, saturated as it is with party influence, political viewpoint is the obvious candidate for that role. Political parties' role in the polity as opinion-forming mechanisms is also expressly recognised in Article 21 of the Basic Law – constitutionally, they do not lead the sort of twilight existence that they traditionally have led in common-law countries. Indeed, some members of the two governing bodies can be found who welcome the extra influence that political outsiders from various lobby groups obtain through the friendship circles, while others see them as a necessary evil;[47] 26% of the members of the Z.D.F.'s Television Council thought that the importance of the "friendship circles" was exaggerated in one survey from the late 1980s.[48] It also true that the *Z.D.F. Agreement*[49] solemnly states that members of the two Councils are not bound by instructions – using similar wording to Article 38 (1) of the Basic Law's comparable proclamation about the status of members of Parliament, a proclamation which is largely nullified by the realities of party discipline. However, the more fluid membership and fewer sanctions available to the "friendship circles" – many people are members whose careers and incomes do not depend upon their following the party line – mean that this fine principle does have some effect in the Z.D.F.'s governing bodies even though it is largely theory rather than practice in relation to Parliament.

Nevertheless, the political parties have succeeded in capturing to some considerable extent the governing bodies of this media institution (and of others not the subject of this chapter), which are meant to be checking up on those very same parties and the governments that they run. This is not atypical of the way in which the German party-state runs. It need hardly be added that the "friendship circles" do not meet in public – nor, at the time of the Court's decision of 2014, did either the Television or the Administrative Council, although the Television Council

46 At p. 120.

47 Buchwald, „Öffentlich-rechtlicher Rundfunk : Institutionen – Auftrag – Programme" in Schwarzkopf (ed.), *Rundfunkpolitik in Deutschland : Wettbewerb und Öffentlichkeit* (Deutscher Taschenbuchverlag, Munich 1989), p. 401; Kepplinger/Hartmann, *Stachel oder Feigenblatt?,* p. 61; Williams, *Broadcasting and Democracy*, p. 125; *cf.* also Hahn, *Aufsicht*, p. 182.

48 Kepplinger/Hartmann, *Stachel oder Feigenblatt?,* p. 61.

49 §§ 21 (9), 24 (5).

did publish agendas and reports on its website[50] – and thus the most obvious way of becoming better informed about and providing oversight of what any of these bodies does is not available.

In his dissenting judgment, Justice Paulus gave further information about how things really work along with one further point of criticism:

> The official meetings largely follow the agreements between the friendship circles. Anyone who does not submit to the dual political structure largely forfeits influence. This may be a means of preventing one-sided television reporting. But aside from that, societal or cultural diversity is not ensured, but rather the triumph of political interests – in themselves not illegitimate – is made possible. The representatives of societal groups are far too dependent upon parties for the achievement of their lobby-group interests to stand up for themselves in debate. Thus television becomes a site for political arguments not an experimental laboratory of diversity. The boards – and thus the broadcasters – adjust to politics, not politics to the functions of the boards.
>
> Oral argument gave illustrations of this. Thus the present Director-General of the Z.D.F. described the functioning of a typical meeting of the Television Council: on the evening beforehand he goes to the friendship circle of the [conservative] Union and his deputy to that of the Social Democrats. On being asked, he assured us that he occasionally does go to the other friendship circle; as they tend to take place in the same hotel but at the same time, participation in both was usually not possible. […] In the Administrative Council, the Director-General negotiates directly with the representative of State governments, who are either State Premiers or from the State Premier's Office.[51]

It should also be added that in Germany in recent years the federal and some State governments have frequently consisted of a Grand Coalition of the two largest parties, the conservative Union and the Social Democrats, which also dominate appointments to the broadcasters' governing bodies. If we compare this state of affairs with the fine principles with which we began, we see, without putting too fine a point on it, a marked gap. Not only has the state failed in its positive duty to ensure the freedom of the media; the arrangements adopted do not even give effect to the negative obligation to avoid political interference.

This unsatisfactory state of affairs might have continued indefinitely had not one of the major parties pushed its luck too far in an incident that forms the final piece of background to the decision of 25 March 2014. The "Brender incident" occurred in 2009 when Nikolaus Brender, the Editor-in-Chief of the Z.D.F., found

50 http://www.zdf.de/zdf-fernsehrat-funktion-vorsitz-und-mitglieder-25100018.html.

51 BVerfGE 136, 9, 62f.

the renewal of his contract blocked by the Z.D.F.'s Administrative Council.[52] Under the *Z.D.F. Agreement* the Editor-in-Chief was appointed by the Director-General with the concurrence of the Administrative Council (§ 27 (2)), the smaller of the two governing bodies with fourteen members. The forces ranged against Herr Brender were led by Roland Koch, the conservative and very outspoken Premier of the State of Hesse, and Edmund Stoiber, a comparably hard-line State Premier from Germany's "deep South", Bavaria. The objections of those two gentlemen were stated to be grounded in a loss of viewers for the main news programme of the Z.D.F. – no less than 26% over the preceding seven years – but it was also impossible to avoid the suspicion that political objections existed. Not that it could be said that Herr Brender was in any way a partisan of the other side of politics; he is perhaps best known for his by now legendary, lengthy and occasionally fierce clash with Social Democrat Chancellor Gerhard Schröder during the discussion of the results on the evening of the federal election of 2005. It may be that Herr Brender's robust independence, lack of pusillanimity in his interactions with politicians as well as his non-participation in the mutual back-scratching among politicians and media people were the true reasons for his downfall. Notably, Herr Brender had refused to attend the "friendship circles".

Although Herr Brender's successor, Peter Frey, was a thoroughly worthy occupant of the Editor-in Chief's chair, the refusal of the Administrative Council to renew Brender's contract in November 2009 was the straw that broke the camel's back: two Social Democratic States, Rhineland-Palatinate[53] followed by Hamburg, commenced the litigation challenging the make-up of the Z.D.F.'s governing bodies that culminated in the decision of 25 March 2014.

---

52 This incident is documented in the following sources, from which the account that follows is largely taken : Degenhart, K&R 2010, 8; Heinicke, KJ 2010, 458; Schäfer, „Die ‚*Causa* Brender' : vom öffentlichen Streit um die Vertragsverlängerung des Z.D.F.-Chefredakteurs zur Diskussion um den politischen Einfluß auf den Rundfunk" Gesellschaft, Wirtschaft, Politik 59 (2010), 111.

53 Kirchberg, K&R 2014, 1137, 1137f states that Rhineland-Palatinate had attempted to achieve reform within the political process, but had failed. It is also worth noting that that State's Premier, the prominent Social Democrat Kurt Beck, was at that time Chairman of the Z.D.F.'s Television Council. See also above, fn 35.

4. The decision of 25 March 2014

a. Majority

The challenge, as a matter of constitutional technicality, was to the sixteen States' statutes that endorsed the *Z.D.F. Agreement*.[54] However, the Court's decision directly invalidated portions of the Agreement itself, above all the provisions mentioned above dividing the membership of the Television Council among the States, the federation, the political parties, the Churches and the Jewish Council as well as the representatives of specified and unspecified societal interest groups. The Court further disapproved of the provision for sixteen unspecified interest-group representatives to be selected by the State Premiers, but not the Premiers' power to select the twenty-five other non-political representatives from specified organisations – rather, it decreed that such representatives could not in future be selected from elected officials (including parliamentarians), officials holding political functions such as mayors[55] or those holding comparable positions in political parties.[56] Furthermore, it decreed that State Premiers could reject names proposed to them by the nominating organisations only if 'particular legal reasons'[57] justified rejection – which reflected the practice anyway,[58] although the existence of a power to reject will inevitably influence, at least on occasions, the shape of proposals made. In each case, the constitutional problem was that the rules as they stood produced insufficient separation between the governing bodies of the broadcasting entity and the state.

The Court also declared, for similar reasons, the make-up of the fourteen-member Administrative Council – the body that had in effect sacked Herr Brender – unconstitutional. This was the first time that the Court had dealt with this body or its equivalents in other broadcasters in any of its decisions on constitutional broadcasting law.[59]

54 Listed at BVerfGE 136, 9, 14f.

55 BVerfGE 136, 9, 40. The judgment left open, and it is consequently unclear how far this prohibition extends down into the ranks of local councils : Hesse/Schneider, NVwZ 2014, 881, 881.

56 BVerfGE 136, 9, 41, 47f.

57 BVerfGE 136, 9, 53.

58 See above, fn 37.

59 Hahn, *Aufsicht*, p. 190.

As sometimes happens in German constitutional law (and also occurs in Canada),[60] the Court declared that the invalidity of the provisions in question would be postponed until 30 June 2015 in order to give the sixteen States responsible for creating the Z.D.F. and determining its constitution – the *Z.D.F. Agreement* – necessary time to come up with replacement rules.

In its decision, the Court re-affirmed (at some length – this is also usual) its previous case law on the need for legislation not merely to avoid trespassing on freedom of opinion, but actively to promote it as a part of securing the right to all Germans, along with its long-held view that the creation of diversity could not be left to the market.[61]

The Court described how these principles cashed out when applied to the composition of the governing bodies of a public broadcaster, and in so doing revealed its deep awareness of the criticisms made of the current arrangements:

> The make-up of the multi-member organs must be aimed at bringing together people with the most diverse possible perspectives and experiences from all areas of communal life. In so doing the legislature must consider in particular the necessity of not reflecting, in the first instance, official and other perspectives and views which are instrumental in the creation of state and political outcomes, but rather bringing to the fore a broad range of views of diverse societal forces. The legislature must ensure that account is taken, in selecting members of the boards, of the most varied groups possible – not merely large ones with an influence on public life but also smaller ones which may not have access to the media – and also that perspectives not coherently organised as interest groups are reflected. The organisation of public broadcasting must be designed, in relation to the make-up of the boards as elsewhere, to give effect to the obligation to provide diverse programming beyond that which private providers offer. The legislature must also comply with equality principles relating to gender as set out in Article 3 II 2 of the Basic Law.
>
> That the governing boards are composed of such groups as are mostly organised in associations does not have the purpose of confiding to them the configuration of programming, let alone making them beneficiaries of the basic right of broadcasting freedom. The oversight committees are rather trustees of the interests of the public. In programming design they are intended to ensure that the persons and bodies responsible allow sufficient time in the whole programme offering to all significant political, world-view and societal forces, even if the variety of them can never be represented completely or even by proxy, even by a board which is appointed in a balanced way from plural groups. The appointment of members using the device of various societal groups does not make them

60 *E.g.* in *Attorney-General for Canada* v. *Bedford* [2013] 3 SCR 1101, 1164f; also authorized by s 172 (1) (b) (ii) of the Constitution of South Africa.

61 On that point, see also BVerfGE 57, 295, 322; Wittemann, (2010) 33 Hastings Int & Comp LR 95, 101.

> representatives of their specific fields, but is merely a means of finding trustees for the public independent of state organs and of bringing in experiences from different sectors of society – thus ensuring that programming does not serve one-sidedly a party, a group, an interest group, a creed or a *Weltanschauung* and that in reporting the views of affected persons, groups of offices are adequately and fairly taken into account.[62]

The Court approved of the appointment of governmental representatives to the governing bodies 'to a narrowly defined extent' and pointed out that they, as politicians, are reliant upon 'open, many-faceted and critical reporting'.[63] On the other hand, the principle requiring broadcasters to be distanced from the state meant that 'the make-up of the [governing] bodies must itself exclude the possibility of an instrumentalisation of reporting in the interests of such actors',[64] *i.e.* politicians. In the result the Court declared that these two principles could be reconciled if the proportion of members of each governing body and their committees who were direct or indirect representatives of the state was limited to one-third.[65] In so doing it took into account 'the power of state-based and particularly party-political communications structures to shape affairs, as currently finds expression in the friendship circles'.[66] Such a limit would ensure that political representatives would have neither a majority nor a veto in relation to decisions, such as the appointment of the Director-General, for which a three-fifths majority is required by the *Z.D.F. Agreement*.[67]

This otherwise fairly arbitrary[68] limit of one-third of political members should be selected, the Court held, in a manner which ensured diversity of views, most obviously by including a variety of parties, although the precise manner of doing so was a matter for the legislature and the Court would ensure only that the

62 BVerfGE 136, 9, 31f.

63 BVerfGE 136, 9, 32.

64 BVerfGE 136, 9, 36.

65 BVerfGE 136, 9, 37, 39.

66 BVerfGE 136, 9, 38.

67 BVerfGE 136, 9, 38.

68 Kirchberg, K&R 2014, 1137, 1138 adds that this limit was a common one in practice in other public broadcasting stations, and perhaps the Court felt that it should not upset their arrangements as well.
The one-third limit is also in accordance with the express statement in Art. 111a II 3 of the Bavarian Constitution that 'the proportion of representatives from the State government, the legislature and the Senate [now abolished] in the supervisory organs must not exceed one-third'. An attempt to apply this to the Z.D.F. failed in BayVerfGH 42, 11 (1989), as the one-third limit was certainly not reached in the Z.D.F. as far as the Bavarian State government and legislature alone were concerned.

principles adopted and the result were within the acceptable range.[69] That was not so at present, which was why the composition of the two governing bodies was held invalid.

The Court, having already, as we saw in the quotation above, found that that the general principles favouring diversity applied as well to the two-thirds of members of the governing bodies who were not to be associated with the state,[70] held that incompatibility rules were required to ensure that these two-thirds were not colonised by politicians: government members, parliamentarians, high political office-holders and party functionaries would all need to be excluded from sneaking in *via* the back door and holding any of the two-thirds of positions reserved for non-state members.[71]

However, the Court accepted that a lower degree of diversity might be acceptable for the fourteen-member Administrative Council, particularly if the decision's principles were adhered to in choosing its members.[72] But this was also not so as the law then stood. It should be recalled that the Administrative Council is elected by the Television Council by a three-fifths majority under § 24 (1) (b) of the *Z.D.F. Agreement*, and the Television Council is itself tainted by excessive political influence, as previously demonstrated.[73] Because 'government members and other representatives of the executive must not have a decisive influence on the choice or appointment of non-state members'[74] of either governing body, the composition of the Administrative Council was therefore also constitutionally invalid because the electoral organ for the Administrative Council was not sufficiently divorced from the state.

However, a clear gap exists here, which can be explained only by necessity: the Court did not say that members of legislatures, as distinct from executives, could not have a decisive influence on the choice of governing bodies' members. For if they could not, who else – aside from the even more political executive government – could act on behalf of a State and choose its representatives? Thus members of State parliaments will count towards the one-third limit of political members if elected to the Television Council, but would be permitted to elect some of that same body's members (and thus also to influence the composition of the Administrative Council). While, unlike with us, State governments' ministers are,

69 BVerfGE 136, 9, 41f.

70 See above, fn 62; BVerfGE 136, 9, 44f.

71 BVerfGE 136, 9, 47–49.

72 BVerfGE 136, 9, 57.

73 BVerfGE 136, 9, 56.

74 BVerfGE 136, 9, 43.

in Germany, not always members of the legislature, and are certainly not required to be, and therefore the executive does not necessarily dominate the legislature by its mere presence and numbers, it is nevertheless the case in Germany also that the legislatures are the place where the government is formed by majority on the floor. State legislatures are therefore, as a rule, just as much under the domination of the governing party or parties as with us, and since the abolition of the Bavarian Senate in the late 1990s none has had an upper House which might have a non-government majority either.

As previously noted in passing, both for the Administrative and Television Councils the Court decreed by five votes to three that greater transparency in their operations was required in the interests of promoting the well-known benefits of transparency such as exposure to scrutiny and ensuring that decisions are taken for proper purposes, not just through behind-the-scenes deals.[75] Clearly the Court had the "friendship circles" in mind here.[76] The Court said:

> What degree of transparency is required for a proper discharge of functions is not indicated in detail in the Constitution. It is the function of the legislature to take care to ensure that in the governing bodies of public broadcasters a balance is found between the principle of public supervision of broadcasting and the confidentiality necessary for effective committee work. In particular it is for the legislature to decide whether the basic principle of public sittings is to apply to the work of the governing bodies. All that is required are rules that ensure a minimum of transparency. This does however include the availability of information about organisational structures, the composition of the boards and their sub-committees as well as future agendas, and also that at least in principle the minutes of meetings are available promptly or that some other way is found of informing the public of the subject of deliberations and their results in a substantial way.[77]

As with a modern legislature, however, publication of the official proceedings and even holding them in public only help the cause of openness to a limited degree if everything is first decided in advance in caucus meetings held behind closed doors.

b. Justice Paulus's dissent

While three Judges dissented on the transparency point, they were clearly content merely to record their disagreement with the new principle and did not reveal their reasons, or even their names. It may be assumed that they did so because

75 BVerfGE 136, 9, 49–51, 55, 57.
76 Kirchberg, K&R 2014, 1137, 1139.
77 BVerfGE 136, 9, 50f.

they were not certain that the decision needed to deal with that point. The only published dissent was that of Justice Andreas Paulus.

He would have gone further than the majority, and in his judgment would have required 'a thorough removal of all state influence in the television governing bodies';[78] 'it is not apparent to me why the presence of the executive in Television and Administrative Councils should be seen to serve the creation and maintenance of broadcasting freedom'.[79]

Justice Paulus also faced, however, the dilemma of selecting staff for his utopia.

> The inclusion of governmental representatives appears [...] to be unnecessary, as the participation of representatives of parliaments and parties can ensure the inclusion of varied political perspectives to the same extent. In their case the danger of political instrumentalisation is lower, as they are not immediately involved in decisions at governmental level, but rather, as members of parliament and participants in political opinion-forming, have a role which is itself independent with respect to the government. On the other hand government members – despite their independence as members of governing bodies – will always be tempted to use their powers of influence to give effect to government policies. Logically they must therefore be totally excluded from membership in the Television and Administrative Councils.[80]

Not everyone will be convinced that party and state can be so easily separated. The logical reaction to this on the part of the executive would be to find backbenchers who are eager for promotion, and thus to please. And despite all this, Justice Paulus further suggested that half of the one-third proportion of executive representatives allowed by the majority, *i.e.* one-sixth, could be just tolerable in the Television Council – but none in the Administrative Council.[81] Where that proposed limit comes from is anyone's guess.

5. Commentary

As can be seen, both Germany and Australia have struggled with the challenge of making a public broadcaster responsible to the public while avoiding the pitfall of making it the creature of those who – nominally – represent the public but are also the chief targets of media scrutiny.

The praiseworthy principles underlying German constitutional broadcasting law can be seen to suffer from multiple structural contradictions in practice

78 BVerfGE 136, 9, 63.
79 BVerfGE 136, 9, 65.
80 BVerfGE 136, 9, 66.
81 BVerfGE 136, 9, 67.

leading to difficulty in implementing them in practice. The overarching one has already been mentioned, namely that the state, *i.e.* politicians, is both responsible for the rules and the danger against the rules must guard[82] – essentially the same difficulty that afflicts Australia. The reverse side of this coin is that politicians are supposedly elected to represent the public and thus should have a role in democratic oversight of public broadcasters, but at the same time it is they that the media are supposed to watch over. Making something subject to constitutional rules as in Germany does not suspend the power relationships that shape the polity – it is important to be realistic and modest about what the law, including constitutional law, can do.

Further contradictions between ideal and reality can be discerned. As the Federal Constitutional Court has pointed out, a political party does not exist for the sake of promoting opinions other than its own, for the promotion of pluralism – it exists to have its views adopted by the public.[83] Interest groups represented by governing bodies, too – despite the fine words of the Federal Constitutional Court about their being trustees for the public,[84] which, given that the Judges are not fools, are hortatory rather than descriptive – do not exist for the general public good but for the sake of the interest they represent, and that is how they usually see their role in public broadcasting bodies as well: they are, and act as, lobby groups.[85] In short, as the Federal Constitutional Court has also pointed out, the method of selection of and the role to be filled by the members of the governing boards are in crass contradiction.[86] No wonder, then, that the product does not match the advertising!

Nor is there any easy solution in sight. There is just no alternative structure standing by to provide an alternative but less politicised source of legitimacy in the selection of members of the governing councils[87] – and indeed Australian experience gives rise to the suspicion that any attempt to create one will immediately run the risk of colonisation by politicians. Nor is there any obvious way of preventing like-minded people from meeting before a formal sitting of a body,

82 Cornils, ZJS 2014, 447, 449; Hahn, *Aufsicht*, p. 163; Schulze-Fielitz in Dreier (ed.), *Grundgesetz Kommentar*, p. 724; Wittemann, (2010) 33 Hastings Int & Comp LJ 95, 137.

83 BVerfGE 60, 53, 67; *cf.* also Huber, „Staatsfreiheit", p. 507.

84 See above, fn 62.

85 Buchwald, „Öffentlich-rechtlicher Rundfunk", p. 403.

86 BVerfGE 83, 238, 334f.

87 Lenski, „Der lange Schatten" at http://www.verfassungsblog.de/lange-schatten-von-art-21-gg-staatsferne-staatsfreiheit-und-machterhalt-im-zdf-staatsvertrag/.

in "friendship circles" or elsewhere. Members of governing councils are likely to have, in the main, recognisable political allegiances, and they cannot be prevented from consulting each other.[88] A final problem is that there is no easy measurable means of determining the success of a public broadcaster comparable to profit or audience share in the private sector (although it will be recalled that the anti-Brender forces tried to use audience share against him – although their argument would doubtless have been that the decline was so precipitous that it could not be simply ignored as too crude a measure of success).

It would, in fact, require a complete change in political culture for any thorough reform to be possible,[89] or some seriously "blue sky" thinking would have to be undertaken – such as considering the selection of boards by a committee consisting of those on whom a high civil honour had been conferred, such as a Knighthood or Companionship in the Order of Australia or a certain class of the equivalent German award, the *Bundesverdienstkreuz*. Such a proposal would be most obviously open to attack as involving elitism and a lack of democratic accountability – which would again raise the tension between making broadcasters accountable to the public while trying to stay away from the only set of elected officials we have, namely politicians. What would really sink any such proposal, however, would be the unwillingness of politicians to let go of control to such an extent. If there were an easy and complete solution to this particular set of problems, no doubt it would have been thought of long ago.

6. Conclusion

In June 2015 the State Premiers signed an amendment to the *Z.D.F. Agreement*,[90] which at the time of writing each of the sixteen State parliaments had either passed into law or were about to do so. With one significant exception, the amendments adhered closely to the minimum standards demanded by the Federal Constitutional Court in its decision of 25 March 2014, and accordingly have effected a substantial but not revolutionary improvement. Even quite mild innovations were not carried out, most notably allowing public-interest groups to nominate themselves for a place on the Television Council as can happen with the Central German Broadcasting network based in Leipzig – an option which the Court had specifically referred to in its decision.[91]

88 Buchwald, „Öffentlich-rechtlicher Rundfunk", p. 402; Degenhart, K&R 2014, 340, 341.
89 Degenhart, K&R 2014, 340, 341; Heinicke, KJ 2010, 458, 462.
90 The copy I am using is that of the Bremen State Parliament, Printed Paper 18/1816.
91 BVerfGE 136, 9, 46; M.D.R.-Staatsvertrag § 19 III, I Nr 16; Cornils, ZJS 2014, 447, 451.

Herr Nikolaus Brender, the man whose sacking in 2009 sparked off the Court case, was reported to have expressed his disappointment, referring to the amendments as 'the work of bureaucrats in State premiers' offices, who wanted it sorted out as noiselessly as possible' and as still leaving much to be desired as far as pluralism was concerned; there had been insufficient public discussion of the topic, he thought, partly because the civil servants had wanted to get it out of the way as quickly and conveniently as possible.[92] Even nine States, those mostly in left-wing hands, added an addendum to the package of amendments stating that they wished to see an early review of whether there was further need for improvement on the pluralism front, with particular reference to the role of State parliaments. That having been said, there was an obvious conflict between the aims of increasing pluralism and decreasing the number of members of the two Councils, which, as noted earlier,[93] were large and perhaps unwieldy by comparison with other broadcasting bodies.'[94]

What, then, were the changes made to the *Z.D.F. Agreement* as a result of the Premiers' agreement in mid-2015? The starting point was the reduction of the Television Council from seventy-seven to sixty, and of the Administrative Council from fourteen to twelve members. In both Councils, exactly one-third – the highest proportion allowed by the Court's decision – were to be political representatives. A ban was introduced on politicians being representatives of interest groups in order to ensure that the one-third limit was not exceeded, and the twelve representatives of political parties in the *Bundestag* were completely deleted. Minor adjustments were also made to the number of representatives of the named interest groups in the Television Council order to achieve the reduction of the number of members.

In the case of the Television Council the twenty governmental members allowed will now consist of one representative for each of the sixteen States, two federal representatives and two from local government; in the case of the Administrative Council, there will be four rather the former five members for the States, none rather than one for the federal government and eight, as previously, from outside the ranks of governments and legislatures.

In one significant point the amendments went beyond what was strictly required. It was noted above that it would be possible for members selected by State legislatures to count as non-governmental; but the amendments stated that, in

92 http://www.deutschlandradiokultur.de/neuer-zdf-staatsvertrag-das-ist-ttip-hoch-drei.1013.de.html?dram:article_id=321219.

93 See above, fn 25.

94 Cornils, ZJS 2014, 447, 451.

future, the interest groups would select their own representatives: there would no longer be any official filter.[95] There were also various minor adjustments to the precise list of named interest groups.

A further innovation was the idea that each of the non-specified interest groups – there continued to be sixteen of them – would be allocated to a specified State for individual nomination. Thus, Baden-Württemberg would select the consumers' representative, Bavaria the representative for digital matters, Berlin the Internet expert, and so on. There is, however, no rule in the *Z.D.F. Agreement* that the representative must be a resident of the State concerned. Notable additions to the list of represented groups included a migrants' representative to be selected by Hesse, Muslims (the State of Lower Saxony) and gays, lesbians, bisexuals, transgender people *etc.* by the State of Thuringia – which, unlike Berlin, for example, is not particularly noted for its sexual diversity. It is a bit of a mystery how this allocation of interest groups to States was arranged. Individual State laws will regulate the manner in which each selection is to take place, which might not always be an easy process. In September 2015 the State Thuringia, which is one of the States involved in Central German Broadcasting, had passed a Bill to amend the *State Media Act*.[96] It provided a new s 53 of the *State Media Act* declaring that, as with Central German Broadcasting, representatives of sexual minority groups with a base in the State would be able to apply for the sole spot reserved for such groups on the Z.D.F.'s Television Council, and the decision among the applicants would be made by the State Parliament.

Rules were also introduced requiring gender balance to be considered and in aid of transparency. In future the Television Council must sit in public unless there is a good reason for a private session such as confidential personnel matters. It remains to be seen whether this will lead to a real increase in public information, let alone participation in its affairs, or whether it will merely drive the real decision-making behind closed doors and render the public sittings a mere formality. A paragraph was also added stating that the members of the Television Council and the Administrative Council are 'trustees for the public' – a phrase clearly taken from the Court's judgment.[97] As already noted, this is more an appeal to a sense of duty than a description of what actually occurs and there is no reason to think that interest groups will suddenly change their approach.

95 See above, fn 26.
96 Gesetz- und Verordnungsblatt für den Freistaat Thüringen, 1 October 2015, p. 134.
97 See above, fn 62.

One further item that remains on the agenda is a review of the governance arrangements of other public broadcasters to ensure that they are in accordance with the principles enunciated by the Court; although its decision of 25 March 2014 applies directly only to the Z.D.F., clearly its principles might well be applied to others. Thus the *Bundestag*'s Committee for Culture and the Media has referred to the principal German state broadcaster, the A.R.D.:

> As well as the work that has just been done as an immediate reaction to the judgment of 25 March 2014 and the consequent need to bring the governance arrangements up to constitutional muster, thought must also be given to whether other public broadcasters' governance, notably that of the A.R.D. (Channel 1), is in accordance with the principles decreed by the Court.[98]

98 Press release available at www.bundestag.de/presse/hib/2014_04/01/263120; Cornils, ZJS 2014, 447, 451.

Justin Malbon

Geo-Pricing of Digital Media: European and Australian Policy Debates Compared

Abstract: Geographically based discriminatory pricing of digital products can affect access to media and media diversity. Geo-pricing tends to be resented by consumers who perceive themselves to be global 'net-citizens'. This chapter explores regulatory debates in Europe and Australia about whether the practice should be supported or constrained.

1. Introduction

Media content delivery was once more controllable than today. Radio and television would broadcast content to a particular region, and not beyond. Creative content contained in physical items such as books, records, CDs and DVDs was sold at set prices within defined geographical borders. For the most part consumers were content with the prices they paid for content and were mostly ignorant of the prices it sold for in other countries. If an interloper were to attempt to disrupt this state of affairs by broadcasting beyond geographical boundaries, or by importing CDs from another country and selling them at a lower price, creative content owners could attack the interloper with the aid of copyright laws that effectively prohibited transnational broadcasting and parallel importing of copyright related products.

Under the old order content owners and providers determined whether specified content would be provided to a particular geographical region (usually a particular country), and if provided, when it would be provided, and at what price. Invariably, different prices would be set for each different geographic location, that is to say providers used **geo-pricing**.

The old order still stands but is increasingly threatened by the internet. It is by inclination mindless of national borders. An email to a next-door neighbour requires about the same effort and financial cost as to someone on the other side of the planet. Creative content in digital form can be transmitted via the internet with equal ease and cost regardless of the recipient's location.

This chapter focuses attention on digital media and the ways providers seek to maintain geo-pricing. **Digital media** includes audio and visual content in a digital format that can be downloaded or streamed. The content includes sports events, television shows, movies, music, e-books, games and software. Pricing of digital media is usually set at a price for a downloadable unit, or a monthly or annual subscription fee for the use of a content providing service. For example, a monthly fee might be set for online access to sports games, televisions shows, movies or music via the provider's platform. Subscription arrangements can also operate for software and games.

Providers typically enforce geo-pricing by purposefully deploying measures to overcome the internet's geographical agnosticism. A common approach is geo-blocking, which involves the provider's computer server identifying a consumer's location from the consumer's internet protocol (IP) address. An IP address is a unique number a device uses to identify it and to communicate with other devices, and is akin to the device's 'mailing address'. The provider's server either refuses to make the sale to the consumer because of the location signalled by their IP address, or it sets a differential price for the product on sale. Providers might also reinforce any technical inhibiters with legal mechanisms, including copyright law, to undertake or threaten legal action to prevent any by-passing of geo-pricing.

The internet threatens geo-pricing strategies in a number of ways. First, consumers are more aware of price differences than before the internet because of the relative ease of product and price comparison, and armed with this knowledge will often seek to purchase a product from a location offering a lower price. Second, they can proceed to purchase unless barriers are placed in their way. Third, consumers often resent being inhibited from purchasing the product at a cheaper price from another location, and will sometimes seek to by-pass any imposed barriers.

Hard battles are being waged by industry players, such as content owners and providers, to maintain geo-pricing. Industry advocates that governments and regulators should maintain and enhance copyright and other laws to prevent parallel importing of digital media, and to prohibit systems and practices that circumvent geo-blocking. To justify their cause, industry portrays their enemies, the circumventers (including consumers), as pirates and thieves.[1] The circumventers will often feel justified in their actions, however, because they resent being denied access to content they demand or resent the 'unfair' prices they are required to pay relative to the prices set for consumers in other locations.

Policy-makers and legislators are caught in the middle of this battle. If they were to be sympathetic to the wishes of their constituents, who are the numerically superior consumers in their jurisdiction, they may well be inclined to characterise geo-pricing as harmful and therefore impose measures to prevent it, or at least not offer it further legislative or regulatory support. If they favour industry they are left to decide whether they should extend prohibitions on circumvention and widen copyright law, or whether they should sit back and leave the market to take care of itself.

The policy directions in Europe and Australia are uncertain and contested. Europe, however, appears to be favouring consumer sentiment, and consequently policy is shifting against geo-pricing for digital media, at least as it arises when both the provider and the consumer are located in a EU member state. European policy and law may in some circumstance characterise intra-EU geo-pricing as anti-competitive and undermining the single European market. In Australia the debate about geo-pricing centres around consumer resentment of the perceived unfairness of geo-pricing in which they are seen to be paying far more than others for digital media. Geo-pricing is sometimes characterised as an 'Australia tax' set by industry.[2] In response to this perceived unfair practice, there are calls for removing parallel importing restrictions on digital media, amending copyright law to allow circumvention, and, as a last resort if these measures do not succeed, banning geo-pricing outright.[3]

The policy debate is important, and has significant implications for industry revenue, and for consumer access to content at 'reasonable' and 'fair' prices. To more fully comprehend the issues at stake it is necessary to understand the nature and dynamics of discriminatory pricing –geo-pricing being a form of discriminatory pricing, which are outlined in Part 2. Linked to discussions about

1 See P Loughlan, 'Pirates, Parasites, Reapers, Sowers, Fruits, Foxes… The Metaphors of Intellectual Property' (2006) 28 *Sydney Law Review* 210 at 217.

2 Parliament of the Commonwealth of Australia, House of Representatives Standing Committee on Infrastructure and Communications, (2013) 'At What Cost? IP Pricing and the Australia Tax' (Canberra) the "IP Review" at vii; and I Harper, P Anderson, S McCluskey and M O'Bryan (2015) *Competition Policy Review Final Report,* Commonwealth of Australia the "Harper Review" at p. 47.

3 Recommendations 4. 5, 8, 9 and 10 of the IP Pricing Review, *above*, at, pp. xii and xiii.

discriminatory pricing are questions about whether it enhances or undermines economic welfare; which is discussed in Part 3. Arguably, it is only reasonably practicable to implement discriminatory pricing, and more specifically for present purposes, geo-pricing, if the seller holds a monopoly or near monopoly position in the relevant market and therefore has a market dominant position and uses that position to exercise market power. If the seller does hold market dominance, it raises anti-competition concerns. This is the locus of the European debate about the geo-pricing of digital media, and is discussed in Part 4.

Given Australian hostility to geo-pricing, the question arises as to whether Australians are in fact paying significantly more for digital media than consumers in comparable high income countries. The discussion in Part 5 points to evidence that both confirms and raises doubt about that. If, however, Australians are required to pay significantly higher prices and they are aware of it, this may prompt some to resent it and seek to circumvent geo-pricing systems, and even engage in illegal downloading and streaming. In apparent response to consumer resentment of perceived unfair pricing policy makers are proposing law reforms to permit parallel importing and circumvention. If these reforms were introduced it could seriously undermine geo-pricing strategies.

Parallel imported products are genuine products imported into a country by someone other than the authorised or licenced distributor or manufacturer.[4] Parallel importing digital media can be contentious because it invariably has associated intellectual property (IP) rights, such as copyright, patent or trademark rights. The IP rights holder might seek to pursue a geo-pricing strategy by setting licensing conditions for the sale of the digital product items which purport to restrict the sale of an item to a specified jurisdiction. For example, the license might only permit a copy of a book, or an ebook to be sold in the US. Laws in another country might reinforce this licence condition by prohibiting the import of items without the rights holder's permission. Laws that permit importation despite any purported license condition restrictions effectively enable parallel importing of the product.

It is posited in this chapter that consumer resentments about the perceived unfairness of geo-pricing are fuelled in part to a growing sense by consumers that they hold a kind of dual citizenship in which they are both citizens of their home country and are 'net-citizens', who are global citizens entitled to access to content available to those located in other countries, and at the best price the global market has to offer. This proposition is discussed in Part 6. Content providers are

4 Harper Review, above note 2 at 166.

not clueless about the potential for their pricing strategies to trigger consumer resentment. Research regarding sellers' responses to potential resentment about pricing is discussed in Part 6.

The normative question raised in conclusion is what ought policy makers and legislators do about geo-pricing. It is proposed in this chapter that public policies and laws should align with broad public conceptions of fairness and equity. These are changing, in large measure because of the internet and the growing self-sense of consumers that they hold dual citizenship as net-citizens entitled to market access on a non-discriminatory basis. Laws and policies ought not, then, support geo-pricing, except to the extent they are based on capacity to pay. That is to say, geo-pricing that sets lower prices for consumers in developing and less developed countries can be supported on the basis of fairness and equity considerations. Such discrimination also aligns with broad public conceptions of fairness.

2. The Nature and Dynamics of Price Discrimination

Price discrimination is a term used by economists to describe the selling of the same product to different customers at different prices when the cost of sale is the same to each of them.[5] Geo-pricing is a form of discriminatory pricing.[6] Discriminatory pricing in its various forms is a widespread practice for selling consumer products, digital or otherwise. Discrimination might be based on a wide array of consumer characteristics, including their age, income, prior purchasing history and geographical location.

As an example of (non geo-pricing) discriminatory pricing; the person sitting next to you in a movie theatre may have paid less for their movie ticket than you if you paid the full adult price and they paid for a concessional student or pensioner ticket. As another example; the person sitting next to you on a commercial flight may have paid less for their ticket than you if, say, they purchased a non-refundable, non-transferrable and non-cancelerable ticket well in advance of the travel day, and you did not. Discriminatory pricing can take various other forms including discount pricing based on customer loyalty, and peak and off-peak pricing for electricity.

Generally, for a discriminatory pricing strategy to work different groups a seller's customers must be prepared to pay different prices for the seller's product. For example, a movie theatre must have some customers prepared to pay a full

---

5 R Posner (2001), *Antitrust Law* 2nd ed, (University of Chicago Press, Chicago) at pp. 79–80.

6 Discriminatory pricing is also known as differential or dynamic pricing.

movie ticket price whilst others such as students and pensioners are paying a lesser price. The students and pensioners should not be able to arbitrage by on-selling their tickets to non-students and non-pensioners. Arbitrage involves consumers purchasing a product unit at its lower price and selling it to consumers who would otherwise pay the seller's higher price. The arbitrage price will be somewhere between the lower price (so the arbitrageur makes a profit) and the seller's higher price (so that the ultimate purchaser benefits from the arbitrage price).

In summary, for price discrimination to operate effectively a number of preconditions need to be met, namely:

- the seller is able to identify different market segments;
- the different segments must have different price elasticities (ie the consumers in one segment has a different willingness to pay than the consumers in another segment);
- the segments must be kept separate (for example, have geographical separation);
- there must be no, or very little opportunities for arbitrage; and
- the seller must have some degree of monopoly power.[7]

A monopolist is often able to exercise monopoly power, otherwise known as market power. This arises if the seller has the ability to earn high profits by raising and keeping the prices of its products substantially above the levels of which those products would be priced in competitive markets. That is, the seller can charge high prices and get away with it. By contrast, in a competitive market, the market will punish a high price seller. Price discrimination allows the monopolist to increase its profit by charging customers a price closer to their willingness to pay than would otherwise be the case if it set a single price.

Economists categorise price discrimination as follows:

> First degree price discrimination. This occurs if the seller is able to evaluate each customer and charge according to that customer's willingness to pay. This is a largely theoretical strategy as it arises if a firm is able to charge the maximum possible price for each unit, enabling it to capture all available consumer surplus for itself. In reality, having such a high degree of market knowledge is often impracticable. It is possible in limited circumstances, for example if a land agent is able to gain detailed information of the potential buyers and assess the willingness to pay of each potential buyer.
>
> Second-degree price discrimination. This involves a group targeting strategy, in which different prices are offered to members of distinct groups. Reduced prices for pensioners and students for movie tickets or public transport are examples of this strategy.

7 T Harford (2007), *The Undercover Economist* (Abacus, London) at pp. 36–45.

> Third-degree price discrimination. This is the so-called 'self-incrimination' strategy. Here the seller offers products that are at least slightly different to each other. The seller, for example, may offer large, medium and small cups of coffee. The difference in the cost of making a large and a small coffee may be trivial, while the price differences are nontrivial. Those with a higher willingness to pay will self-select the higher cost cup of coffee.[8]

The practical difficulties of giving effect to first degree discrimination are to an extent being overcome with the aid of so called 'big data'. This usually involves a seller collecting extensive data on their customers' prior purchasing patterns, internet searching histories and other information about their income, and so forth. The seller's computer system will make assessments about each customer's willingness to pay and vary prices, or make product recommendations (sometimes at variant prices) accordingly. Researchers at Northeastern University in Boston undertook a study of automated recommendations made on a number of sites such as those operated by Netflix, Amazon and Yelp.[9] These sites offer personalised recommendations to users. A site may operate an algorithm which takes the uses history of prior searches into account to make a personalised recommendation for a product or service. The Northeastern University researchers found that in many cases the recommendations may be to the users' disadvantage by manipulating the products shown. The recommendations may involve steering users to higher priced products. This usually involves placing the higher-priced recommended products at the top of the recommendation list. The recommendations may also engage in another form of price discrimination by altering the price of products for different users.

More specifically the researchers found:

- Cheaptickets and Orbitz implement price discrimination by offering reduced prices on hotels to 'members'.
- Expedia and Hotels.com engage in a process that steers a subset of users towards more expensive hotels.
- Home Depot and Travelocity personalise search results for users on mobile devices.
- Priceline personalises search results based on a user's history of clicks and purchases.[10]

8 Above at pp. 36–45.

9 A Hannak, G Soeller, D Lazer, A Mislove and C Wilson, (2014) 'Measuring Price Discrimination and Steering on E-commerce Web Sites', ACM *Proceedings of the 2014 Conference on Internet Measurement Conference*, 305.

10 Above at 306.

3. Economic Welfare and Price Discrimination

Detractors and supporters of geo-pricing for digital media will often enlist economic arguments to justify their positions. This is possible in part because there are differences of opinion amongst economists as to the economic virtue of price discrimination. Opinion does, however, tend to the view that in many cases the practice is not economically damaging, and may be economically beneficial in particular cases. Care should be taken, however, to avoid making generalised *a priori* claims about the beneficial effects or otherwise of price discrimination. Meaningful assessments will usually require considering the facts of the particular product and marketplace being considered.

Generally, price discrimination is considered to be good if it enhances overall consumer welfare. Consumer welfare refers to the individual benefits derived from the consumption of goods and services in a market. Theoretically, individual welfare is an individual's own assessment of her satisfaction at purchasing a product at a given price. Measuring consumer welfare therefore requires information about individual preferences.[11] Economic assessments are complicated by the need for the assessor to determine whether the assessment of consumer welfare is made from the perspective of the market as a totality or from the perspective of a particular individual consumer. Welfare effects may also depend on whether the discriminatory pricing increases or decreases total output. According to Evans et al

> Economic theory shows that price discrimination can, in principle, be pro-competitive or anti-competitive depending on its impact on aggregate output. Price discrimination is welfare-enhancing when it facilitates access to the market for consumers with lower willingness to pay.[12]

Under a standard economic model, supply and demand for units of a product can be graphically represented with price on a vertical axis, quantity on a horizontal axis, and supply and demand curves being represented within the two axes. Typically, as price increases demand decreases, and vice versa. In a competitive market the unit price for a product will be the point at which the quantity of the product demanded will equal the quantity supplied, resulting in economic equilibrium. The demand curve can be seen as representing a statistical distribution of consumers' willingness to pay for the product. If every consumer had the same willingness to pay for a unit, the demand 'curve' would in fact be flat, and the seller would capture the entire consumer surplus with a uniform price.

---

11 https://stats.oecd.org/glossary/detail.asp?ID=3177.

12 D Evans, A Padilla and M Salinger (2006) 'A Pragmatic Approach to Identifying and Analysing Legitimate Tying Cases' 27 *European Competition Law Review* 535 at p. 563.

Consumer surplus can be illustrated with this example: assume I am willing to pay $800 for the 'vinyl collection 1970–78' of music recordings of the band Black Sabbath but I do not have to because the seller is offering it for sale at $500 a copy. The consumer surplus for this copy of the vinyl collection is $300. There may be other buyers willing to pay a price that is more than the $500 sale price. The total sum of the amounts consumers are willing to pay in excess of the $500 sale price equals the total consumer surplus. This reflects the total amount of 'enjoyment' consumers get, net of the price they actually paid. According to economic theory, consumer surplus comprises the uncompensated positive externalities in the market for production.

Consumer surplus is not necessarily a problem if the unit price for the product is above the marginal cost for producing and selling it. In this situation the seller will benefit despite not capturing the consumer surplus.

In practice the demand 'curve' will be curved and rarely if ever flat. As a result, a uniform price will not capture all the consumer surplus. The usual aim of price discrimination is to capture as much consumer surplus as possible by setting different prices for a product, with higher prices being set for consumers with a high willingness to pay, and a lower price for consumers with a lower willingness to pay.

Another economic concept for understanding the dynamics of price discrimination is 'producer surplus'. This is the total of seller's profits above the cost and a reasonable return on capital invested in producing the product. Say, for example, the unit price is $40 and there are sufficient buyers of the product at that price to enable the seller to cover the cost of production and sale and to make a reasonable return on investment. If the seller sells each unit at $45, the amount of $5 multiplied by the number of buyers who purchased the product would equal the producer surplus.

If a monopolist is able to discriminate between consumers on the basis of their willingness to pay, it would be able to turn some of the consumer surplus into producer surplus. Put another way; assume there are three groups of consumers – Group A who are willing to pay a relatively high price for a product, Group B who have a lesser willingness to pay than Group A, and Group C who have the lowest willingness to pay for the product. Assume the monopolist sets prices according to each group's willingness to pay. The price for Group A will reduce the Group members' consumer surplus, which in turn will increase the producer surplus for sales to those consumers. Assume that the price set for members of Group B is a 'competitive price' (i.e. the price the seller would set in a competitive marketplace). There would be no producer surplus for these sales. If the monopolist only sold to Groups A and B, then Group C would effectively be deprived of the benefit or enjoyment of the product. If, however, the monopolist was able to separately sell the product to Group C at a price they were willing to pay, and that price is greater than the marginal cost of selling the product to them, it will be a win for both of them. The monopolist would increase total output, and the pricing strategy would increase total welfare.

The overall consumer welfare benefits can be starkly illustrated with the example of a pharmaceutical company that produces a life-saving drug. It might sell the drug at a relatively high price in high income countries in which consumers have a high willingness to pay for the drug. However, this price would effectively exclude patients in low income countries where they have a lower willingness (and capacity) to pay. Price discrimination would enable the drug to be sold at a high price in high income countries and low prices in low income countries, thereby increasing overall consumer welfare.

4. European Responses to Geo-Pricing

European concerns about geo-pricing predate the establishment of the European Union by the 1957 Treaty of Rome. For instance, an earlier 1952 Treaty instituting the European Coal and Steel Community included a provision against price discrimination similar to provisions of the subsequent Treaty of Rome.

Article 85 of the Treaty of Rome prohibits agreements and concerted practices that are likely to affect trade between member States that results in the prevention, restriction or distortion of competition. The prohibited practices include 'the application to parties to transactions of unequal terms in respect of equivalent supplies, thereby placing them at a competitive disadvantage'.[13] Article 86 prohibits an enterprise taking improper advantage of a dominant position by undertaking that activity. The Treaty of Rome does not define price discrimination. However, Article 86, as interpreted by the European Court of Justice, results in some forms of price discrimination being considered abuses of a dominant position.[14] The Court considered whether Article 86 was breached in two cases where discriminatory pricing was at issue; in *United Brands*[15] and *Tetra Pak II.*[16]

---

13 Treaty establishing the European Economic Community (1957), Article 85(d).

14 D Geradin and N Petit (2005) 'Price Discrimination Under EC Competition Law: The Need for a Case-By-Case Approach' The Global Competition Law Centre Working Papers Series; College of Europe, Brugge, Global Competition Law Centre Working Paper 07/05 https://www.coleurope.eu/system/files_force/research-paper/gclc_wp_07-05.pdf at p. 4.

15 *United Brands Company v Commission of the European Communities* (1978) 4 ECR 207.

16 *Tetra Pak International SA v Commission of the European Communities* (1994) ECR 755.

In *United Brands* a seller unloaded bananas at Rotterdam and Bremen and sold them to distributors and ripeners from various Member States at significantly different prices. The terms and conditions of sale included a clause that had the effect of preventing parallel importing from one Member State to another. As a first step the European Court of Justice was required to decide as a question of fact whether the United Brands was in a market dominant position. The Court found this to be the case, and proceeded to the second step which required it to determine whether United Brands abused its dominant position by its geo-pricing strategy.

In taking the first analytical step, the Court found that United Brands, had a market share of about 45% in the relevant geographic and product markets. The Court emphasised, however, that market dominance was not measured solely by market share. It took account of other factors to find market dominance, including United Brands' vertically integrated structure, technical expertise and product differentiation. The Court also noted that there were formidable barriers to entry into the banana trade because of the enormous capital outlay a potential competitor would be required to make to enter the market.

Given that United Brands had market dominance, the question became whether it was abusing its position by imposing differential prices for the same product. The Court found that United Brands acted to prejudice customers and affected trade between member States, in particular by partitioning national markets.[17] The Court also found, in effect, that only a firm with considerable market power can successfully engage in United Brands' conduct.[18] Thus, the successful imposition of geo-pricing by a firm can suggest it is abusing its market dominance.

In *Tetra Pak II* the seller sold machines and cartons for packaging liquid foods and charged considerably different prices for them across member States. The firm held a share of about 92% of the market for aseptic carton packaging and about 50% of the non-aseptic market. The European Commission found it had engaged in market partitioning and was charging considerably lower prices in some locations, such as Italy. On appeal, the ECJ confirmed the Commission's findings.

According to Geradin and Petit these cases did not find geo-pricing itself to be unlawful, rather they found it was possible to abuse market dominance by engaging in geo-pricing.[19] They argue that Article 86(c) should only be applied to the

---

17 *United Brands Company v Commission of the European Communities* above note 15 at para 159.

18 M FitzPatrick (1979), '*United Brands Company v. Commission of the European Communities*: Window to Price Discrimination Law in the European Economic Community', 1 *Northwestern Journal of International and Business* 338 at 342.

19 D Geradin and N Petit above note 14 at p. 41.

limited circumstances where a non-vertically integrated dominant firm price discriminates between customers (usually local distributors) with the effect of placing one or more of them at a competitive disadvantage relative to other customers. They argue this principle should not be applied simply because pricing strategies are being used that are designed to harm the dominant firm's competitors.[20]

The issue of circumventing geo-blocking came to the fore in the 2011 European Court of Justice decision of *Football Association Premier League Ltd and Karen Murphy*.[21] The case involved the Football Association Premier League, which administers the English Premier League and licenses broadcasting of games on a country by country basis. Licensee television broadcasters were required to encrypt their satellite signals, which is a form of geo-blocking. A number of British pubs started using decoder cards issued by a Greek broadcaster for subscribers resident in Greece. The pubs effectively circumvented the Football Association's geo-pricing strategy. Various parties were prosecuted for breaching UK copyright law, which effectively rendered it a criminal offence to import decoder cards. The Association also brought civil actions for the use of the decoder cards. The High Court of Justice of England and Wales referred a number of legal questions to the European Court of Justice. The ECJ ruled that the Greek decoding devices were not 'illicit devices' under the Conditional Access Directive 98/84/EC, even though some were purchased using a false name and address and were in breach of contractual terms permitting their use only for private purposes. In addition, the legislation was found to be contrary to the Treaty on the Functioning of the EU as it had the effect of preventing people resident outside the Member State of the broadcaster from gaining access to the broadcast services. The legislation by prohibiting the import, sale and use of the foreign decoding cards was contrary to the freedom to provide services and could not be justified either by the objective of protecting intellectual property rights or by the objective of encouraging the public to attend football stadiums. In this case geo-pricing was found, in effect, to be undermining the single European market.

Intra-EU geo-pricing of digital media is further threatened by the European Commission's Digital Single Market Strategy announced on 6 May 2015. One major issue the Strategy seeks to deal with concerns the pricing practices of online suppliers—in particular the charging of different prices in different Member States.[22]

---

20 *Above* at p. 8.

21 (2011) C-403/08 and C-429/08.

22 http://ec.europa.eu/priorities/digital-single-market_en.

The Strategy comprises three policy areas, including establishing better online access to digital media. The policy aims include 'tackling geo-blocking' and it claims that:

> Geo-blocking leaves many Europeans unable to use the online services available in other EU countries, or redirects them to a local store with different prices. This is often done without any justification. Such discrimination cannot exist in a single market.[23]

As an indication of the EU Commission's attitudes to intra-EU geo-pricing, Commissioner Vestager announced during a 2015 speech in Berlin that the European Commission is investigating alleged geo-blocking of certain video games sold online for personal computers.[24] She stated that the Commission's goal is to identify what hampers competition in e-commerce when sales straddle national borders.

Commissioner Vestager's expressed opposition to intra-EU geo-pricing appeared to be inspired in part by consumer resentment of the practice. She seemed to be attempting to channel the broad sense of consumer resentment by stating that:

> I, for one, cannot understand why I can watch my favourite Danish channels on my tablet in Copenhagen – a service I paid for – but I can't when I am in Brussels.
>
> Or why I can buy a film on DVD back home and watch it abroad, but I cannot do the same online.
>
> Think of a French tourist who buys a pair of Italian shoes in Rome. Why is she re-routed to a French website when she tries to buy them online from home?
>
> It is very difficult to explain this to the people and, at the same time, make the point that we are all residents of the EU and consumers in the same internal market.[25]

The Commissioner claimed that a well-functioning Digital Single Market could add about €340 billion to the GDP of the Union. Consequently, she said, 'Our task as competition enforcers is making sure that the Digital Single Market is a place where all players – large and small – can compete on the merits of their products'.[26]

In late 2015, the Commission proposed a Regulation 'on ensuring the cross-border portability of online content services in the internal market'.[27] The Regulation

---

23 http://ec.europa.eu/priorities/digital-single-market/better-online-access-digital-goods-and-services_en.

24 M Vestager (2015) 'Competition Policy for the Digital Single Market: Focus on E-Commerce' http://europa.eu/rapid/press-release_SPEECH-15-4704_en.htm.

25 *Above.*

26 *Above.*

27 Brussels, 9.12.2015, COM(2015) 627.

will only come into force if adopted by at least 28 Member States. The Explanatory Statement to the proposed Regulation states that:

> Consumer demand for the cross-border portability of online content services is substantial and expected to grow. However, when people travel in the EU, they frequently cannot enjoy such cross-border portability or can do so only to a limited extent. The absence of, or problems with, cross-border portability of online content services in the EU results from the licensing practices of right holders and/or the commercial practices of service providers.
>
> This proposal aims to remove barriers to cross-border portability so that the needs of users can be met more effectively as well as promoting innovation for the benefit of consumers, service providers and right holders. The proposal introduces a common approach in the Union while maintaining a high level of protection for right holders. In doing so, it contributes to the functioning of the internal market as an area without internal borders, where the freedom to provide and to receive services shall be ensured.

The Preamble suggests that the Regulation is aimed at broadcasters that prevent their subscribers from accessing and using their service outside the territory for which the service provider holds the licence.[28] It states that their conduct cannot be justified on the basis of protecting their IP rights.[29] The Regulation also aims at enabling cross-border portability of online content services so that consumers can have continued access while they are temporarily outside their home state.[30]

5. Australian Resentment of Geo-Pricing

The Australian policy debate about geo-pricing of digital media played out in two forums over recent times; before the Australian National Parliament's House of Representatives Standing Committee on Infrastructure and Communications (the IP Pricing Review) in 2013[31] and the 2015 Harper Review.[32]

The IP Pricing Review was focused on geo-pricing of digital media and found, amongst other things, that Australian consumers often pay much more for IT products than their counterparts in comparable economies. It found that in many cases Australian consumers were paying 50% to 100% more for the same product than US consumers.[33] The Review Committee found the price differences could

28 Above at paragraph 10.
29 *Above* at paragraph 11.
30 *Above* at paragraph 18.
31 The IP Pricing Review, above note 2.
32 The Harper Review, above note 2.
33 The IP Pricing Review above, note 2 at p. vii.

not be explained by the cost for sellers of doing business in Australia, particularly for digitally delivered content. It hinted at the resentment this arouses by observing that Australian consumers often referred to the pricing difference as the 'Australia tax'.[34] The Committee concluded that high IT prices make it harder for Australian businesses to compete internationally and can be a significant barrier to access and participation for disadvantaged Australians.[35]

The Committee claimed the prices of digital media are 'substantially higher than what might be expected as a consequence of any costs arising from delivery in the Australian market'.[36] It found that of a comparison of more than 150 products there was an average price difference of 50% in the Australian price relative to the overseas sales price (usually the price the products were sold that in the US market). For instance, the median price difference between the Australian price and the overseas price was 49% higher for Adobe products and 67% higher for Microsoft products. More than 70 online music products were compared, which revealed a median difference of 67%. 70 downloadable games were found to have a median price difference of 61% between Australia and US prices. The price of more than 120 e-books were compared revealing a median price difference of 13%.[37]

These findings were consistent with those of the consumer organisation Choice, which stated in its submission to the Committee that it had compared the prices of more than 200 products, finding that there were average price differentials of more than 50% compared with US prices for digital media.[38] More specifically Choice:

> ... compared the prices of more than fifty software products, focusing on Microsoft and Adobe, comparing Australian and US prices, using data collected in 2008 and in mid-2012. Across more than thirty Microsoft software products, Choice data showed consistently higher prices in Australia for substantially identical products, with Australians paying an average 49 per cent more than US customers. According to Choice, Microsoft Office products, including Microsoft Word, Excel, and Access were more than 30 per cent more expensive in Australia, while the various iterations of Microsoft's popular Windows 7 operating system were 40 to 50 per cent more expensive.[39]

---

34 The Harper Review, above note 2 at p. 47.

35 The IP Pricing Review at p. vii.

36 *Above* at pp. 3–4.

37 Above at pp. 17–18. The Standing Committee acknowledged that making price comparisons is an inexact science – see pp. 17–19. See also Australian Productivity Commission Research Report (2009), 'Restrictions on the Parallel Importation of Books' (Commonwealth Government, Canberra) at para 4.2.

38 The IP Pricing Review, above at p. 18.

39 *Above* at p. 23.

Choice also found that the price for individual music tracks downloadable from Apple's iTunes store had a price mark-up of 67%, with Australians being charged 51% more for a downloadable album.[40] Substantial price mark-ups were also found to apply for downloadable games and e-books.[41]

The Committee admitted, however, to limitations in its analysis because it could not gain access to statistical data that would allow for systematic comparisons of IT pricing, and noted that the Australian Productivity Commission experienced similar problems in data collection during the course of its 2011 report on the Australian retail industry.[42]

Although the Committee recognised that 'businesses must remain free to set their own prices in a market economy', it nevertheless made recommendations which it claimed would sharpen competition in Australian IT markets. It was hopeful that this would place downward pressures on IT prices.[43] Its recommendations included that:

- parallel importation restrictions under the *Copyright Act* be removed;[44]
- the *Copyright Act* anti-circumvention provisions be amended to clarify and ensure that consumers have the right to circumvent technological protection measures that control geographic market segmentation;[45]
- a law exempting some anti-competitive practices that would otherwise be prohibited be repealed.[46] These exemptions apply to the licensing of trademarks, designs, copyrights and patents;[47]
- as a last resort, if there was 'persistent market failure' despite these proposed reforms, geo-blocking be banned and any contract or terms of service that sought to enforce geo-blocking be rendered void.[48]

The Harper Review endorsed the Committee's recommendations and stated that it:

---

40 *Above* at p. 29.

41 *Above* at pp. 30–33.

42 *Above* at p. 20. The Committee was referring to the Australian Productivity Commission Inquiry Report (2011) 'Economic Structure and Performance of the Australian Retail Industry', Report 56 (Australian Government, Canberra) at p. 89.

43 *Above* at p. viii.

44 *Above* at p. xii.

45 Recommendation 5, IP Pricing Review, above at p. xiii.

46 Section 51(3) *Competition and Consumer Act 2010.*

47 The IP Pricing Review, above note 2 at, p. xiii. The s. 51(3) exemption does not, however, apply to the monopolisation and resale price maintenance provisions of the Act.

48 *Above* at p. xiii.

> ...supports moves to address international price discrimination through market solutions that empower consumers. These include removing restrictions on parallel imports and ensuring that consumers are able to take legal steps to circumvent attempts to block their access to cheaper legitimate goods.[49]

Harper found that parallel importing restrictions benefit local producers by shielding them from international competition.[50] Consistent with the recommendations of the IP Pricing Review Committee, Harper recommended the removal of restrictions on parallel importing unless it could be shown that the benefits to the community outweigh the costs and the objectives of the restrictions can only be achieved by restricting competition.[51]

The IP Pricing Review Committee hinted at the nature and reasons for Australian resentment of geo-pricing of digital media. For instance, it claimed that it is 'generally accepted that Australians have tolerated higher prices for a range of goods for much of their history 'because of Australia's geographical remoteness, comparatively small and scattered population and an historically weak Australian dollar'.[52] However, the internet has since allowed Australian consumers to engage in a global marketplace where they 'became increasingly aware of prices in comparable overseas markets', leading to many becoming 'frustrated by, regional pricing strategies that prevent them from taking advantage of cheaper prices overseas'.[53] According to one witness before the Committee, Australian consumers had previously been willing to pay more for products relative to consumers in other countries because they had been relatively unaware of the price differences: 'But now we have access to international prices, and purchases are fast and simple a higher dollar has made saving and people taking advantage of that'.[54]

It is possible, however, that the Committee's findings about the pricing of digital media has become at least partly obsolescent, even within three years of its report. The Australian dollar declined by more than 30% over that time relative to the US dollar, which itself diminished price differences between the US and Australia in some cases. In addition, sectors of the digital media marketplace underwent rapid transformation. For instance, there was a marked increase in subscribers to music

49 The Harper Review, above note 2 at 354.

50 *Above* at 47.

51 *Above* at p. 48.

52 Parliament of the Commonwealth of Australia, House of Representatives Standing Committee on Infrastructure and Communications, (2013) 'At What Cost? IP Pricing and the Australia Tax' (Canberra), at p. 3.

53 *Above* at p. 3. See also pp. 11 and 12.

54 *Above* at p. 12.

streaming and downloading services.[55] Typically, for a monthly fee subscribers can listen online or download music of their choice.

There are a number of providers of music subscription services including Spotify, Apple Music, Google Play Music, Rdio, Tidal, Rhapsody, Xbox Music, Deezer, Napster, Mog and Rara. Many of the services offer their subscribers access to a vast catalogue of over 20 million songs. The value of the digital music business in 2014 totalled $US6.9 billion worldwide.[56] In the US revenues for digital music were $US3.5 billion and accounted for 71% of the US recorded music market in 2014.[57] These revenues included those from streaming services. Subscription income increased by 33.5% from the previous year.[58] According to a 2015 report by the music industry association, the International Federation of the Phonographic Industry, the 'defining positive characteristic of the global music market in early 2015 is the continued surge in consumer uptake of streaming services', with the number of paying subscribers worldwide increasing by 46.4% during 2014.[59]

It appears that providers such as Spotify and Apple Music, have non-exclusive rights to provide the music in their online catalogues. Non-exclusivity appears to result in none of the service providers being able to exercise market power, and consequently are unable to set monopoly prices. That is to say, it appears to be a competitive marketplace.

I undertook a quick survey of prices for a number of subscription services for digital media in early 2016. I compared prices to gain of sense of whether geo-pricing was being applied to a number of forms of digital media. The survey was of a very limited nature, and therefore the claims made about what it reveals are necessarily very modest. I compared prices in a number of geographical locations for leading providers for film and TV programs (Netflix), music (Apple Music and Spotify) and software (Microsoft Office). Using a virtual private network (VPN) I was able to fool the service provider's computer system into believing I was located in a particular country of my choosing. I then attempted to find out the monthly fee for their subscription service. This proved to be no easy task in some cases as some services require a potential subscriber to join the service before the pricing is revealed. In any event, I used my best endeavours to locate

55 International Federation of the Phonographic Industry (2015) 'Digital Music Report 2015: Charting the Path to Sustainable Growth' www.ifpi.org/downloads/Digital-Music-Report-2015.pdf.

56 *Above at p. 22.*

57 *Above at p. 14*

58 *Above at p. 9.*

59 *Above at p. 15.*

the price, but given some of the difficulties I faced, there is a risk of error in some instances. I viewed prices as at 15 January 2016 in Australia, Germany, the UK and the US as these are all relatively high income countries and therefore it can be reasonably assumed that consumers have an approximately equal capacity and willingness to pay for the products. I then converted the price to the US dollar rate as at 15 January 2016 to enable meaningful price comparability. The results are as set out in the table below.

Product	**Country**	**Price** (in local currency)	**Price** converted to $US
Netflix HD up to 2 screens	Australia	$11.99	$8.22
	Germany	€7.99	$8.72
	UK	£5.99	$8.54
US allows unlimited screens	US	$8.99	$7.99
Apple Music	Australia	$11.99	$8.22
	UK	£9.99	$14.24
	US	$9.99	$9.99
Spotify premium	Australia	$11.99	$8.22
	Germany	€9.99	$10.90
	UK	£9.99	$14.24
	US	$9.99	$9.99
Microsoft Office home	Australia	$11.99	$8.22
	Germany	€10	$10.91
	UK	£5.99	$8.54
	US	$9.99	$9.99

A comparison purportedly made by a member of the 'Spotify Community' of the monthly subscription fee for Spotify's premium service as at 25 July 2012 revealed the following:[60]

60 https://community.spotify.com/t5/Help-Accounts-and-Subscriptions/Cost-of-Spotify-Premium-for-different-countries-in-relation-to/td-p/133098.

Country/Region	Monthly subscription fee at local currency	Fee converted to $US
Australia	$11.99	$12.50
Europe	€9.99	$12.50
Denmark	99 Danish kroners	$16.64
Norway	99 Norwegian kroners	$17
Sweden	99 Swedish kroners	$15
Switzerland	12.95 Swiss francs	$13.50
UK	£9.99	$15.80
US	$US9.99	$9.99

From these very limited surveys it can be concluded that the price differences between the locations examined are for the most part not substantial. Generally, Australian prices were not significantly higher than US prices; indeed, in some cases the Australian prices were lower than US. Caution needs to be applied in comparing these prices as like for like comparisons might not always exist. For instance, the Netflix catalogue is substantially larger for US consumers than for those in Australia.[61] These pricing observation are underscored by another examination I made. I took the book that was at the top of the New York Times bestseller list for mid-January 2016, which was *The Girl on the Train* by Paula Hawkins, and compared the prices Amazon was selling the ebook (ie its Kindle) version in various locations. Amazon was selling the book on 15 January 2016 at its Kindle store for $US11.99 for US located purchasers, £6.99 for UK located purchasers and $Aus9.89 for Australian located purchasers. Converting those prices to US dollars resulted in the US price being $11.99 for US purchasers, $9.90 for UK purchasers and $6.78 for Australian purchasers. If anything, the comparison showed price discrimination against US purchasers. It is possible that these price comparisons are further complicated if Amazon uses first degree price discrimination. If so, the possibility cannot be ruled out that Amazon offers the same e-book to different consumers in the same geographical location at different prices, which are determined by an algorithm that sets prices based on its calculation of an individual consumer's willingness to pay.

Why then is there such a difference between the prices observed by the IP Pricing Review and the more recent observations I made? In response, the Committee's surveys were far more extensive than mine, suggesting there is little basis

61 N Healey (2015) 'Netflix Australia: What we know' CNet.com www.cnet.com/au/news/netflix-australia-what-we-know/#!

for comparison. However, my survey gives some grounds for pause. It suggests that there may be changes in pricing strategies as some sellers are shifting towards offering their products on a subscription basis rather than a one-off sale, or are offering both the option to subscribe or make one-off purchases. Microsoft, for instance, has recently shifted its strategy to a subscription model for its Windows operating system. For some decades Microsoft held market dominance for operating systems for personal computers. Wingfield notes, however, that Microsoft is dramatically changing its strategy for the sale of its Windows operating system. It is not charging customers to upgrade to Windows 10, which Wingfield opines 'shows how power dynamics in the tech industry have changed'.[62] He notes that companies like Google have crept into Microsoft's business with free software and services subsidised by its advertising business. Meanwhile Apple have made upgrades to its applications and operating systems for free, earning its money from hardware sales. Microsoft is also facing difficulty in penetrating the smart phone environment.

Despite having reasons to believe that some markets for digital media have become competitive, resulting in price reductions and a lessening of geo-pricing strategies, it may remain the case that Australians are paying substantially higher prices in other digital media markets. If so, concerns about the impact of geo-pricing on Australian consumers remain. However, despite the strong recommendations of both the IP Pricing Review and the Harper Review, no measures have been introduced to date to give effect to the recommendations.

6. Seller Anticipation of Resentment over Pricing

Market dominant sellers may consider themselves relatively impervious to consumer resentment about differential pricing as buyers are faced with take-it-or-leave-it choices. In such conditions there are no competitors that can benefit from any resentment of the seller's pricing strategy. However, given how dynamic the online marketplace is, such (arrogant) disregard of consumer sentiment may risk the sowing the seeds of future business decline if market conditions change so as to enable new entrants. In such cases the incumbent cannot count upon customer loyalty, and indeed risks a flight of customers who resent the treatment they suffered when the incumbent was market dominant.

---

62 Nick Wingfield 'Windows 10 Signifies Microsoft's Shift in Strategy' 19 July, 2015 www.nytimes.com/2015/07/20/technology/windows-10-signifies-microsofts-shift-in-strategy.html?_r=0.

Intriguingly, consumer resentment towards differential pricing is context dependent. Differential pricing *per se* is not necessarily resented. For instance, differential pricing of cinema tickets is generally not resented, presumably because providing discounts for pensioners and students is seen as a reasonable proxy for determining capacity to pay. The general assumption of consumers appears to be that students and pensioners are likely to have lower incomes and therefore a reduced capacity to pay, and therefore it is fair to offer them a discount. In the case of cheap airfares it would seem that this is generally considered fair because no-one is excluded from purchasing the cheap tickets, providing they accept the somewhat onerous ticket conditions, including non-transferability and luggage weight restrictions that apply.

It appears, however, that consumers resent it if they perceive the seller is taking unfair advantage of them or of a particular set of circumstances (eg where there is a flood leading to a food shortages and the seller hikes up the prices of food) and engages in some form of price 'gouging'. Gouging involves charging whatever the market can bear.

As a somewhat astounding example of an attempt at price discrimination, Fisher refers to a 1999 report in which the Coca-Cola Company tested vending machines that would increase the price of Coke when the outside temperature rose. Unsurprisingly the vending machines provoked strong resistance from users during testing and Coca-Cola abandoned introducing them to the market.[63]

In a 1986 study by Kahneman, Knetsch, and Thaler they asked participants whether particular hypothetical pricing practices were fair.[64] They found that many respondents regarded it unfair for a firm to raise the price of an item whose demand increased as a result of a change in the weather. The respondents did, however, perceive a firm's conduct to be fair if price rises were due to increases in the price of inputs in producing and providing the product.[65] Conversely, respondents did not regard it fair for prices to stay constant when costs fall.[66] Rotemberg observes more generally that:

63 W Fisher (2007) 'When Should we Permit Differential Pricing of Information?' 55 *University of California Law Review* 1 at 10.

64 D Kahneman, J Knetsch, and R Thaler (1986), 'Fairness as a Constraint on Profit: Seeking Entitlements in the Market' 76 *American Economic Review*, 728 at 734.

65 *Above* at 733.

66 See P Dickson and R Kalapurakal (1994), 'The Use and Perceived Fairness of Price-Setting Rules in the Bulk Electricity Market' 15 *Journal of Economic Psychology* 427.

> Whether sincere or not, altruistic behavior by firms can explain two important pricing phenomena even if consumer utility functions are quite standard. The first is that groups that are generally regarded as poor (students, the elderly) often obtain goods at lower prices. By contrast, third-degree price discrimination that is based on differences in elasticities of demand is frequently regarded as unfair, and is sometimes deterred by negative customer reactions. The second is that, even when prices do change, prices seem to be more responsive to changes in factor cost than to changes in demand that have the same effect on marginal cost.[67]

Consumer resentment of first degree price discrimination gains confirmation in a 2005 study by Turow, Feldman and Meltzer. They put a series of questions to a nationally representative sample of 1,500 adults who used the internet during month prior to the survey.[68] Their study revealed that consumers incorrectly believe that sellers cannot charge them different prices based on what they know about them.[69] Their study also offers support for the proposition that consumers resent geo-pricing. When asked: 'It would bother me to learn that other people pay less than I do for the same products' 76% agreed or strongly agreed and 22% disagreed or strongly disagreed.[70] When respondents were also asked whether 'It's okay if an online store I use charges different people different prices for the same products during the same hour?' 11% agreed or strongly agreed and 87% disagreed or strongly disagreed.[71] When respondents were asked whether 'Websites should be required to let customers know if they charge different people different prices for the same products during the same hour'? 84% agreed or strongly agreed and 14% disagreed or strongly disagreed.

Sellers, it appears, are sensitive to the risk of consumer resentment when designing their pricing strategies. Iyer and Schoar observed that sellers are reluctant to increase their prices in certain circumstances. One explanation for this behaviour they offer is that 'firms avoid price changes for fear of being seen as price gouging. For example, if buyers have a preference for fairness, firms will restrain from making big price changes since buyers might perceive these as a sign that

67 J Rotemberg (2011), 'Fair Pricing' 9 *Journal of the European Economic Association* 952 at 953.

68 J Turow, L Feldman and K Meltzer (2005), 'Open to Exploitation: America's Shoppers Online and Offline. A Report from the Annenberg Public Policy Center of the University of Pennsylvania, http://repository.upenn.edu/asc_papers/35 at p. 4.

69 *Above* at p. 3.

70 *Above* at p. 3.

71 Above at p. 22.

the seller is trying to take advantage of them; especially if they cannot observe the reason for the price change'.[72]

Rotemberg refers to studies in which firms were asked why they keep their prices rigid. The studies revealed that sellers tend to say they do so to avoid antagonising their customers. He hypothesises that consumers will regard the firm as fair if it acts in a seemingly altruistic way. He suggests that firms are able to appear to be acting altruistically if they conduct themselves in a way that is based on fear of angry customer reactions to perceived unfair pricing. That is, firms can minimise resentment over pricing if they internalise customer emotions, 'and particularly the disappointment and regret that consumers feel when the price they face is higher than a price that was previously available to them'.[73]

Triggering resentment can risk the loss of potential buyers, who may in some instances refuse to make a purchase even if the refusal leaves them worst off. There are a number of studies that confirm the existence of this behaviour. As Iyer and Schoar observe:

> ...the literature on contracts as reference points suggests that buyers might feel "aggrieved" if they are asked to accept changes in contract terms, since they anchor on the original contract. In response, they might not be willing to renegotiate the terms, even if this makes them worse off ex post or leads to break down of trade.[74]

Resentment, then, is framed by a consumer's perception of 'fairness'. Pricing that appears to be based on customers' capacity to pay (eg cinema tickets), or responds to increases or decreased in cost inputs in production and delivery are generally perceived as fair. However, perceived price gouging and taking unfair advantage of a situation (such as a sudden shortage), or lifting prices without apparent justification as seen to be unfair. Studies of consumer attitudes to pricing mentioned above also suggest that differential pricing that is not based on perceived capacity to pay, but rather on what the seller can get away with charging, is also seen as unfair. The internet has made price comparisons across geographical locations more transparent, thereby inciting the kinds of resentment mentioned in the

---

72 R Iyer and A Schoar (2014) 'Contract Renegotiation and Fear of Price Gouging' Mimeo, MIT. http://jeffd.scripts.mit.edu/riyer/docs/Fear_gouging_3.pdf at p. 2. See also Anderson, E., Simester, D., 2010. "Price Stickiness and Customer Antagonism," *Quarterly Journal of Economics*, 125(2), 729–765.

73 J Rotemberg above, note 67 at 952.

74 R Iyer and A Schoar above, note 72 at p. 1. See also H Yuan and S Han (2011) 'The Effects of Consumers' Price Expectations on Sellers' Dynamic Pricing Strategies' 48 *Journal of Marketing Research* 48.

Australian IP Pricing Review[75] and hinted at by EU Commissioner Vestager in her Berlin speech.[76]

It can be speculated that consumers using the internet perceive themselves to be a kind of dual citizen; a citizen of their country and a global net-citizen. Net-citizenry may be perceived as entitling the citizen to be as unconstrained by national borders as the internet itself when they seek information, engage in online conversations, send and receive emails, engage with social media and shop for goods and services, including digital media. The digital media marketplace may well be perceived to be global, and not nationally bound. This perception may have arisen despite the fact that for decades, if not centuries, creative content distribution outlets were nationally based, and pricing was related to national boundaries.

Geo-pricing of creative content, which was once broadly seen by consumers to be fair and reasonable (or at least tolerable) is now perceived to be unfair – at least in an online environment. Sellers that resist this reframing of fairness risk provoking consumer resentment. It seems that legislators are conscious of this reframing of fairness, and are backing the perceived interests of consumers.

7. Conclusion

A normative question arises as to how policy makers and legislators ought to respond to geo-pricing. Public policy seeks to advance socially and economically fair, just and equitable outcomes, or ought to do so. Some fair, just and equitable values such as enhancing competition are enduring whilst others are contingent, context dependent and dynamic. Conceptions of social and economic fairness and justice regarding geo-pricing are being reframed by the internet. The internet is global, whilst geo-pricing reinforces the notion that the world, and consequently markets, are defined and circumscribed by national borders. Increased capacities for consumers to view prices in other locations, along with the ready capacity to shop across borders if constraints are not put in their way, combined with a growing self-sense of being net-citizens with an entitlement to act as members of a global community and a global marketplace is reframing conceptions of fairness which are undermining the basis for geo-pricing.

Public policy values of fairness and equity are informed by broader public conceptions of those values. Evidence of public conceptions of fairness regarding discriminatory pricing can be found in behavioral studies, some of which are

---

75 IP Pricing Review, above note 2.

76 M Vestager (2015), 'Competition Policy for the Digital Single Market: Focus on E-Commerce' http://europa.eu/rapid/press-release_SPEECH-15-4704_en.htm.

referred to above in Part 6. It may be surmised from these studies that geo-pricing is in many instances seen as a form of gouging by sellers who are effectively operating as monopolists. Sellers engaging in geo-pricing invariably call upon the support of policy makers and legislators to extend copyright and to prohibit parallel importing and other forms of circumvention. A reframing of the fairness parameters as described in this chapter suggests that laws and policies that operate in the way sought by geo-pricers are increasingly out of step.

If these postulations hold, there is nevertheless scope for some degree of geo-pricing that complies with the re-framed conceptions of fairness. The pricing comparisons reported in this chapter are deliberately limited to high income, or relatively high income, countries. The prices reported are doubtless far too high – in a fairness sense – for consumers in non-high income countries, such as those in developing and less developed countries. The high income nation prices would exclude them from the market. Consumer welfare measured on a world-wide scale would be increased if lower prices for digital media were set for consumers with a low willingness and capacity to pay. Developing and less developed countries are a reasonable proxy for a low willingness to pay.

The public policy implications are that setting objectives and laws that enable geo-pricing by providing copyright protections, prohibiting parallel importing and circumvention in circumstances where the geo-pricing sets differential pricing based on whether the location is in a developed, developing or less developed country are acceptable because they meet the fairness criteria.

Although EU law and policy is framed around anti-competition concerns and the desire to strengthen the EU as a single market, they are not inconsistent with the fairness postulates put in this chapter. The EU debate tends, however, to confine itself to a Eurocentric view, and is largely ill-inclined to consider how geo-pricing should be dealt with regarding non-European sellers. The Australian debate is more explicitly framed around notions of fairness. There is, however, a need to finesse the public policy debate in Australia, Europe and other places to allow for geo-pricing based on the relative wealth of nations.

List of authors

Dr. Duns, John
Associate Professor, Law School, Monash University

Dr. Fleischer, Romy Nicole
Solicitor, Noerr LLP Dresden
Law tutor and research fellow, Philipps University Marburg

Dr. Gounalakis, Georgios
Professor, Philipps University Marburg
Member of the Commission on Concentration in the Media (KEK)

Dr. Kling, Michael
Professor, Philipps University Marburg

Dr. Malbon, Justin
Professor, Law School, Monash University;
Adjunct Research Fellow, Australian Centre for Intellectual Property in Agriculture;
Visiting Scholar, Law School, Cambridge University;
Visiting Fellow, Wolfson College, Cambridge;
Visiting Fellow, European University Institute, Florence, Italy

Dr. Rodrick, Sharon
Senior Lecturer, Law School, Monash University

Dr. Röß, Simon
Research fellow and law tutor, Philipps University Marburg

Dr. Taylor, Greg
Honorary Professor, Philipps University Marburg;
Associate Professor, Graduate School of Business and Law, R.M.I.T. University, Melbourne

Dr. Windholz, Eric
Senior Lecturer, Law School, Monash University;
Associate, Monash Centre for Commercial Law and Regulatory Studies

Schriften zum Medien-, Urheber- und Wirtschaftsrecht

Herausgegeben von Prof. Dr. Georgios Gounalakis

Band 1 Thomas Lang: Immaterialgüterrechtliche Lizenzierung und kartellrechtliche Verhaltenskontrolle. Eine Untersuchung der Reichweite gemeinschaftskartellrechtlicher Eingriffsbefugnisse in Immaterialgüterrechtspositionen vor dem Hintergrund der schutzrechtsspezifischen wettbewerblichen Ausschließlichkeit. 2009.

Band 2 Anna-Karina Bonacker: Der Widerruf von Fernabsatzverträgen am Beispiel der Internetauktion eBay. 2009.

Band 3 Rainer Jürgen Scharf: Der unbefristete Widerruf internetbasierter Verträge. Zugleich ein Beitrag zur Dogmatik des § 355 BGB. 2009.

Band 4 Sebastian Gorski: Effizienz, Wahlfreiheit und Gleichbehandlung? Eine Untersuchung der Einführung von Wettbewerb zwischen musikalischen Verwertungsgesellschaften durch die Europäische Kommission. 2009.

Band 5 Daniel Walter: Die rechtliche Behandlung der Erbringung unbestellter Leistungen nach § 241a BGB. 2009.

Band 6 Richard Helwig: Die Kompetenz der Europäischen Gemeinschaft zur Schaffung eines europäischen Medienkonzentrationsrechts. Notwendigkeit, Voraussetzungen und Reichweite einer möglichen Regulierung zur Sicherung von Medien- und Meinungsvielfalt in Europa. 2009.

Band 7 Bettina Yunis: Alternative Streitbeilegung über elektronische Datennetze. 2011.

Band 8 Andreas Walter: Störerhaftung bei Handeln Dritter. 2011.

Band 9 Andreas Zenner: Die zivilrechtliche Verantwortlichkeit des Abschlussprüfers für den Bestätigungsvermerk. 2011.

Band 10 Kristine Wagner: Die Privatkopie als urheberrechtliche Schrankenregelung. 2011.

Band 11 Ina Lutz: Testierfreiheit und Pflichtteilsrecht im spanischen *Código Civil* im Vergleich mit dem deutschen Bürgerlichen Gesetzbuch. Unter besonderer Berücksichtigung von Immobilienerbschaften. 2011.

Band 12 Heiko Drebes: „Datenschutz" für Unternehmen im B2B? Schutz der Daten des geschäftlichen E-Business im Spannungsfeld zwischen technisch-organisatorischer und rechtlicher Regulierung. 2012.

Band 13 Heiko Zimmer: Zugriff auf Internetzugangsdaten. Unter besonderer Berücksichtigung der Verhältnismäßigkeit einer verdachtsunabhängigen Vorratsdatenspeicherung. Eine Interessenabwägung zwischen Datenschutz, Strafverfolgung und Urheberrecht im Internet. 2012.

Band 14 Ricarda Leffler: Der strafrechtliche Schutz des Rechts am eigenen Bild vor dem neuen Phänomen des Cyber-Bullying. Eine Untersuchung der Normanwendungs- und Auslegungsprobleme der strafrechtlichen Bildnisschutzvorschriften bei deren Verletzung im Rahmen von Internetdelikten. 2012.

Band 15 Nadine Kristin Keil: Verdachtsberichterstattung. Medienberichterstattung über Straftatverdächtige. 2013.

Band 16 Alexandra Sommerhoff: Meinungsvielfalt und Medienkonvergenz. Die Sicherung der Meinungsvielfalt in Deutschland und Großbritannien. 2013.

Band 17 Christoph Wege: Roman und Persönlichkeitsrecht. Ein partikulardogmatischer Entwurf. 2013.

Band 18 Florian Jäkel: Netzneutralität im Internet. Verfassungsrechtliche Aspekte und Sicherungsmechanismen. Zugleich ein Beitrag zu Kommunikations- und Medienfreiheiten im Internet. 2013.

Band 19 Lars Querndt: Selektivvertrieb und eBay-Versteigerungen. Die kartellrechtliche Zulässigkeit des eBay-Ausschlusses aus dem Selektivvertrieb in Vertragshändlerverträgen und Markenlizenzen unter besonderer Berücksichtigung des Markenrechts. 2014.

Band 20 Catherine M. Manley: The Trademark Paradox. Trademarks and Their Conflicting Legal and Commercial Boundaries. 2015.

Band 21 Arne Neubauer: Internetvertrieb im Kartellrecht. Eine kritische Auseinandersetzung mit herstellerseitigen Vertriebsbeschränkungen. 2015.

Band 22 Kristin Grimm: Lizenzketten im Urheberrecht. Zum Schicksal der Unterlizenz nach Beendigung des Hauptlizenzvertrages. 2016.

Band 23 Georgios Gounalakis / Greg Taylor (eds.): Media Diversity Law. Australia and Germany Compared. 2016.

www.peterlang.com